OCCASIONAL PAPER **238**

Stabilization and Reform in Latin America:
A Macroeconomic Perspective on the Experience Since the Early 1990s

Anoop Singh, Agnès Belaisch, Charles Collyns, Paula De Masi,
Reva Krieger, Guy Meredith, and Robert Rennhack

INTERNATIONAL MONETARY FUND
Washington DC
2005

Production: IMF Multimedia Services Division
Figures: Jorge Salazar
Typesetting: Alicia Etchebarne-Bourdin

Cataloging-in-Publication Data

Stabilization and reform in Latin America: a macroeconomic perspective on the experience since the early 1990s/Anoop Singh . . . [et al.]—Washington, D.C.: International Monetary Fund, 2005.

   p. cm.—(Occasional paper); 238
   Includes bibliographical references.
   ISBN 1-58906-250-7

   1. Latin America—Economic policy. 2. Latin America—Economic conditions. 3. International Monetary Fund—Latin America. I. Singh, Anoop. II. Occasional paper (International Monetary Fund); no. 238.

HC123.S73 2005

Price: US$25.00
(US$22.00 to full-time faculty members and
students at universities and colleges)

Please send orders to:
International Monetary Fund, Publication Services
700 19th Street, N.W., Washington, D.C. 20431, U.S.A.
Tel.: (202) 623-7430   Telefax: (202) 623-7201
E-mail: publications@imf.org
Internet: http://www.imf.org

recycled paper

Contents

Foreword ix

Preface xi

Executive Summary xiii

    Taking Stock xiii
    Fiscal Sustainability xv
    Monetary and Exchange Rate Regimes xvi
    Latin American Financial Systems and Financial Dollarization xvii
    External Vulnerabilities xviii
    Future Priorities and Role of IMF xix

I   **Introduction** 1
    References 2

II   **Taking Stock** 3

    Main Economic and Social Outcomes 3
    Explaining the Outcomes 11
    Conclusion 23
    References 23

III   **Fiscal Sustainability** 26

    Lack of Short-Term Policy Constraints 26
    Common Fragilities 28
    Underlying Weaknesses 31
    Fiscal Lessons, Policy Responses, and Challenges 40
    References 41

IV   **Monetary and Exchange Rate Regimes** 45

    Overview 45
    Alternative Approaches to Monetary Stabilization 45
    Macroeconomic Impact of Exchange Rate-Based Stabilization
        Plans 48
    Effects on Other Elements of Reform Programs 56
    Exit and Regime Change 56
    Lessons, Policy Responses, and Challenges 57
    References 59

V   **Latin American Financial Systems: Crises and Reforms** 63

    Key Characteristics of Latin American Financial Systems 63
    Underlying Weaknesses 70

Banking Crises and Reforms 73
Lessons, Policy Responses, and Challenges 77
References 77

VI Financial Dollarization in Latin America **79**

Causes 79
Managing the Risks 85
Lessons, Policy Responses, and Challenges 87
References 88

VII External Vulnerabilities **90**

Disappointing Outcomes of Trade Liberalization 90
Capital Flows to Latin America 99
Low Trade Shares and Volatile Capital Flows Amplified
Vulnerabilities 101
Lessons, Policy Responses, and Challenges 101
References 103

VIII Lessons and Priorities for Future Agenda **106**

Looking Back 106
Disappointments 107
Explanatory Factors 107
Priorities for Future Agenda 108
IMF Role: Supporting Growth Agendas 112
References 114

Boxes

2.1. Latin America: Labor Market Reforms 18
2.2. Latin America: Impediments to Business Activity and Growth 22
3.1. Chile's Fiscal Consolidation in 1990s 29
3.2. Tax Amnesties in Argentina 33
3.3. Infrastructure Spending and Growth in Latin America 36
4.1. Exchange Rate Experience in Central America 50
4.2. Cyclical Impact of Exchange Rate-Based Stabilization Plans 54
5.1. Finance for Growth: Experiences in Chile and Mexico 65
5.2. Do Brazilian Banks Compete? 68
5.3. Taxation of Financial Transactions in Latin America 71
5.4. Vulnerabilities from Offshore Banking 75
5.5. Cross-Border Financial Integration: Banking in Central
America 76
7.1. NAFTA: Benefits and Challenges 97

Tables

ES1. Latin America: Policy Indicators, 1992 and 2002 xiii
ES2. Selected Latin American Countries: Real Per Capita GDP,
1998–2003 xiv
ES3. Latin America: Incidence of Poverty xiv
ES4. Selected Latin America Countries: Total Change in Public
Infrastructure Spending, 1990 to 2000 xv
ES5. Selected Latin American Counties: Foreign Exchange Deposits xvii
2.1. International Comparison: Growth in Real Per Capita GDP 5
2.2. Real Per Capita GDP, 1998–2003 7
2.3. Consequences of Crisis: Current Account Adjustment 9

2.4. Latin America: Incidence of Poverty — 9
2.5. IMF Arrangements in Latin America, 1989–2004 — 15
2.6. International Comparison: Corruption Perception Index — 21
3.1. Selected Latin American Countries: Composition of Public Debt, 2000 — 30
3.2. Selected Latin American Countries: Real Effective Exchange Rates and Foreign Currency Debt — 30
3.3. Selected Latin American Countries: General Government Tax Revenues — 32
3.4. Selected Latin American Countries: Value-Added-Tax (VAT) Revenue Productivity — 34
3.5. Selected Latin American Countries: Cost of Tax Collection, 1998 — 34
3.6. Selected Latin American Countries: Earmarked Spending, 2002 — 34
3.7. Selected Latin American Countries: Estimates of Implicit Pension Debt in 1990s — 39
4.1. Monetary Stabilization Plans: Objectives and Timing — 47
4.2. Pre- and Post-Stabilization Inflation and Exchange Rate Developments — 49
4.3. Latin America: Increases in Central Bank Independence — 51
5.1. International Comparison: Financial Systems, 2003 — 64
5.2. Selected Latin American Countries: Structure of Banking Systems — 67
5.3. Selected Latin American Countries: Assets and Loans of Public Banks — 67
5.4. International Comparison: Bank Performance Indicators — 69
5.5. Three Latin American Countries: Bankruptcy Frameworks — 72
5.6. Latin America: Fiscal Costs of Banking Crises in 1990s — 74
6.1. Dollarization Indicators, 2001 — 79
6.2. Selected Latin American Countries: Deposit and Loan Dollarization — 80
6.3. Selected Latin American Countries with Low Dollarization: Risk-Management Arrangements — 83
6.4. Latin America: Offshore Deposits — 84
6.5. Selected Highly Dollarized Latin American Countries: Risk-Management Arrangements — 86
7.1. Latin America: Regional Integration Initiatives, 1990–Present — 92
7.2. International Comparison: Export Performance in Latin America and Asia — 93

Figures

ES1. Latin America: Inflation — xiv
ES2. Four Latin American Countries: Public Debt — xv
ES3. Four Latin American Countries: Real Effective Exchange Rates — xvi
ES4. International Comparison: Exports of Goods and Services — xviii
2.1. Selected Latin American Countries: Inflation Performance — 4
2.2. Selected Latin American Countries: Growth Performance — 6
2.3. Latin America: Real GDP — 7
2.4. Selected Latin American and Asian Countries: Per Capita Incomes Compared with United States, 1950–2000 — 7
2.5. Selected Latin American Countries: Output Volatility — 8
2.6. Selected Latin American Countries: Consequences of Crisis for Real GDP Growth — 8
2.7. Latin America: Incidence of Poverty and Extreme Poverty — 10
2.8. Latin America: Economic Growth and Poverty Reduction, 1990–2001 — 11

2.9. Global Indicators 12
2.10. Emerging Market Spreads 13
2.11. Latin America: Emerging Market Bond Spreads 14
2.12. Latin America: IMF-Supported Arrangements 14
2.13. Latin America: Contribution of Reforms to Economic Growth 17
2.14. Latin America: Structural Reform Indices 17
2.15. International Comparison: Per Capita Income and Governance, 2000 20
2.16. Latin America: Governance Ratings, 1985–2001 21
2.17. International Comparison: Governance Indicators, 2001 21
3.1. International Comparison: Government Net Debt, 1996 27
3.2. Selected Latin American Countries: Public Sector Balances 27
3.3. Selected Latin American Countries: Public Debt 28
3.4. International Comparison: Cyclical Sensitivity of Primary Balance 28
3.5. Brazil: Composition of Spending 35
3.6. Selected Latin American Countries: General Government Expenditure on Wages and Infrastructure 37
3.7. Brazil: Public Sector Primary Balance 37
3.8. Argentina: "Fiscal Skeletons" and Primary Balance 38
3.9. Argentina: "Fiscal Skeletons" and Public Debt Paths 38
4.1. Latin America: Fiscal Deficits and Inflation, 1980–2001 46
4.2. Latin America: Exchange Rate Developments 48
4.3. Inflation Under Alternative Stabilization Plans 52
4.4. Latin America: Real Effective Exchange Rates 53
4.5. Inflation Targeting in Latin America 58
5.1. Latin America: Boom and Bust in Credit Growth 63
5.2. Interest Spread in Latin America 69
5.3. Comparative Savings and Loan Ratios in Mid-1990s 70
5.4. Strength of Financial Regulatory Environment in Selected Countries 74
6.1. Selected Latin American Countries: Deposit Dollarization and Inflation, 1990–2001 81
6.2. Real Interest Rates in Selected Highly Dollarized Countries 82
6.3. Real Interest Rates in Non-Dollarized Countries 82
6.4. Public Sector Deficits in Highly Dollarized Countries 84
6.5. Selected Latin American Countries: Inflation and Real Bilateral Exchange Rate Volatility, 1990–2002 85
6.6. Selected Latin American Countries: Reserve Coverage of Foreign Currency Deposits 85
7.1. Trade and Financial Integration Across Developing Regions, 1975–99 90
7.2. Selected Latin American Countries: Average Tariffs 91
7.3. International Comparison: Exports of Goods and Services 92
7.4. Selected Latin American Countries: Trade Openness, 2002 94
7.5. Selected Latin American Countries: Herfindahl Index for Exports 94
7.6. Selected Latin American Countries: Commodity Exports 94
7.7. Latin America: Net Private Capital Flows 99
7.8. Selected Latin American Countries: Net Foreign Direct Investment (FDI) Flows 100
7.9. International Comparison: External Debt 102
7.10. Selected Latin American Countries: External Debt, 2000 102

The following symbols have been used throughout this paper:

. . .   to indicate that data are not available;

—   to indicate that the figure is zero or less than half the final digit shown, or that the item does not exist;

–   between years or months (e.g., 1997–98 or January–June) to indicate the years or months covered, including the beginning and ending years or months; and

/   between years (e.g., 1997/98) to indicate a fiscal (financial) year.

"n.a." means not applicable.

"Billion" means a thousand million.

Minor discrepancies between constituent figures and totals are due to rounding.

The term "country," as used in this paper, does not in all cases refer to a territorial entity that is a state as understood by international law and practice; the term also covers some territorial entities that are not states, but for which statistical data are maintained and provided internationally on a separate and independent basis.

Foreword

The 1980s were described as a lost decade for Latin America and led to a spate of reform programs being introduced across the region at the start of the 1990s. In spite of this, the 1990s, too, were a decade of disappointment. Most countries grew at rates well below their potential, making poverty reduction as elusive as ever. There were capital account and currency crises in several countries.

This study is an attempt to analyze what went wrong and why, and to draw lessons for the future. Why have growth rates been so low? Why did so many countries in the region fail to maintain the confidence of the international financial markets? And what are the economic policy implications of the failures of the 1990s?

Latin America's short-term economic prospects currently look more promising than they have for some time. As the global economy strengthens, a pickup in activity is well under way in most countries in the region, after two years of weakness. This study comes at an important juncture, since it is easier to tackle underlying economic weaknesses and introduce reforms when the outlook is more buoyant.

But reforms need to be carefully targeted, to deliver macroeconomic stability that will increase resilience to outside shocks and so make it possible to sustain higher growth rates and thus reduce poverty. By identifying where reforms fell short, or where they were not followed through, this study should help policymakers to avoid the shortcomings of the 1990s and set Latin America on a path of sustainable, more rapid growth.

Anne O. Krueger
First Deputy Managing Director
International Monetary Fund

Preface

This study was prepared by a staff team under the direction of Anoop Singh, Director of the Western Hemisphere Department. The other principal members of the team involved in the preparation of this report included Agnès Belaisch, Charles Collyns, Paula De Masi, Reva Krieger, Guy Meredith, and Robert Rennhack.

Many other staff members of the Western Hemisphere Department as well as of other IMF departments provided valuable inputs and technical expertise on a variety of issues, and helped in identifying and organizing data sources, at different stages of preparation. Among these, we would like to especially acknowledge Geoffrey Bannister, Nigel Chalk, Martine Guerguil, Lorenzo Giorgianni, Graham Ingham, Eliot Kalter, Hans Peter Lankes, Alex Lehmann, Saúl Lizondo, Ousmene Mandeng, Jorge Márquez-Ruarte, Steven Phillips, Markus Rodlauer, Alfred Schipke, Ricardo Velloso, Andy Wolfe, and Philip Young.

The authors are indebted to the research and administrative assistants in the Western Hemisphere Department and, in particular, to Lita Ali, Alfred Go, Elena Pinillos, and Carolina Worthington for providing outstanding administrative and organizational support, and to Victor Culiuc, Bruce Culmer, Genevieve Mendiola, and Gustavo Ramirez for excellent research assistance. Paul Gleason of the External Relations Department edited the manuscript and coordinated production of the publication.

The paper has been reviewed internally and externally. Without implicating these reviewers for the analysis and views expressed in the paper, we would like to especially thank and acknowledge the detailed comments received from Anne Krueger, Agustín Carstens, Guillermo Le Fort, Luis Martí, Murilo Portugal, and Roberto Steiner. In addition, this paper has benefited from discussions with former Managing Director Horst Köhler and, in its formative stage, with Eduardo Aninat, former Deputy Managing Director. We are also grateful for comments on the scope and content of the paper, at various stages of its preparation, from a number of distinguished experts outside the IMF, including Javier Comboni, Vittorio Corbo, David de Ferranti, Sebastian Edwards, Dennis Flannery, Pablo Guidotti, Arnold Harberger, Roberto Junguito, Guillermo Perry, and John Williamson.

The views expressed in this paper, as well as any remaining errors, are solely the responsibility of the authors and do not necessarily reflect the views of the International Monetary Fund, the IMF Executive Directors, or national authorities.

Executive Summary

Taking Stock

Initial results of policy reforms in the late 1980s and early 1990s were promising. Inflation was quickly brought down after stabilization plans were introduced, and this achievement has since endured (Table ES.1 and Figure ES.1). Real growth accelerated in the first half of the 1990s, and social indicators began to improve. The external environment in the early 1990s also contributed to the improved performance, as cyclical weakness in the industrial countries contributed to a surge in capital flows to Latin America.

These improvements were not sustained, however. Persistent macroeconomic volatility and recurring financial crises contributed to capital account reversals and a weakening in growth later in the decade, culminating in the crises of 2001–2002. Real per

Table ES1. Latin America: Policy Indicators, 1992 and 2002

	1992		2002	
	Number of countries	GDP share (percent)	Number of countries	GDP share (percent)
Inflation[1]				
Low < 10 percent	3	2.3	12	82.5
10–20 percent	2	1.9	3	3.0
High > 20 percent	12	95.9	2	14.5
Dollarization (share of dollar deposits)				
High > 50 percent	3	4.9	9	20.3
< 50 percent	14	95.1	8	79.7
Public debt/GDP (percent)				
High > 40 percent	9	50.4	15	97.9
25–40 percent	5	24.0	1	0.7
< 25 percent	3	25.7	1	1.3
Exports/GDP (percent)				
High > 25 percent	7	11.9	10	23.7
< 25 percent	10	88.1	7	76.3
Exchange rate flexibility[2]				
Inflexible	13	55.0	10	13.0
Flexible	4	45.0	7	87.0
Corruption Perception Index[3]				
More corrupt than sample median	13	81.9	12	52.8
Less corrupt than sample median	4	18.1	5	47.2

Sources: IMF, World Economic Outlook database; Reinhart and Rogoff (2002); and Transparency International.

Note: Countries covered are Argentina, Bolivia, Brazil, Chile, Colombia, Costa Rica, Ecuador, El Salvador, Guatemala, Honduras, Mexico, Nicaragua, Panama, Paraguay, Peru, Uruguay, and Venezuela.

[1] The 1992 column reports average inflation during 1981–92.

[2] Based on Reinhart and Rogoff (2002) de facto reclassification of exchange rate arrangements. Flexible exchange rates include free floats and managed floats. Inflexible regimes include all other arrangements (i.e., formal dollarization, currency boards, fixed regimes, bands, crawling pegs, and crawling bands).

[3] Compiled by Transparency International. For 1992, the index is an average for 1988–92.

Figure ES1. Latin America: Inflation[1]
(Annual percentage change)

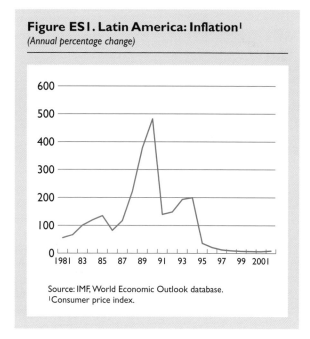

Source: IMF, World Economic Outlook database.
[1]Consumer price index.

capita GDP in the region stagnated over the period 1998–2003 (Table ES.2).

Trends in poverty and income inequality have not improved substantially over the past decade. Poverty rates initially declined from their peaks in the late 1980s, but progress was not sustained as economic activity stagnated (Table ES.3). Moreover, income inequality in Latin America remains very high by international standards, undermining support for market reforms and trust in government institutions.

These setbacks reflected both external shocks and domestic vulnerabilities. From an external perspective, the favorable conditions in the early 1990s dete-

riorated as rising interest rates in the United States and weakening investor confidence triggered a sharp reversal in capital inflows. With regard to domestic policies, on the macroeconomic side, inflexible exchange rate regimes were not adequately supported by fiscal and structural policies. They also encouraged balance-sheet mismatches and informal dollarization. Export growth did not keep pace with capital flows, exacerbating vulnerabilities. In combination, these factors created a macroeconomic and financial structure that was highly exposed to external and internal shocks, and sensitive to shifts in market confidence.

From an institutional and structural perspective, reforms were uneven and remained incomplete. More progress was made with measures that had low up-front costs, such as privatization, relative to reforms that promised greater long-term benefits, such as improving macroeconomic and labor market institutions, and strengthening legal and judicial systems. Insufficient emphasis was placed on ensuring that the benefits of reforms were broadly shared, thus jeopardizing popular support for them.

The consequences of incomplete reforms were felt in the latter part of the decade. The growth momentum slowed, as the transitory effects of earlier reforms waned. At the same time, external financing flows—an important element in fueling Latin American growth—dried up as the crises in emerging market financing were compounded by rising risk aversion. Persisting macroeconomic vulnerabilities, slowing growth, and limited popular support for corrective measures then undermined investor confidence, precipitating crises in a wide range of countries. Only Chile and Mexico, which had gone furthest in addressing underlying vulnerabilities, were able to successfully resist the difficult conditions.

The region is now recovering from the financial market pressures of 2002. Strengthening political resolve in many countries to address the immediate

Table ES2. Selected Latin American Countries: Real Per Capita GDP, 1998–2003
(Average annual percentage change)

Latin America	−0.1
Argentina	−2.6
Bolivia	0.1
Brazil	0.0
Chile	1.1
Colombia	−0.9
Ecuador	−0.3
Mexico	1.3
Peru	0.3
Uruguay	−2.7
Venezuela	−4.9

Source: IMF, World Economic Outlook database.

Table ES3. Latin America: Incidence of Poverty[1]
(Percent of population)

	1990	2000	2001	2002	2003
Poverty	48.3	42.4	43.1	44.0	44.4
Extreme poverty	22.5	18.1	18.5	19.4	20.0

Source: United Nations, Economic Commission for Latin America and the Caribbean (ECLAC).
[1]Data for 2003 are estimates. Poverty rates are calculated using the cost-of-basic-needs method, which establishes a poverty line based on the cost of a basic food basket. For details, see ECLAC (2001).

macroeconomic vulnerabilities—combined with an ongoing global recovery, strong commodity prices, and favorable emerging market conditions—has contributed to the region's registering a strong growth performance in 2004.

For the recoveries to be sustained, however, these economies must be made more crisis resistant. Priorities include strengthening fiscal management, lowering public debt, consolidating inflation-targeting frameworks to sustain low inflation with exchange rate flexibility, deepening domestic financial intermediation, and pursuing trade liberalization. In each of these areas, crucial institutional building should be emphasized to assure the sustainability of policies.

Restoring growth momentum will also require giving renewed impetus to broader structural reforms. Emphasis must be placed on measures with longer-term growth payoffs, especially those encouraging the building of stronger institutions of governance. Improvements in the business environment and labor market reforms are also needed to raise investment and structural flexibility.

Fiscal Sustainability

Many countries in the region shared a common vulnerability in the 1990s—rising levels of public debt, weak financing structures, and a long history of debt crises. Although pre-crisis debt/GDP ratios in the range of 40–50 percent were not notably high by international standards, they concealed important weaknesses:

- debt ratios drifted up during the 1990s, even when economic conditions were good, owing to lack of immediate policy constraints and ambiguous criteria for determining sustainability (Figure ES.2);

- a lack of credibility led to reliance on dollar- or interest-linked debt, leaving debt stocks vulnerable to sharp jumps in the face of financial pressures and movements in real exchange rates;

- weak fiscal institutions impeded implementation of corrective measures; and

- government debt was also boosted by crisis support to financial institutions, realization of other contingent claims, and recognition of fiscal "skeletons."

Rising debt ratios were symptomatic of deeper weaknesses in fiscal systems:

- narrow revenue bases were combined with weak collection mechanisms and frequent tax amnesties (Argentina had averaged one amnesty per year since 1990);

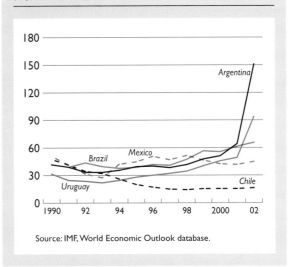

Figure ES2. Four Latin American Countries: Public Debt
(In percent of GDP)

Source: IMF, World Economic Outlook database.

- there were rigidities in current spending, including a large share of spending subject to earmarking and statutory floors, and generally inflexible arrangements with subnational levels of government; and

- weak fiscal institutions encouraged overreliance on ad hoc and temporary adjustment measures.

- These weaknesses increased the difficulty of undertaking fiscal consolidation. When such measures were taken, they often implied cuts in public infrastructure spending, increases in distortionary taxes, and compression of social spending (Table ES.4). These actions were detrimental to longer-term growth and popular support for reforms.

Table ES4. Selected Latin American Countries: Total Change in Public Infrastructure Spending, 1990 to 2000
(Percent of GDP)

Argentina	−3.6
Brazil	−2.7
Chile	1.6
Mexico	−2.1
Average for Latin America	−1.8

Sources: IMF, Fiscal Affairs Department; and International Finance Corporation.

Although countries have responded to the fiscal lessons of the 1990s at differing speeds and to varying degrees, many positive changes in fiscal policy are already under way and bearing fruit. The current cyclical upturn has afforded countries the opportunity to strengthen policies and has yielded stronger fiscal positions and room in budgets to provide additional support to the poor.

Thus, in the recent period, many countries have implemented important policy measures:

• A number of countries have increasingly sought to strengthen fiscal institutions by adopting fiscal rules and budget procedures as a means of ensuring fiscal discipline. For example, in Brazil, a series of reforms, including the Fiscal Responsibility Law approved in 2000, have improved fiscal transparency and encouraged fiscal consolidation.

• Countries are also taking a broader view of the fiscal situation so as to better measure and monitor the overall fiscal position, including the treatment of public/private investment projects. Moreover, the accounting treatment of public pensions has also improved, with several countries undertaking reforms to reduce the long-term fiscal burdens of aging populations.

• Countries are making progress in improving public-debt structures by moving toward longer-term, fixed-rate domestic debt that do not entail the types of vulnerabilities introduced particularly by foreign currency-denominated debt.

• Efforts are also under way in many Latin American countries to increase the flexibility of budget structures—by strengthening tax administration, reducing tax revenue earmarking, and curtailing the use of minimum spending floors—to eliminate the tendency for fiscal policy to be conducted on a procyclical basis.

Monetary and Exchange Rate Regimes

The majority of countries in the region achieved inflation control by adopting exchange rate-based stabilization plans. By 1992, only a handful of countries had exchange regimes that could be considered flexible. Stabilization programs yielded initial success: inflation came down quickly from high levels, while output expanded in response to a consumption boom.

Inflexible exchange rate systems, however, lacked an exit strategy. Although economic activity initially increased as a result of capital inflows, competitiveness was undermined over time by real exchange rate appreciation (Figure ES.3).

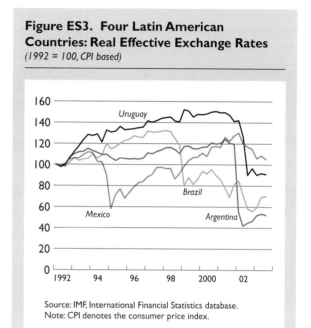

Figure ES3. Four Latin American Countries: Real Effective Exchange Rates
(1992 = 100, CPI based)

Source: IMF, International Financial Statistics database.
Note: CPI denotes the consumer price index.

To be sustainable, exchange rate-based stabilization programs needed support in the form of highly prudent fiscal policies, greater wage and price flexibility, and trade deepening. In practice, however, the adoption of such exchange rate regimes did not, in itself, discipline other policies, and inconsistencies arose. Corrective actions to the exchange rate became increasingly difficult to take as financial pressures intensified, leading to crises and forced exits from the exchange regimes.

Inflexible exchange rate regimes hampered the implementation of other aspects of reform plans. Associated capital inflows reduced fiscal discipline, allowed unsound financing of deficits, and fueled lending booms that led to banking crises. They also limited the scope for offsetting the contractionary impact of fiscal adjustments through monetary easing. The effects of trade liberalization on exports were suppressed by overvalued real exchange rates.

Some countries instead pursued monetary stabilization by adopting objectives for inflation while allowing greater exchange rate flexibility. These approaches were often supported by measures to increase central bank independence. In these cases, reductions in inflation tended to be steadier than under exchange rate-based plans, since resulting imbalances and policy inconsistencies were less pronounced and crisis-driven changes in the monetary regime were avoided.

Overall, there are many reasons to be optimistic about the region's transition to a new, low-inflation environment and the adapted policy frameworks for sustaining it.

- Many countries in the region have moved toward inflation-targeting frameworks. Combined with greater central bank independence and flexible exchange rate regimes, such frameworks have contributed to the credibility of low-inflation environments and have proven resilient in the face of turbulent external conditions, including contagion from neighboring countries.

- Inflation targeting is still evolving in Latin America, and there remain considerable challenges to ensuring that this approach becomes entrenched. For lasting success, it is important to have a well-established macroeconomic policy framework, policy instrument independence, and a sound and developed financial system.

- Latin American countries are making steady progress in putting in place these necessary conditions to support a full-fledged inflation-targeting framework. For example, there is continued movement toward new formal institutional frameworks that extend central bank independence and restrict or prohibit central bank financing of government deficits. Communications policies have also improved.

- Other key challenges for Latin American countries in implementing full-fledged inflation targeting include (i) the possible pressures to suspend inflation targets when growth is particularly weak; (ii) generally continued fiscal dominance; (iii) a high degree of sensitivity to exchange rate fluctuations, especially in conditions of high (spontaneous) dollarization, that could conflict with inflation-targeting objectives; and (iv) persisting vulnerabilities in many cases in financial systems.

Latin American Financial Systems and Financial Dollarization

Financial sector reforms in the early 1990s often focused on deregulation, privatization, and liberalizing foreign entry. Supporting prudential frameworks proved inadequate, however, since they were generally aimed at narrow definitions of balance-sheet matching and capital adequacy, as opposed to sound overall risk management.

Structural impediments to domestic financial deepening remained significant. They included heavy unremunerated reserve requirements, taxes on financial transactions, inadequate mechanisms for enforcing creditors' rights, and insufficient competition among financial intermediaries.

Regulatory forbearance, strong capital inflows, and weak risk-assessment mechanisms contributed to a series of banking crises from 1994 onward. Resolution of these crises often involved an increased concentration of bank assets in government securities. Subsequently, regulations have been tightened while credit to the private sector has remained stagnant.

Informal dollarization of banking systems rose during the 1990s in countries where macroeconomic policies lacked credibility (Table ES.1 and Table ES.5). Banks offset the immediate balance-sheet risk by lending in dollars, but borrowers generally lacked dollar income streams. Eventual exchange rate depreciation led to widespread loan defaults and a second series of banking crises. With bank soundness jeopardized, runs on dollar deposits could not be easily halted by central banks lacking sufficient foreign exchange reserves.

Full legal dollarization also entailed risks. In Ecuador, the adoption of this strategy has placed a heavy burden on maintaining fiscal policy discipline and taking steps to ensure a more flexible economic structure.

Latin America's experience since the early 1990s has demonstrated the importance of sound and resilient financial systems in reducing vulnerabilities and supporting sustained growth. Most Latin American countries are continuing their efforts to address the weaknesses in their financial system, revive and sustain credit flows, and create greater resilience to shocks:

- Most Latin American countries have continued to strengthen banking sector regulations and supervi-

Table ES5. Selected Latin American Countries: Foreign Exchange Deposits
(In percent of total deposits)

	1990	2001
Argentina	47	74
Chile	16	12
El Salvador	4	100
Guatemala	0	5
Honduras	2	33
Mexico	10	8
Nicaragua	40	71
Paraguay[1]	34	64
Peru	63	74
Uruguay[2]	89	92

Sources: Central bank statistical publications; and IMF staff estimates.
[1]For Paraguay, 1990 column refers to 1996 data.
[2]Loan ratio for Uruguay includes only lending to residents.

sion. In particular, loan classification and provisioning standards have been tightened; capital-adequacy levels have been raised; corrective-action frameworks are being introduced to ensure more rapid response to emerging problems; and the power and independence of financial regulators have been bolstered.

- It is also recognized that there needs to be greater reliance on market discipline to ensure prudent behavior, including by limiting coverage of deposit-insurance systems and improving financial transparency.

- For those countries where banking crises have erupted in recent years—for example, Argentina, Ecuador, and Uruguay—efforts must continue to rehabilitate or resolve failed banks.

- A broader range of initiatives is also needed and is under way to foster the expansion of efficient and long-term credit intermediation as well as to deepen capital markets.

- Dollarization has provided a means through which countries with low macroeconomic policy credibility are able to resist capital flight and hold savings within the domestic financial system. Highly dollarized countries are, however, subject to heightened liquidity and credit risks.

- Authorities in highly dollarized countries in Latin America have been addressing these risks by making efforts to achieve stronger macroeconomic policies so as to boost confidence in holding and transacting in the domestic currency. To address short-term risks of dollarization, some countries have built up international reserves and arranged lines of credit to be drawn on in times of stress. Also, some countries have amended prudential rules to reflect the risks associated with dollarization.

External Vulnerabilities

Although most Latin American economies liberalized trade in the late 1980s and early 1990s, the impact in terms of increasing openness was typically limited (see Figure ES.4):

- Tariff rates in the region declined substantially, but still-high tariffs and nontariff barriers and the need to liberalize trade in essential infrastructure services have meant that the region has made less progress than others in opening to trade.

- Increasing recourse to regional trade arrangements, including Mercosur, while encouraging intraregional trade, did not vigorously promote export growth outside of Latin America.

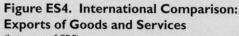

Figure ES4. International Comparison: Exports of Goods and Services
(In percent of GDP)

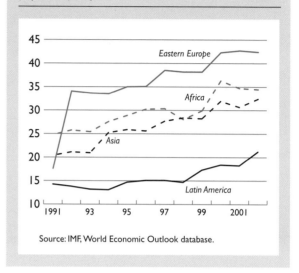

Source: IMF, World Economic Outlook database.

- Latin American countries continue to face barriers to export to industrial country markets, particularly for agricultural products.

- Little progress was made in strengthening trade institutions and infrastructure—weaknesses that have tended to hinder trade.

- The region's weak and volatile macroeconomic environment discouraged trade and investment, and inflexible nominal exchange rates and real exchange rate appreciation limited incentives for export diversification.

The main exceptions to this weak trade performance were Chile—which has opened its economy aggressively and achieved sound macroeconomic policies at an early stage—and Mexico, which has benefited from the North American Free Trade Agreement (NAFTA) and other free-trade agreements.

Although the trade share of most Latin American countries rose only slowly in the 1990s, capital flows surged. This resulted in ratios of foreign debt and debt-servicing payments to exports that were among the highest in the world. Debt-servicing payments rose as market confidence waned, but, with low export/GDP ratios, large depreciations in the real exchange rate were needed to achieve offsetting improvements in the trade balance. Yet such depreciations themselves raised interest payments (in dollars) relative to domestic incomes, leading to a vicious circle.

Prudential guidelines in developed markets did not encourage differentiation among emerging market borrowers according to risk. In addition, lenders tended to limit apparent risks by investing in short-term and/or foreign currency debt. Shifting these risks to borrowing governments did not reduce overall risk, however, but transformed it into (less visible) default risk. When the implications of this practice were belatedly recognized in markets, jumps in yield spreads fueled crises.

In recent years, considerable progress has been made by many Latin American countries in reducing the mismatch between low trade openness and high capital account openness. Their efforts have been centered on pursuing trade liberalization through multiple channels while building greater financial resilience.

- Latin American countries are actively participating in World Trade Organization (WTO) negotiations for a new development round; forging bilateral and regional agreements with the United States and the European Union; and continuing negotiations for the Free Trade Agreement of the Americas.

- Nonetheless, there remains considerable scope for Latin American countries to encourage trade opening—and to benefit thereby—by unilaterally easing their own restrictions, particularly with regard to tariff escalation, nontariff barriers, and restrictions on services trade.

- More broadly, continued emphasis on developing trade institutions is critically important for supporting trade growth and openness. Further development of transportation infrastructure—such as roads and ports—will help to alleviate bottlenecks in a number of countries.

Although volatile capital flows remain problematic for Latin America, progress continues to be made throughout the region in strengthening financial systems and underlying macroeconomic frameworks to create greater resilience to shocks.

- Many countries have taken steps to improve risk-management practices of financial institutions by adapting prudential regulations and improving supervision to conform with international best practices, and strengthening the broader institutional framework of the financial sector by improving accounting standards and auditing procedures.

- Adopting more flexible exchange rates in many Latin American countries has improved their flexibility in responding to external shocks.

Future Priorities and Role of IMF

In defining priorities for the future agenda, embracing institutional change is critical for the sus-

tainability of policies. Strengthening of institutions is needed to successfully implement both macroeconomic and structural policies. This is consistent with recent research that points to institutional factors outweighing factor accumulation in explaining cross-country differences in per capita income.

In the macroeconomic area, there are two key priorities:

- Many countries have recently adopted inflation targeting, which appears to be a promising means of conducting monetary policy in the region. It will be important, however, for policymakers to reinforce the underlying institutional framework for inflation targeting by supporting central bank independence and setting out clear performance objectives. In other countries that choose to continue with inflexible exchange rate systems, owing to individual circumstances, fiscal and structural policies need to be strong enough to absorb shocks and sustain these systems.

- Debt in many Latin American countries remains high and needs to be brought down and its composition shifted away from short-term, floating-rate, and foreign currency-linked debt. To enhance the credibility of sustained fiscal policy, it is critical to strengthen fiscal institutions and fiscal transparency, and improve government expenditure management and tax administration. As experience has taught, without broader institutional change, efforts to bring down debt levels in an enduring way will be unsuccessful. A strong political consensus is needed to move in this direction, however, especially because constitutional change may be necessary to implement many of the related reforms.

An agenda for broad-based structural reform—and, in particular, institutional reform—is needed to support macroeconomic policies. The priorities for the structural reform agenda include the following:

- Achieving sound and resilient financial systems in Latin America is a key element in reducing Latin America's vulnerability to crisis, reviving credit flows, and sustaining growth. There is continued need to improve financial sector regulation and supervision, and adopt measures to increase reliance on market mechanisms.

- Despite considerable efforts it made to liberalize trade in the 1990s, Latin America's trade opening proceeded relatively slowly. There is much scope to advance Latin America's trade openness through both domestic and international efforts. Internationally, the benefits of achieving multilateral liberalization through a successful Doha round cannot be overstated. Meanwhile, many countries in Latin America are improving their market access through bilateral trade agreements. At the same time, there is clearly room—domestically—for countries in the region to curtail continuing protectionist practices and improve the competitiveness of regional trade agreements. For these initiatives to bear fruit, however, Latin American countries must also address remaining problems with trade-related institutions and infrastructure—particularly customs administration and legal uncertainties.

- Labor market reforms were notably absent from the structural reform agendas of the 1990s. Reforms are needed to amend institutional arrangements, such as high severance costs and restrictions on temporary hiring, that act as barriers to entry and exit as well as to ensure the availability of efficient social safety nets and educational programs to reengage workers. Labor market flexibility is especially necessary to facilitate the kind of intersectoral mobility needed to enable countries to benefit fully from globalization.

- An improved and more strategic role of the state is essential. Corruption and weak governance in Latin America have tended to undermine market activity, with the resulting burden falling most heavily on the poor. Further efforts to confront these weaknesses and remove costly distortions in the regulatory and incentive structure would improve the investment climate, help attract new private investment, and create a firmer foundation for economic activity.

Moving forward in both areas—macroeconomic and structural—will require popular support. Such support will be promoted by providing social safety nets and reducing corruption. Forging a deeper political consensus will be a sine qua non for moving in this direction. The IMF and the other international financial institutions, together with the broader international community, can play key roles in helping develop such a consensus.

In the wake of recent financial crises, the IMF has strengthened its role in crisis resolution and prevention. Much progress has been made in this regard, especially in drawing lessons from the crises in emerging markets and expanding the tools of crisis prevention, especially improving transparency; developing a new framework of internationally agreed standards and codes for monetary, fiscal, and financial policies; and deepening IMF surveillance of key risks and vulnerabilities. Crisis resolution has been helped by the growing acceptance of collective-action clauses. These initiatives have catalyzed improved transparency across the region and helped lessen contagion risks.

There is room to do more. Increased emphasis on the IMF's surveillance role will help these new initiatives become entrenched. An intensified surveillance role should include casting "a fresh pair of eyes" over the substance of the dialogue with country authorities and ensuring that the program's timetable is carefully adhered to, especially for countries involved in prolonged programs.

Reducing the risk and incidence of crises is only part of the essential agenda. Similarly, the IMF, working in close coordination with the other international financial institutions, can further sharpen its focus on policies that will deliver faster growth, raise living standards, and reduce poverty. As indicated above, such a policy agenda needs to emphasize institutional change and reform, and broad country ownership of such an agenda will be increasingly important.

The IMF and the other international financial institutions will need to do more to nurture the adoption of such an agenda, through adapting conditionality and developing an outreach strategy. The IMF, working in close coordination with the World Bank and the Inter-American Development Bank (IADB), can play a larger role in developing the broader consensus that is needed. There is room to be more proactive in working with government at all levels, legislatures, and the private sector to explain the lessons the IMF has learned from experience and building stronger country ownership of policies. At the same time, the IMF needs to persist with its strengthened surveillance of vulnerabilities stemming from public debt, balance-sheet exposures, financial sector weaknesses, and exchange rate arrangements. Helping the region increase investments in public and private infrastructure within a strong framework of debt sustainability is also a priority.

In addition, the international community needs to reflect on establishing sufficient external incentives or anchors that could catalyze the process of domestic institutional building. Greater trade openness and development of international agreements (such as NAFTA) can directly help remove domestic impediments to reforms and boost institutional development.

I   Introduction

Latin America's economic prospects heralded new promise in the early 1990s, as ambitious programs were introduced to promote macroeconomic stability and market-based reforms. In the context of increasingly democratic political systems, the adoption of policies broadly consistent with the so-called Washington Consensus reflected a broad shift away from the interventionist and inward-looking policies followed in the past.[1] At the beginning of the 1990s, Latin America also benefited from a "fresh start" in the form of debt reduction through the Brady Plan. Together, these developments held out the promise that Latin America could overcome a history of default and embark on a high-growth path of the type seen in East Asia.

Although the specifics of the stabilization and reform programs differed importantly across countries, there were many important common elements. The programs were generally aimed at establishing macroeconomic discipline and centered on ending the inflationary financing of government deficits. To promote transparency and credibility, monetary policy was typically constrained by a commitment to a fixed exchange rate. Complementing stabilization policies were structural reforms that generally focused on increasing the role of market forces through privatization and deregulation, while economic openness was promoted through removal of currency restrictions and liberalization of trade and capital flows, including for foreign direct investment. Extensive restrictions on domestic financial systems were eased, and market access to foreign institutions was increased.

The region's economic performance in the first half of the 1990s appeared to validate many of the high initial expectations. Inflation came down dramatically. With the debt overhang resolved and reforms under way, private capital inflows resumed. In conjunction with more liberalized domestic financial markets, domestic spending rose and per capita output growth accelerated to an average of almost 2½ percent per year during 1990–95, after contracting through the 1980s. Social indicators, such as life expectancy, infant mortality, and poverty, registered visible improvements.

Signs of fragilities became evident, however, with Mexico's "tequila" crisis in 1994–95 and contagion to the other major economies in the region. Subsequently, during the latter part of the 1990s, in the wake of the Asian and Russian crises, investor appetite for global risk declined; and the consequent sudden reversals of capital inflows accentuated inherent vulnerabilities in many Latin American economies. Economic and financial crises recurred in Brazil and Ecuador (1999), Argentina (2001), and Brazil and Uruguay (2002); and other countries in the region also came under pressure. Real per capita GDP contracted by more than 1 percent, on average, during 1997–2002; and the improvement in social indicators came to a halt in many countries, although, encouragingly, Chile and Mexico were generally able to resist these pressures and maintain positive growth.

In view of these setbacks, important questions have been raised about why the reform programs in Latin America did not yield larger and more lasting benefits. This study assesses the experience with economic reform programs in Latin America since the early 1990s and draws lessons for future policy priorities. In particular, the paper identifies the achievements and disappointments of the period; seeks to better understand the explanatory roles of both external factors and domestic policies (especially macroeconomic policies); points to the responses of the region to the experience of the 1990s; and assesses key future challenges, including those for the IMF and the international community. It emphasizes the experiences of the larger emerging market countries, such as Argentina, Brazil, Chile, and Mexico, given their economic importance inside and outside the region, while also drawing on the experiences of a wider range of countries. It surveys the literature, reviews the empirical evidence, and aims to

---

[1]The reform policies included fiscal discipline, reordering public expenditure toward basic health and education, tax reform, market-determined interest rates, a competitive exchange rate, trade liberalization, openness to foreign direct investment, privatization, deregulation, and improved property rights. See Williamson (1990).

bring together the results of other studies undertaken inside the IMF.

There was substantial and prolonged IMF and other international financial institution involvement in the region during this period, including through financial arrangements and surveillance. This relationship, however, is not a main aim of this study, enabling it to remain focused on the policy outcomes, explanatory factors, and lessons for setting future priorities. Separate assessments of the IMF's relationship with countries in the region are being made by the IMF's Independent Evaluation Office (IEO) and researchers outside the IMF.[2] Such an assessment requires a different methodology from that followed in this paper to, for example, analyze to what extent policies followed were influenced by IMF involvement, and to compare actual outcomes with those under a counterfactual scenario assuming no relationship with the IMF.

This study finds that stabilization and structural reforms did boost growth, although the effects were smaller and less long-lived than originally hoped. One frequent weakness of reform plans was that the initiatives were not coordinated in a mutually reinforcing way—for instance, by strengthening financial supervision while liberalizing financial regulations or enhancing regulatory oversight while privatizing public enterprises. Another was that reforms were sometimes unbalanced, in that initiatives in some key areas, such as increasing flexibility in labor markets, were limited compared with those that were easier to implement, such as privatization and deregulation. On the macroeconomic side, exchange rate-based anchors were not supported by fiscal prudence. As a result, the initial benefits that resulted from stabilization and structural reform policies were eroded later in the decade by financial

instability. In retrospect, it is clear that macroeconomic policies did not sufficiently crisis-proof these economies in the face of challenging internal and external environments.

This study begins by taking stock of the main outcomes of the stabilization and reform programs and reviews the explanatory factors. Subsequent chapters seek to understand these mixed results from a macroeconomic perspective, to identify lessons from this experience, and to assess the region's responses to these lessons and future challenges. Although a broad range of economic, political, social, and institutional influences have had an impact, this study concentrates on the key policy areas that lay at the heart of stabilization and reform programs—notably, fiscal, monetary, financial, and trade policies. The final section draws broad lessons and points to future challenges, including those for the IMF and the other international financial institutions.

References

Hutchison, M., and I. Noy, 2004, "Macroeconomic Effects of IMF-Sponsored Programs in Latin America: Output Costs, Program Recidivism and the Vicious Cycle of Failed Stabilizations," forthcoming in the *Journal of International Money and Finance.*

International Monetary Fund, Independent Evaluation Office, 2002, *Evaluation of Prolonged Use of IMF Resources* (Washington: International Monetary Fund). Also available on the Web at *http://www.imf.org/external/np/ieo/2002/pu/#intro.*

———, 2003, *The IMF and Recent Capital Account Crises: Indonesia, Korea, and Brazil* (Washington: International Monetary Fund).

———, 2004, *Report on the Evaluation of the Role of the IMF in Argentina, 1991–2001* (Washington: International Monetary Fund).

Mussa, Michael, 2002, *Argentina and the Fund: From Triumph to Tragedy* (Washington: Institute for International Economics).

Williamson, John, 1990, "What Does Washington Mean by Policy Reform?" in *Latin American Adjustment: How Much Has Happened?* ed. by John Williamson (Washington: Institute for International Economics).

---

[2]There is a growing literature published, both within and outside the IMF, that analyzes the economic impact of IMF programs. Prominent examples of this literature with particular relevance to the Latin American experience include Hutchison and Noy (2004); IMF, Independent Evaluation Office (2002, 2003, 2004); IMF (2003); and Mussa (2002).

II Taking Stock

Starting in the late 1980s, most Latin American countries began introducing market-based structural reforms in a range of areas, especially international trade, the financial sector, the tax system, and state enterprises. These policies were aimed at increasing the role of market forces, after years of government intervention, and promoting greater integration with the global economy. Structural reforms were combined with measures aimed at establishing financial and macroeconomic stability, primarily by disciplining monetary policy and emphasizing fiscal sustainability.

This section reviews the main outcomes of the stabilization and structural reform programs and assesses the factors, both external and internal, that contributed to these results. To summarize, although reform programs were instrumental in arresting high inflation and sustaining inflation at a low level, and providing an initial boost to growth, the 1990s were another period of considerable disappointment for the region. The main economic and social outcomes eventually fell well short of expectations in terms of permanently boosting growth and reducing poverty and income inequality. External factors can partially explain this outturn, particularly in the late 1990s. Their impact was magnified, however, as these shocks interacted with domestic rigidities and macroeconomic vulnerabilities, leading to renewed bouts of financial instability. The structural aspects of reform programs yielded up-front benefits but were not comprehensive and enduring enough to catalyze sustained growth. In particular, the institutional framework for conducting market-based activity was generally neglected.

Main Economic and Social Outcomes

Inflation

Inflation control was the most notable success of the stabilization and reform programs of the 1990s, in stark contrast to Latin America's long history of high inflation and sporadic bouts of hyperinflation. At the end of the 1980s, regional inflation hit nearly 500 percent, with even higher peak rates in Brazil and Argentina (Figure 2.1). Under these conditions, the economic, social, and political costs of uncontrolled inflation became starkly evident. High and volatile inflation undermined macroeconomic stability and growth, and exacerbated income inequality and poverty. Financial intermediation was disrupted; resources were increasingly devoted to unproductive activities; relative prices became distorted; and confidence in longer-term economic prospects and the direction of policies was undermined.

Against this background, a strong public consensus emerged that inflation should be reduced to low levels. Most Latin American countries, especially those with past records of hyperinflation, initially elected to disinflate through exchange rate-based stabilization plans.[3] Although the choice of firmness of the exchange rate arrangement varied across countries, ranging from Argentina's adoption of a currency board under its convertibility plan to crawling pegs in countries such as Brazil and Mexico, the general strategy yielded impressive reductions in inflation. Countries that opted for more flexible strategies with multiple intermediate objectives—for example, the approach taken in Chile—tended to experience more gradual reductions in inflation; generally, these countries had lower initial rates of inflation and benefited from the retention of greater policy flexibility.

By the end of the 1990s, only two Latin American countries had inflation rates of more than 10 percent, and the regional average had dropped to well below 10 percent. The importance of this achievement should not be underestimated. Gains in inflation control have proved to be enduring, even when exchange rate-based stabilization plans ultimately became unsustainable. Even though the transition to more flexible monetary arrangements, notably inflation targeting in the context of floating exchange rate systems, was accompanied by initial financial instability and sharp exchange rate depreciations, the in-

---

[3]Given that monetary anchors had failed to control inflation, exchange rates were viewed as a more effective anchor that would introduce credibility to policy that the central bank lacked under a discretionary framework. These issues are discussed in more detail in Section IV.

Figure 2.1. Selected Latin American Countries: Inflation Performance
(Annual percentage change in consumer price index)

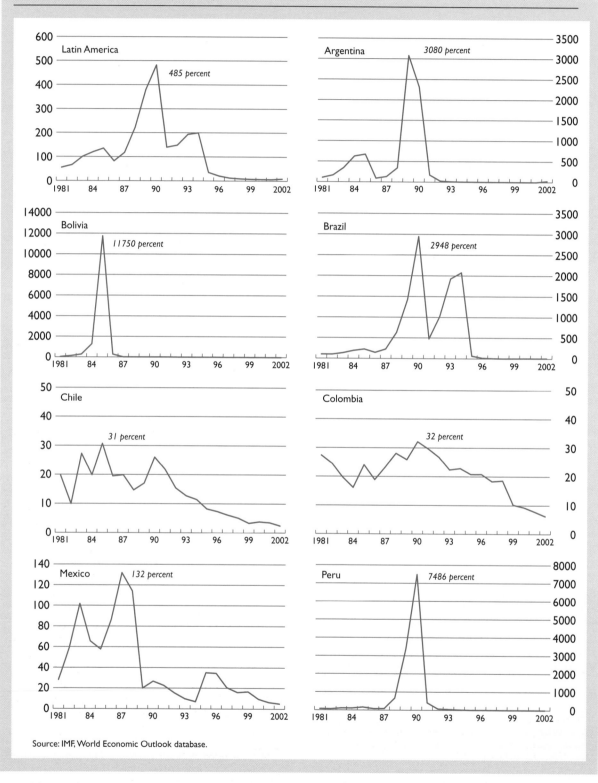

Source: IMF, World Economic Outlook database.

Table 2.1. International Comparison: Growth in Real Per Capita GDP
(Annual percent change)

	1981–90	1991–97	1998–2003
Latin America	−0.6	2.5	−0.1
Industrial countries	2.5	1.4	1.8
Other developing countries	1.9	2.6	3.3
Asia	4.8	6.5	4.8
Other Asia[1]	2.8	4.1	1.1
Eastern and Central Asia Europe	1.2	0.7	2.6
Middle East	−1.3	1.3	1.8
Sub-Saharan Africa	−0.6	−0.5	0.7

Source: IMF, World Economic Outlook database.
[1]Excluding China and India.

creased credibility of commitments to low inflation reduced the pass-through of these shocks. For example, the financial crises in Mexico (1994–95), Brazil (1999 and 2002), and Argentina (2002) caused only transitory increases in inflation of a magnitude much smaller than the spikes observed in the 1980s.[4]

Economic Growth

A key objective of the stabilization and structural reforms of the 1990s was to permanently boost growth following the dismal performance in the previous decade (Table 2.1). During the 1980s, per capita GDP fell at an average annual rate of about ½ of 1 percent, with nearly all Latin American countries experiencing negative growth—although Chile and Colombia were notable exceptions.[5]

Following the reforms implemented in the late 1980s and early 1990s, annual real per capita GDP growth in the region initially picked up to 2½ percent, on average, during 1991–97. This improvement reinforced confidence in the payoff to reforms, even though growth in this period still fell well short of the achievements of some other fast-growing regions, particularly Asia, as well as of Latin America's own performance in the 1960s and 1970s.

Aggregate per capita income growth rates for the region masked considerable cross-country variation, however (Figure 2.2). The strongest performances were seen in those countries that aggressively pursued reform agendas early on. Indeed, annual per capita income growth for 1990–97 averaged more than 6 percent in Chile, nearly 5 percent in Argentina, and more than 3 percent in Peru.

In the event, Latin America's economic revival was short-lived. By the late 1990s, growth in the region began to deteriorate. Beginning with the worldwide contagion from the Asian and Russian crises in 1997–98, financial strains intensified in the region, and real per capita GDP stagnated during 1998–2003. Again, there was considerable variation across countries. For example, incomes contracted sharply in Argentina, Uruguay, and Venezuela, and more moderately in Colombia and Ecuador, while staying roughly flat in Brazil, Bolivia, and Peru (Table 2.2). The only countries experiencing positive per capita income growth over this period were Chile and Mexico—in Mexico's case, this partly reflected the transformation of its economy associated with the North American Free Trade Agreement (NAFTA) and the benefits resulting from strong U.S. growth in the late 1990s.

Viewed relative to a longer period, Latin America's growth performance over the past two decades is somewhat disappointing. Essentially, since the region's last period of rapid growth in the 1960s and 1970s, there has been minimal change in per capita GDP (Figure 2.3). The fastest-growing country—Chile—has been able to raise its per capita income at an average annual rate of 3.1 percent, making it a star performer in the region but still falling well below rates seen in the East Asian countries. Consequently, countries in the region have generally not been able to close the relative income gap with advanced economies (Figure 2.4).[6]

---

[4]There is emerging evidence that the pass-through of exchange rate depreciations to inflation has been falling in Latin America. See, for example, Carstens and Werner (1999), Mihaljek and Klau (2001), and Belaisch (2003).

[5]For a discussion of the factors that contributed to the fall in growth during the 1980s, see Loayza, Fajnzylber, and Calderón (2003).

---

[6]A recent report by Brazil's Ministry of Finance estimated that per capita income in Brazil is currently just as far from the North American level as it was in 1960. See Brazil, Ministry of Finance (2003).

Figure 2.2. Selected Latin American Countries: Growth Performance
(Annual percentage change in per capita real GDP)

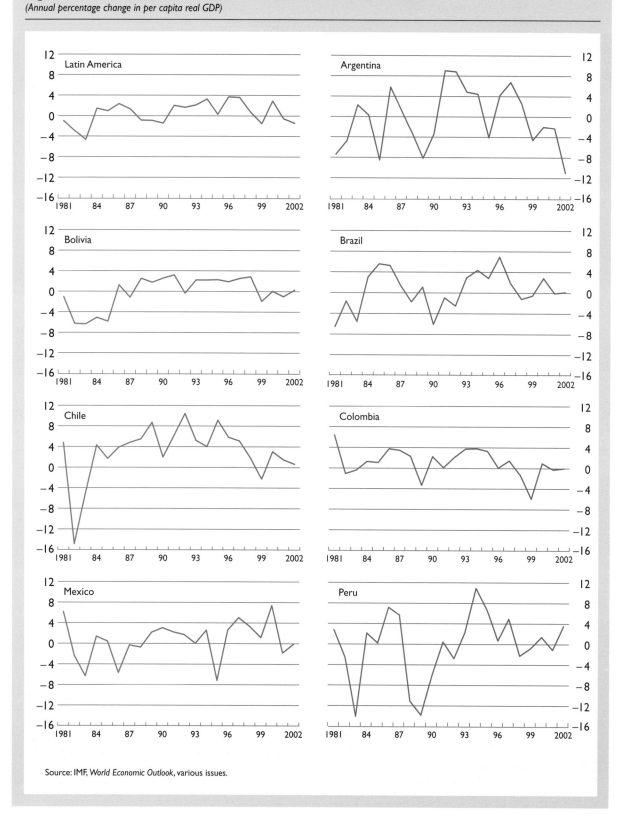

Source: IMF, *World Economic Outlook*, various issues.

Table 2.2. Real Per Capita GDP, 1998–2003[1]
(Average annual percent change)

Latin America	–0.1
Argentina	–2.6
Bolivia	0.1
Brazil	0.0
Chile	1.1
Colombia	–0.9
Ecuador	–0.3
Mexico	1.3
Peru	0.3
Uruguay	–2.7
Venezuela	–4.9

Source: IMF, World Economic Outlook database.
[1]Data for 2003 are estimates.

Figure 2.3. Latin America: Real GDP
(Annual average growth, in percent)

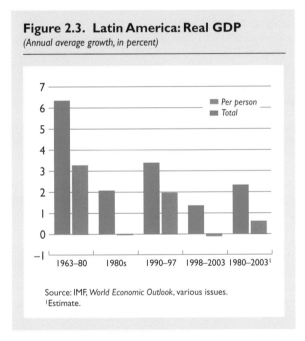

Source: IMF, *World Economic Outlook*, various issues.
[1]Estimate.

Figure 2.4. Selected Latin American and Asian Countries: Per Capita Incomes Compared with the United States, 1950–2000
(Percent)

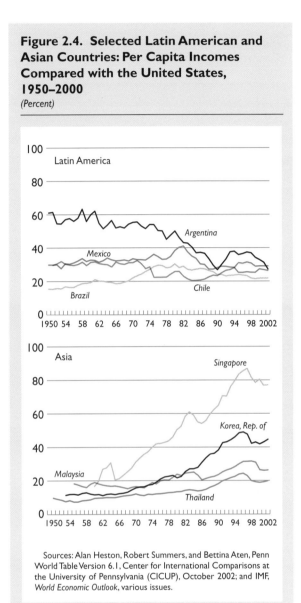

Sources: Alan Heston, Robert Summers, and Bettina Aten, Penn World Table Version 6.1, Center for International Comparisons at the University of Pennsylvania (CICUP), October 2002; and IMF, *World Economic Outlook*, various issues.

With slower GDP growth in the latter part of the 1990s, employment also suffered, particularly for wage earners.[7] The quality of new jobs deteriorated, with many concentrated in microenterprises or self-employment at relatively low wages.[8] The share of the informal sector—defined as employment without access to social benefits or unemployment protection—rose to around 50 percent of total employment in Latin America.[9] As explained in what follows,

rigidities in the tax framework in many countries (especially distortionary payroll taxes), combined with inflexible labor market policies, contributed to the rise of informal employment, with adverse feedback effects on government revenues and pension systems.

In addition to weak growth, a continuing feature of Latin American economic performance has been high macroeconomic—especially output—volatility associated with recurrent crises (Figures 2.5 and 2.6). For example, in Ecuador and Mexico, real GDP fell by

---

[7]See Stallings and Peres (2000).

[8]See Stallings and Peres (2000) and Saavendra (2003).

[9]An even higher proportion is engaged outside the formal sector in Brazil, where the share of informal employment has steadily

increased over the past decade, with negative effects on productivity and real wages. See Brazil, Ministry of Finance (2003).

Figure 2.5. Selected Latin American Countries: Output Volatility
(Standard deviation of annual percentage change)

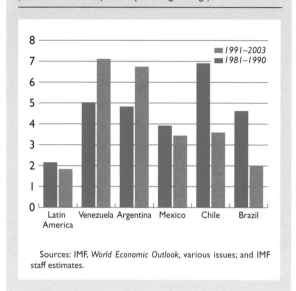

Sources: IMF, *World Economic Outlook*, various issues; and IMF staff estimates.

Figure 2.6. Selected Latin American Countries: Consequences of Crisis for Real GDP Growth[1]
(Annual percentage change)

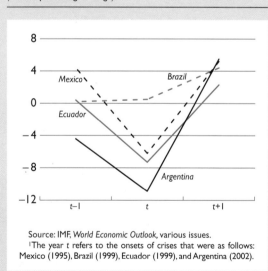

Source: IMF, *World Economic Outlook*, various issues.
[1]The year *t* refers to the onsets of crises that were as follows: Mexico (1995), Brazil (1999), Ecuador (1999), and Argentina (2002).

7¼ and 6¼ percent, respectively, in the first year of their crises; in Argentina, output declined by more than 11 percent in 2002. Over this period, Brazil was the only country in the region that did not experience a sharp drop in output in the wake of its financial

crises (in 1999 and 2002), although its growth rate dropped close to zero in both episodes.[10] Where initial output losses were steep, it should also be noted that subsequent recoveries were relatively rapid and strong, certainly in comparison with the region's experience in the late 1970s and early 1980s.

Imbalances between the openness of the trade and capital accounts have contributed to output volatility. Improvements in the trade balance following exchange rate depreciations could only partially offset the collapse in domestic demand during crisis periods, given limited trade openness. Generally, the turnarounds experienced in net exports largely reflected import compression as opposed to higher exports (Table 2.3). For example, Mexico's import volumes dropped by 26 percent in 1995, while export volumes rose by less than half as much. Over time, exchange rate effects became more important, as evidenced by surges in export volumes in most countries in the year following the crisis. The limited immediate buffer provided by changes in trade flows underscored the vulnerabilities created by the surge in capital flows, relative to trade flows, in the region in the 1990s.

Poverty and Income Inequality

Despite the enduring reductions in inflation since the early 1990s, the region has generally not been able to secure improvements in poverty and income inequality, fueling discontent with the reform process. Although poverty rates initially declined from their peaks at the beginning of the decade following the debt crises of the 1980s, progress was not sustained, especially in the context of stalled growth and financial crises in the latter part of the 1990s.[11] By 2003, about 44 percent of households in Latin America fell below the poverty line, and almost 20 percent were in extreme poverty (Table 2.4). In absolute terms, the number of poor grew by about 14 million over the decade to reach 214 million in 2002.[12]

---

[10]Kochhar, Lane, and Savastano (2003) survey the crisis experiences in Ecuador (1999), Mexico (1995), Brazil (1999), Indonesia (1998), Thailand (1998), Malaysia (1998), the Republic of Korea (1998), Russia (1998), and the Philippines (1998). Almost all were characterized by a sharp drop in output in the first year, led by a collapse in domestic demand.

[11]Poverty statistics vary considerably, depending upon the underlying methodology used. See Székely, Lustig, Cumpa, and Mejia-Guerra (2000) for a discussion. In this section, poverty data are based on those compiled in ECLAC (2002). For a discussion of poverty trends, see ECLAC (2002). Morley (2001) and ECLAC (1997) provide various explanations for the persistence of poverty in the region.

[12]World Bank data, which define poverty as those people living on less than $1 per day, show similar poverty trends. Based on this alternative definition, the poverty rate in Latin America edged

Table 2.3. Consequences of Crisis: Current Account Adjustment

Country	Year t	Change in Current Account (percent of GDP)		Export Volume Growth (percent)		Import Volume Growth (percent)	
		t	$t+1$	t	$t+1$	t	$t+1$
Ecuador	1999	17.5	−1.1	0.2	−5.3	−45.7	14.3
Mexico	1995	6.5	−0.2	12.1	21.0	−26.4	24.7
Brazil	1999	−0.5	0.6	5.8	11.5	−10.7	12.1
Brazil	2002	2.9	2.5	7.9	15.7	−12.3	−3.7

Sources: Kochhar and others (2003); and IMF staff estimates.

Table 2.4. Latin America: Incidence of Poverty[1]
(Percent of population)

	1990	2000	2001	2002	2003
Poverty	48.3	42.4	43.1	44.0	44.4
Extreme poverty	22.5	18.1	18.5	19.4	20.0

Source: United Nations, Economic Commision for Latin America and the Caribbean (ECLAC).

[1]Data for 2003 are estimates. Poverty rates are calculated using the cost-of-basic-needs method, which establishes a poverty line based on the cost of a basic food basket. For details, see ECLAC (2001).

Aggregate poverty rates also mask considerable variation across and within countries (Figure 2.7). In general, more rapid growth was associated with greater success in improving indicators of human development (Figure 2.8). But social policies also played a role. For example, during the 1990s, the poverty rate declined by more than 10 percentage points in Brazil and Chile as social spending was raised; education indicators improved; and new, targeted antipoverty programs were introduced. In contrast, the poverty rate rose by 9 percentage points in Venezuela and changed little in Ecuador, Colombia, Guatemala, Honduras, Nicaragua, and Paraguay—all countries where poverty rates remain in excess of 60 percent.[13] Moreover, within

countries, poverty is particularly high among indigenous people, especially in Bolivia, Guatemala, and Peru. Although indigenous people represent about 8 percent of the population in Latin America, they make up 25 percent of those living in extreme poverty.

Income inequality in Latin America remains extremely high by international standards, representing a serious social problem.[14] During the 1990s, the average Gini coefficient was 0.52 in Latin America, compared with 0.34 in member countries of the Organization for Economic Cooperation and Development (OECD), 0.33 in Eastern Europe, and 0.41 in Asia.[15] Estimates suggest that inequality trended up-

down from 11.3 percent of the population in 1990 to 9.5 percent in 2001, the most recent year for which data are available. In absolute terms, over the same period, the number of people living in poverty rose by about 500,000 people to 49.8 million. For a discussion of World Bank methodology and data, see World Bank (2003c and 2001).

[13]Poverty rates increased sharply in both Argentina and Uruguay in 2001–2002 following financial crises. ECLAC (2003) estimates that poverty in Argentina doubled to 45 percent in 2002 from its 1999 level. Similarly, in Uruguay, poverty is estimated to

have increased to 15 percent from about 9 percent in 1999. In Colombia, the impact of higher social expenditures was offset by displacements caused by the ongoing internal conflict.

[14]Deininger and Squire (1996); see also Morley (2001). Empirical evidence suggests that the dominant factor in explaining differences in inequality is the level of education. See Menezes-Filho (2001).

[15]See World Bank (2003b), Deininger and Squire (1996), and Morley (2001). The Gini coefficient (which ranges from 0 to 1) measures inequality; the higher the coefficient, the higher the level of inequality.

Figure 2.7. Latin America: Incidence of Poverty and Extreme Poverty[1]
(In percent of population)

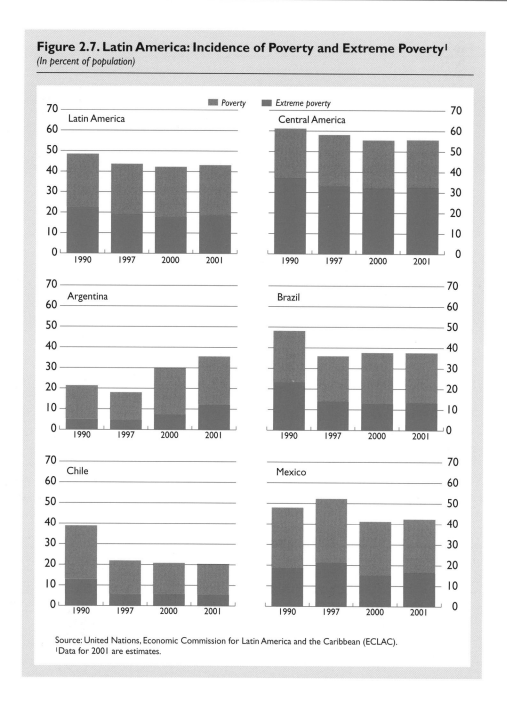

Source: United Nations, Economic Commission for Latin America and the Caribbean (ECLAC).
[1]Data for 2001 are estimates.

ward over the 1990s, although at a slower rate, with the greatest increases occurring in Argentina and Bolivia.[16] Although inequality cuts across all groups, recent evidence by the World Bank points to particularly marked differences according to race and eth-

nicity. The situation in Brazil has been starkly reported by the Ministry of Finance, which notes that income inequality has not appreciably improved over the past 30 years, and that the richest 10 percent of individuals account for 44 percent, whereas the poorest 10 percent account for only 1 percent, of the country's income.[17]

[16]Székely (2001) estimates income inequality trends based on regression estimates for each country, where the dependent variable is the Gini coefficient and the independent variable is a time trend.

[17]Brazil, Ministry of Finance (2003).

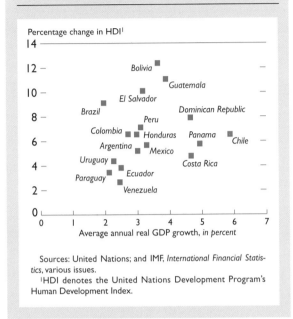

Figure 2.8. Latin America: Economic Growth and Poverty Reduction, 1990–2001

Percentage change in HDI[1]

Average annual real GDP growth, *in percent*

Sources: United Nations; and IMF, *International Financial Statistics*, various issues.
[1]HDI denotes the United Nations Development Program's Human Development Index.

Pervasive inequality in Latin America has had negative consequences for the political economy of the region.[18] Evidence suggests that inequality leads to greater violence and weak institutions, and hampers a country's ability to respond to economic shocks.[19] In addition, higher income inequality has made it more difficult to reduce poverty for a given rate of economic growth.

As well as lowering overall output, macroeconomic volatility may have had adverse effects on income and wealth inequality in the region, as the poor have typically been less able to adapt to economic shocks (Pfeffermann (2002)). In addition, Lustig (1995) argues that economic turmoil forces the poor to sell land or other assets to finance their children's education, undermining their ability to generate income. Lustig and Arias (2000) provide evidence that crises have tended to increase poverty, with the incidence remaining higher even after the crisis has passed. In addition to their obvious social costs, crises indirectly jeopardized the sustainability of reform programs by undermining popular support for them.

---

[18]For a detailed discussion, see World Bank (2003b).

[19]Evidence on the effect of inequality on growth is mixed. The studies surveyed in Benabou (1996) and Perotti (1996) suggested that higher inequality tended to reduce future growth, but Forbes (2003) finds that this result is reversed when different measures of inequality are used on panel data.

Explaining the Outcomes

External Shocks and Domestic Vulnerabilities

Why did the eventual results of stabilization and structural reform policies fail to match the high expectations of the early 1990s? The external environment played a significant role, especially as Latin American countries generally remained vulnerable to the volatilities that stemmed from the economic cycle in industrial countries and shifts in sentiment toward emerging market financing.[20] There is broad consensus that these global factors, combined with domestic vulnerabilities, led to a degree of volatility in capital flows that was the single most important factor determining outcomes.[21]

Economic activity in the industrial countries, notably the United States, affected Latin America through its impact on trade and capital flows. The evidence strongly suggests that the effects on capital flows overwhelmed the trade impact, both during upswings and downturns, reflecting the region's capital market opening in a context of still-low export-to-GDP ratios.[22] Thus, cyclical slowdown and monetary easing in the industrial countries during 1989–93 enabled the acceleration of capital flows to fast-growing emerging markets in the first half of the 1990s, dominating any negative impact on the region's exports (Figure 2.9). Later in the 1990s, the dominant external influences were upward pressure on interest rates, as activity strengthened in industrial countries, compounded by contagion from emerging market crises in Asia and Russia during 1997–98, which weakened the confidence of global investors.

With external financing having played an important role in fueling Latin American growth in the early 1990s, and a lack of progress in deepening domestic financial markets, these economies were highly vulnerable to shifts in global market sentiment. This was particularly the case for countries that had adopted rigid exchange rate systems while, at the same time, accumulating significant short-term external debt. Together, these conditions led to an environment that was prone to a cascading loss of market confidence.

The succession of emerging market crises is identified in Figure 2.10. The first significant disturbance

---

[20]The analysis early in the decade of Calvo, Leiderman, and Reinhart (1992) presaged many of the subsequent difficulties with external shocks and capital flows to the region.

[21]See Calvo and Reinhart (1999).

[22]Stallings and Peres (2000) provide evidence that economic growth in the region is more closely linked with capital inflows than with trade flows. Fernandez-Arias and Panizza (2001) find that an increase in private net capital flows of 1 percentage point of GDP boosts growth by almost ½ of 1 percentage point.

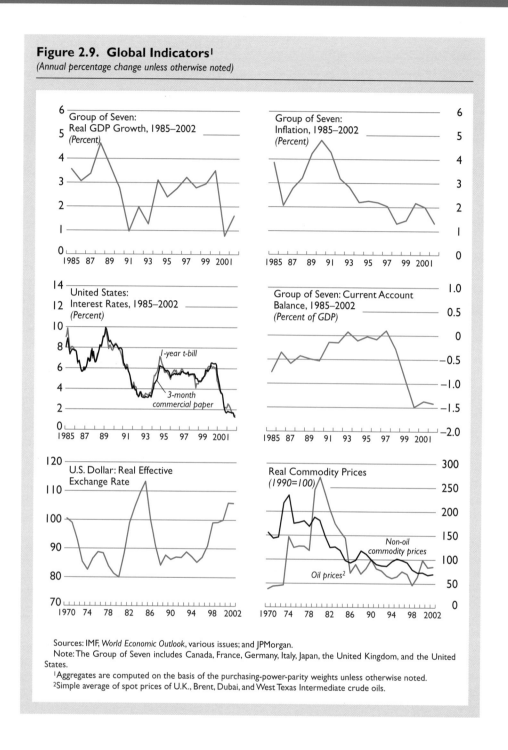

Figure 2.9. Global Indicators[1]
(Annual percentage change unless otherwise noted)

Sources: IMF, *World Economic Outlook*, various issues; and JPMorgan.
Note: The Group of Seven includes Canada, France, Germany, Italy, Japan, the United Kingdom, and the United States.
[1]Aggregates are computed on the basis of the purchasing-power-parity weights unless otherwise noted.
[2]Simple average of spot prices of U.K., Brent, Dubai, and West Texas Intermediate crude oils.

in emerging markets in the 1990s was the Mexican peso crisis in late 1994. In this instance, the underlying causes reflected both a deterioration in the external environment, particularly rising U.S. interest rates, and domestic factors, including political shocks, exchange rate overvaluation, financial sector fragilities in a context of a large external financing need, and a highly vulnerable structure of financing.

As a result, the broader impact on other emerging markets was transitory, and global yield spreads quickly returned to the low levels observed before the Mexican crisis (Figure 2.11).[23] Indeed, the re-

[23]Immediate contagion from Mexico was experienced by Argentina, whose fixed exchange rate regime was tested, and successfully defended, in April 1995.

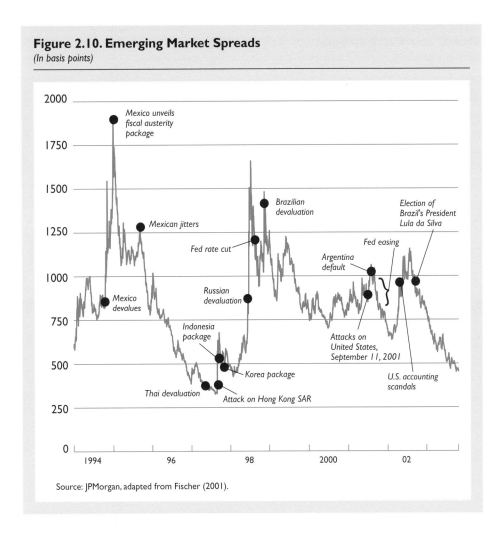

Figure 2.10. Emerging Market Spreads
(In basis points)

Mexico unveils fiscal austerity package

Mexican jitters

Brazilian devaluation

Election of Brazil's President Lula da Silva

Fed rate cut

Fed easing

Argentina default

Mexico devalues

Russian devaluation

Indonesia package

Attacks on United States, September 11, 2001

Korea package

Thai devaluation

Attack on Hong Kong SAR

U.S. accounting scandals

Source: JPMorgan, adapted from Fischer (2001).

silence of other markets with respect to the Mexican crisis tended, if anything, to reinforce confidence in the strength of their fundamentals, leading to further capital inflows through 1996.

The onset of the Asian crisis in mid-1997, however, had a much more pervasive impact on emerging market financing. In particular, it highlighted the vulnerabilities of economies that appeared to have relatively sound fundamentals to shifts in market sentiment when external liabilities were significant and exchange rate regimes were inflexible. The Russian debt default in August 1998, followed by the Long-Term Capital Management (LTCM) crisis, further underscored these vulnerabilities. Yield spreads in emerging markets jumped, especially at longer maturities, prompting borrowers to shift into increasingly short-term debt as emerging market financing virtually dried up during this period.

Although all countries in Latin America were affected by these changes in external conditions, countries with stronger policy fundamentals and flexibility resisted the strains better. Chile, for example, had

significantly reduced external debt during the 1990s, creating fiscal room for maneuver while moving to an increasingly flexible exchange rate regime. Even though Chile's growth in the late 1990s was affected by higher global interest rates and spillovers from elsewhere in the region, a financial crisis was avoided, and fiscal and monetary policies remained on track.[24] Other countries with weaker domestic policies and greater vulnerabilities, however, suffered a series of crises, notably Brazil (1999 and 2002), Ecuador (1999), Argentina (2001), Uruguay and Paraguay (2002), and Venezuela (2003).

Indeed, perhaps the most vexing issue since the early 1990s has been the slow progress of most Latin American countries in establishing greater financial resiliency and sufficient macroeconomic policy flex-

[24]Nevertheless, there was also a notable slowdown in Chile's total factor productivity growth over this period. Although there is not yet a consensus on the sources of this slowdown, it appears to have been at least partly due to a fading of the effects of structural reforms, for instance in education (Beyer and Vergara, 2002).

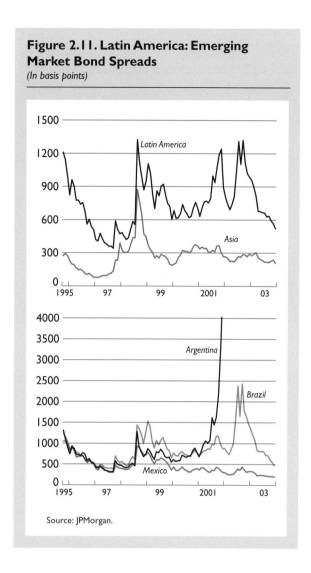

Figure 2.11. Latin America: Emerging Market Bond Spreads

(In basis points)

Source: JPMorgan.

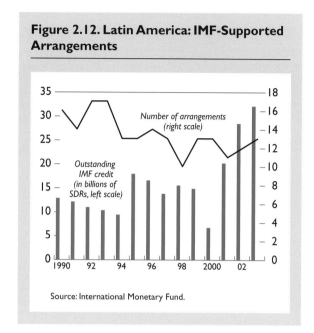

Figure 2.12. Latin America: IMF-Supported Arrangements

Source: International Monetary Fund.

crisis in the region. Most importantly, dependence on foreign capital inflows created growing balance-sheet mismatches in the public and private sectors, as foreign currency-denominated debt accumulated, leaving countries exposed to shifts in global market sentiment. Shocks that destabilized the exchange rate then undermined financial stability, creating a vicious circle of feedback effects that magnified the impact on growth. The health of domestic financial systems closely mirrored the boom-bust cycles of capital flows, compounding macroeconomic volatility. After a period of rapid growth in the early 1990s, credit generally collapsed after the mid-1990s, with only Chile being able to maintain a more even pattern of credit growth.

Absorbing external shocks would have required a much stronger fiscal policy and institutional framework than most countries in the region—other than Chile—had developed. Instead, with a tendency toward procyclical fiscal behavior in Latin America, fiscal policy was an additional source of—rather than a solution to—macroeconomic volatility.[26] Thus, government spending generally increased in response to a pickup in growth and declined when financing sources dried up.

ibility to cushion the impact of economic shocks, particularly from external sources. In these circumstances, the recurrence of macroeconomic volatility and financial stress was inevitable, perpetuating reliance on IMF and other international official financing support (Figure 2.12 and Table 2.5).[25] These episodes of recurring financial volatility disrupted growth, exacerbated poverty, and contributed to "reform fatigue" in several cases.

Several domestic vulnerabilities contributed to the recurrence of macroeconomic stability and financial

---

[25]Not all programs were framed in a crisis context, however. It should be noted that a number of arrangements with the IMF were precautionary in nature, in the sense that these countries did not expect to use IMF resources. The Poverty Reduction and Growth Facility (PRGF) programs were in support of poverty reduction and growth agendas, and were not necessarily responses to financial crises.

---

[26]The underlying problem was the lack of fiscal restraint when economic conditions were favorable, which, in turn, led to debt accumulation. When economic conditions deteriorated and market access disappeared, the only options were fiscal restraint or a return to the reliance on inflationary financing of fiscal deficits seen during the 1980s.

Table 2.5. IMF Arrangements in Latin America, 1989–2004[1]

	Type of IMF Program	Beginning Date	Expiration Date	Amount Agreed (In percent of quota)	Amount Drawn (In percent of total package)
Argentina	SBA	Nov. 89	Mar. 91	66.0	69
	SBA	Jul. 91	Mar. 92	70.1	56
	SBA	Mar. 92	Mar. 96	361.2	100
	SBA	Apr. 96	Jan. 98	46.8	85
	EFF[2]	Feb. 98	Mar. 00	135.3	—
	SBA/SRF[2]	Mar. 00	Jan. 03	800.0	58
	SBA	Jan. 03	Aug. 03	102.7	100
	SBA	Sep. 03	Sep. 06	424.2	23
Bolivia	PRGF	Jul. 88	May 94	...	100
	PRGF	Dec. 94	Sep. 98	80.0	100
	PRGF	Sep. 98	Jun. 02	80.0	63
	SBA	Apr. 03	Jun. 04	50.0	75
Brazil	SBA	Aug. 88	Feb. 90	...	33
	SBA	Jan. 92	Aug. 93	102.6	9
	SBA/SRF[3]	Dec. 98	Sep. 01	600.0	73
	SBA/SRF[2]	Sep. 01	Sep. 02	400.0	94
	SBA/SRF	Sep. 02	Mar. 05	901.7	63
Chile	SBA	Nov. 89	Nov. 90	15.0	100
Colombia	EFF	Dec. 99	Dec. 02	252.8	—
	SBA[2]	Jan. 03	Jan. 05	200.0	—
Costa Rica	SBA	May 89	May 90	50.0	—
	SBA	Apr. 91	Sep. 92	40.0	76
	SBA[2]	Apr. 93	Feb. 94	17.7	—
	SBA	Nov. 95	Feb. 97	43.7	—
Dominican Republic	SBA	Aug. 91	Mar. 93	35.0	100
	SBA	Jul. 93	Mar. 94	20.0	53
	SBA	Aug. 03	Aug. 05	200.0	20
Ecuador	SBA	Sep. 89	Feb. 91	73.0	36
	SBA	Dec. 91	Dec. 92	79.8	25
	SBA	May 94	Dec. 95	79.3	57
	SBA	Apr. 00	Dec. 01	75.0	100
	SBA	Mar. 03	Apr. 04	50.0	40
El Salvador	SBA	Aug. 90	Aug. 91	40.0	—
	SBA[2]	Jan. 92	Mar. 93	46.6	—
	SBA	May 93	Dec. 94	37.5	—
	SBA[2]	Jul. 95	Sep. 96	30.0	—
	SBA[2]	Feb. 97	May 98	30.0	—
	SBA[2]	Sep. 98	Feb. 00	30.0	—
Guatemala	SBA	Oct. 88	Feb. 90	50.0	43
	SBA[2]	Dec. 92	Mar. 94	34.1	—
	SBA[2]	Apr. 02	Mar. 03	40.0	—
	SBA[2]	Jun. 03	Mar. 04	40.0	—
Honduras	SBA	Jul. 90	Feb. 92	45.0	100
	PRGF	Jul. 92	Jul. 97	70.0	71
	PRGF	Mar. 99	Dec. 02	121.0	69
Mexico	EFF[3]	May 89	May 93	320.0	88
	SBA[3]	Feb. 95	Feb. 97	688.4	73
	SBA	Jul. 99	Nov. 00	120.0	63
Nicaragua	SBA	Sep. 91	Mar. 93	59.9	42
	PRGF	Jun. 94	Jun. 97	125.0	17
	PRGF	Mar. 98	Mar. 02	155.0	77
	PRGF	Dec. 02	Dec. 05	75.0	29

Table 2.5 *(concluded)*

	Type of IMF Program	Beginning Date	Expiration Date	Amount Agreed *(In percent of quota)*	Amount Drawn *(In percent of total package)*
Panama	SBA	Feb. 92	Sep. 94	72.6	74
	SBA	Nov. 95	Mar. 97	56.4	100
	EFF	Dec. 97	Jun. 00	80.2	33
	SBA[2]	Jun. 00	Mar. 02	31.0	—
Peru	EFF[3]	Mar. 93	Mar. 96	218.4	63
	EFF[2]	Jul. 96	Mar. 99	64.4	53
	EFF[2]	Jun. 99	Feb. 01	60.0	—
	SBA[2]	Mar. 01	Jan. 02	20.1	—
	SBA[2]	Feb. 02	Feb. 04	39.9	—
Uruguay	SBA	Dec. 90	Mar. 92	57.9	9
	SBA[3]	Jul. 92	Jun. 93	30.5	32
	SBA[2]	Mar. 96	Mar. 97	44.4	—
	SBA[2]	Jun. 97	Mar. 99	55.5	91
	SBA[2]	Mar. 99	Mar. 00	31.1	—
	SBA[2]	May 00	Mar. 02	48.9	100
	SBA/SRF	Apr. 02	Mar. 05	694.4	69
Venezuela	EFF	Jun. 89	Mar. 93	281.0	52
	SBA[3]	Jul. 96	Jul. 97	50.0	36

Sources: IMF, Finance Department and Policy Development and Review Department.
Notes: SBA = Stand-By Arrangement, EFF = Extended Fund Facility, PRGF = Poverty Reduction and Growth Facility, SRF = Supplemental Reserve Facility.
[1]Data are as of January 31, 2004.
[2]Precautionary on approval.
[3]Program turned precautionary.

Weaknesses in Structural Reform Programs

Resisting external shocks, reducing macroeconomic vulnerabilities, and building a new growth momentum would have required strong domestic reforms. Successive studies have indicated that the initial reforms in Latin America generally had an impact on growth, but one that declined as improvements in capital, labor input, and total factor productivity were not sustained (Figure 2.13). During 1991–93—the period of fastest reforms—growth picked up, but when the reform process slowed (Figure 2.14), the growth effect diminished as well.[27] Fernandez and Montiel (1997) point out that a more lasting recovery in Latin American growth would have materialized if there had been broader and deeper implementation of reforms. There was also a tendency to attribute a disproportionate amount of the early pickup in growth to structural reforms, as opposed to cyclical factors. For example, the evidence presented in Lora and Barrera (1997) suggested that the reforms implemented during the first half of the 1990s had a substantial effect on productivity, investment, and growth.[28] In contrast, more recent studies based on longer time series indicate that the early estimates may have overstated the benefits of the reforms.[29]

The evidence also does not suggest a link between structural reforms and reductions in poverty and in-

---

[27]Some studies have analyzed the interaction between structural reforms and macroeconomic stabilization. For example, Ocampo (2004) observes that the most aggressive structural reformers also introduced strong stabilization policies that reinforced the initial results—for example, Chile and Peru in the early 1990s, with Argentina also having been viewed as a strong reformer in this period. Over time, however, rigid stabilization frameworks tended to undermine the effects of reforms. Lora and Panizza (2002) finds that the extent of reforms has tended to differ more across policy areas than across countries.

[28]The Lora and Barrera (1997) estimates suggested that structural reforms had boosted growth by 1.9 percentage points, or a total of 2.2 percentage points if macroeconomic stabilization plans were also included. Other early studies also concluding that the reforms had a positive and significant impact on growth include Fernandez-Arias and Montiel (1997); Easterly, Loayza, and Montiel (1997); and IADB (1997).
[29]Lora and Panizza (2002), as well as Stallings and Peres (2000) and Escaith and Morley (2000), conclude that the reforms had a smaller and less robust effect on growth than had previously been thought.

come inequality. Based on household survey data, Behrman, Birdsall, and Székely (2001) find that reforms in the areas of external trade, capital account liberalization, tax reform, privatization, and labor market reform did not affect poverty and inequality, whereas financial sector reforms may have had a negative effect. Birdsall and Székely (2003) conclude that greater reliance on market dynamics failed to create opportunities for the poor to generate income. Deininger and Squire (1998) emphasize the potential importance of land reform in Latin America for reducing inequality.

Looking back, it is clear that the structural reform agenda was too narrow in scope and comprehensiveness. Some key areas were neglected, notably making the labor market more flexible, and improving education systems and opportunities. Insufficient attention was given to developing and strengthening institutions, which, recent evidence indicates, play a decisive role in raising growth. And, finally, political economy factors were generally neglected. Inadequate emphasis was placed on combining growth with improvements in social conditions and sustained progress in reducing poverty, which undermined efforts to build and maintain a broad consensus in favor of reforms.

Labor Markets

Labor market reforms have been almost universally neglected across Latin America. Although a full analysis is beyond the scope of this paper, Box 2.1 presents evidence that Latin America's labor market rigidities are generally greater than in other regions. A notable exception is Chile, which made reform of labor legislation an early priority in the 1990s, helped by the popular consensus on restoring labor rights that had been restricted by the previous, military government.[30] In other countries, however, restrictive labor markets contributed to the structural inflexibility of economies that ultimately undermined rigid exchange rate systems. Civil service employment practices were resistant to change. High payroll taxes (including social security contributions) further distorted the policy framework and discouraged employment in the formal sector. As a result, unemployment rates have remained persistently high and informal labor markets have flourished, undermining public finances, productivity, real wages, and growth.

---

[30]The importance of labor market reforms in Chile's early reform efforts is discussed in Foxley (2003). Foxley points out the benefits of establishing a permanent tripartite dialogue between the government, the private sector, and labor organizations.

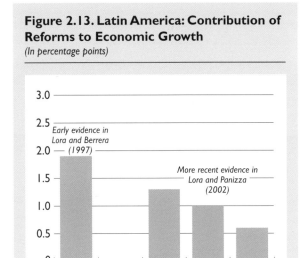

Figure 2.13. Latin America: Contribution of Reforms to Economic Growth
(In percentage points)

Sources: Lora and Berrera (1997); and Lora and Panizza (2002).

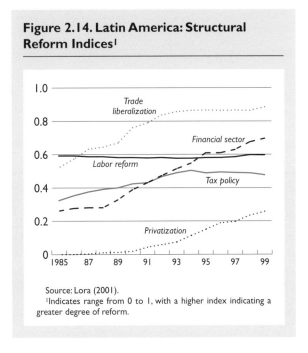

Figure 2.14. Latin America: Structural Reform Indices¹

Source: Lora (2001).
¹Indicates range from 0 to 1, with a higher index indicating a greater degree of reform.

Institutions and Governance

Measures to strengthen institutions and governance were also not aggressively pursued in the reform agendas of most Latin American countries. Over the last decade, evidence has accumulated on the importance of sound institutions in fostering efficient markets, prudent macroeconomic policies, and

Box 2.1. Latin America: Labor Market Reforms

Although economic reforms in other policy areas during the 1990s were uneven within and across countries, labor market reforms across Latin America tended to be widely neglected. Throughout the decade, unemployment rates were persistently high, even when economic growth picked up early on.[1]

One of the major shortcomings of Latin America's labor markets is institutional rigidities. In order to compare the restrictiveness of labor markets internationally, Botero and others (2003) construct an index of legal job protection based on grounds for dismissal, notice and severance payments, and whether the right of job security is anchored in the constitution. Although stronger provisions for job security in poorer countries reflect, to some degree, inadequate social safety nets, Latin America's labor laws are the most restrictive even when compared with those of other low-income regions. A notable exception is Chile, which scored substantially better than the region overall. Of course, this measure has limitations as an indicator of actual practice, as opposed to legal principles, and thus may overstate the gap between Latin America and other regions.

The failure to address labor market rigidities in the context of structural reforms and macroeconomic stabilization during the 1990s was particularly detrimental, given the region's move toward less flexible exchange rate systems. Failure to reform labor markets had the following consequences:

- The benefits of other structural reforms—such as privatization, deregulation, and price liberaliza-

tion—were not fully reflected in more efficient resource allocation, undermining the region's growth potential;

- The creation of skilled jobs in the formal economy was curtailed, contributing to an increase in the wedge between wages in high- and low-paying jobs;

- Growth in the informal labor market (covering employment on temporary and fixed-term contracts) was encouraged, promoting noncompliance with existing labor laws, adversely affecting productivity, and undermining public finances;

- The adjustment to economic shocks was made more difficult, as was reflected in deeper and longer economic downturns; and

- In terms of distributional consequences, labor market practices have favored those who profit from labor market protection, such as skilled white males, over women; unskilled workers; and, in some countries, indigenous populations.[2] Consequently, inequalities worsened.

The absence of broad-based labor market reforms and persistently high unemployment rates not only had adverse macroeconomic and distributional consequences but also contributed to reform fatigue and, ultimately, the rejection of economic reforms

---

[1]For a comprehensive discussion of labor market issues in Latin America, see IADB (2004).

[2]At the micro level, a number of studies show that some of the existing inequalities in Latin America are directly related to distributional aspects of the labor markets. See, for example, World Bank (2003b).

---

effective policy responses to shocks (Figure 2.15).[31] The lack of progress in institutional reforms in Latin America is now seen as one important reason why the improvements in macroeconomic and financial policies were not sustained throughout the period.

The widespread restoration of democracy in the region during the 1980s was a major achievement, but did not translate into substantial progress in

strengthening governance (Figure 2.16). Democratic accountability increased progressively, but most countries in the region continued to suffer from a "crisis of representation," reflecting a combination of frustration with political institutions and low confidence in politicians.[32] National legislatures in Latin America were generally seen as fragmented and ineffective. The absence of mechanisms to manage conflict and build consensus hindered policy implementation and undermined credibility, as was vividly demonstrated in Argentina and Venezuela in 2002–2003. Moreover, some groups were able to capture the political process for their own benefit, skewing the distribution of the benefits of reforms. This exacerbated income inequality, with episodes of political violence and illegal activities increasing.

---

[31]For recent evidence on the importance of strong governance and institutions in fostering sustained growth, see IMF (2003); Rodrik, Subramanian, and Trebbi (2002); Kaufmann and Kraay (2002); Hall and Jones (1999); and Rodrik (1999). Institutions are found to be important because of their role in determining transaction costs and facilitating market activity; supporting structural reforms; and promoting incentives for productive activities, such as the accumulation of skills or the development of new goods, rather than redistributive activity, such as rent seeking, corruption, or theft.

[32]Dominguez (1997).

International Comparison: Index of Labor Market Rigidity
(0 = low, I = high)[1]

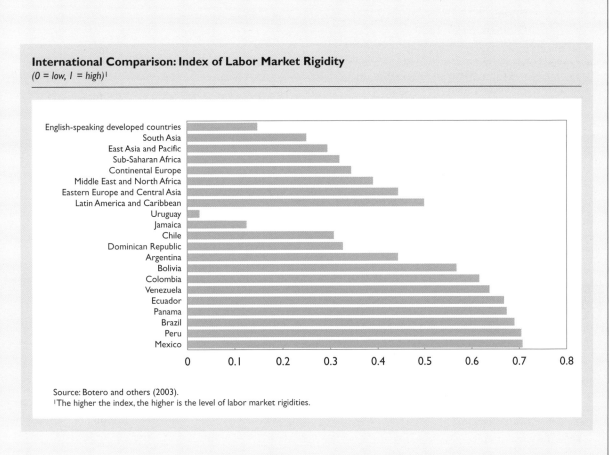

Source: Botero and others (2003).
[1]The higher the index, the higher is the level of labor market rigidities.

by large groups of society. Unemployment remains a major challenge for the region—for example, a 2001 Latinobarometer survey revealed that unemployment is considered to be the number one economic problem in Latin America, ahead of corruption and poverty.[3]

―――――――
[3]See Latinobarometer (2001).

Latin America also lagged in the area of government effectiveness, reflecting to some extent the low accountability of government agencies in a number of countries—although institutions in Uruguay, Chile, and Costa Rica are notable exceptions. These weaknesses have limited and, in some cases, distorted the effects of reforms. For example, poor control over the spending of subnational entities severely affected the efficiency gains expected from decentralization.

The rule of law in Latin America is relatively weak and has deteriorated in recent years to such an extent that some of its countries' levels of compliance are among the lowest in the world, reflecting in many cases underground and drug-related activity (Figure 2.17). This has imposed high security costs on formal economic activity in several countries. Moreover, economic crises have led to a general deterioration in public safety. Judicial systems are often weak and

highly politicized, which undermines confidence in property rights, hampers the introduction of new reforms, and increases lending risks.

Corruption remains a formidable problem in the countries of Latin America, as in other emerging market countries (Table 2.6). Several Latin American countries are ranked among the most corrupt in the world, including Bolivia and Ecuador. A notable exception is Chile, which ranks above the OECD average.

In addition to these shortcomings in governance and in protecting property rights, countries' incentive structures have further impaired institutional environment for business activity. Extensive bureaucracy has led to an excessive and uncertain regulatory environment and, together with weak enforcement of the rule of law and corruption, has discouraged both domestic and foreign private investment. A weak institutional environment for business activity is a common prob-

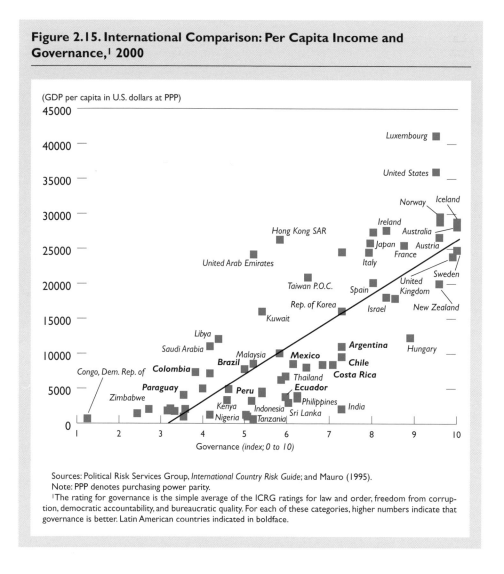

Figure 2.15. International Comparison: Per Capita Income and Governance,[1] 2000

(GDP per capita in U.S. dollars at PPP)

Governance (index; 0 to 10)

Sources: Political Risk Services Group, *International Country Risk Guide*; and Mauro (1995).
Note: PPP denotes purchasing power parity.
[1]The rating for governance is the simple average of the ICRG ratings for law and order, freedom from corruption, democratic accountability, and bureaucratic quality. For each of these categories, higher numbers indicate that governance is better. Latin American countries indicated in boldface.

lem in many developing and emerging market countries, including those in many parts of Latin America, with cumbersome regulations on key aspects of business activity—for example, starting and closing a business, managing a workforce, enforcing contracts, and getting credit (Box 2.2).

Weaknesses in Macroeconomic Policy Frameworks

The macroeconomic policy agendas in the early 1990s aimed at reversing the legacy of hyperinflation, state intervention in economic policy, and import substitution by emphasizing fiscal and monetary discipline, financial strengthening, and greater openness to the world. These policy frameworks suffered, however, from inconsistencies and imbalances in their implementation and sequencing, and from the

lack of strong institutions to ensure their sustainability. Early successes with reforms may have led to complacency about longer-term payoffs, and implementation was not systematic and sustained. Ultimately, reforms were overwhelmed by repeated financial crises and rising social discontent.

Fiscal Reforms and Privatization

It was generally recognized that the success of stabilization programs rested on restoring fiscal discipline. In practice, however, political economy considerations and complacency during the early recoveries caused fiscal positions to weaken—instead of strengthen—in most countries during the 1990s, as is discussed in Section III. Most importantly, the growth period of the early 1990s was not used to build surpluses and develop countercyclical policies

Figure 2.16. Latin America: Governance Ratings, 1985–2001

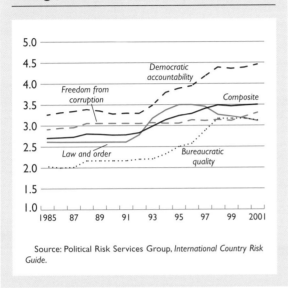

Source: Political Risk Services Group, *International Country Risk Guide.*

Figure 2.17. International Comparison: Governance Indicators,[1] 2001

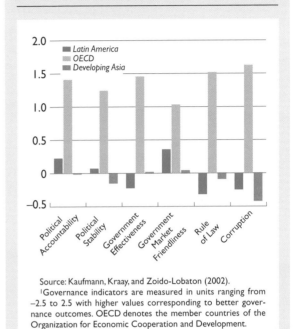

Source: Kaufmann, Kraay, and Zoido-Lobaton (2002).
[1]Governance indicators are measured in units ranging from –2.5 to 2.5 with higher values corresponding to better governance outcomes. OECD denotes the member countries of the Organization for Economic Cooperation and Development.

Table 2.6. International Comparison: Corruption Perception Index
(0 = most corrupt; 10 = least corrupt)

	2001
Latin America average	3.7
Chile	7.5
Brazil	4.0
Colombia	3.8
Mexico	3.7
Argentina	3.5
Venezuela	2.8
Nicaragua	2.4
Ecuador	2.3
Bolivia	2.0
Other emerging markets	4.3
OECD	7.2

Source: Transparency International.
Note: OECD denotes the member countries of the Organization for Economic Cooperation and Development.

(except in Chile). Instead, new imbalances quickly developed, as spending commitments (including those of subnational governments in some countries) outstripped revenue efforts; privatization receipts were not used to pay down debt or anchor improved social benefits; and quasi-fiscal deficits were allowed to emerge. Institutions for revenue collection and expenditure management remained weak. Privatization programs (emphasized in Bolivia, Brazil, and Argentina) were generally successful in securing sustained improvements in service, but their implementation emphasized short-term revenue maximization and—particularly for utilities—sometimes proceeded ahead of the improvements in the regulatory framework needed to ensure adequate competition.[33]

Monetary and Exchange Rate Policies

The adoption of exchange rate-based stabilization plans in many countries initially succeeded in bringing inflation down quickly and generating growth. In the absence of the necessary supporting policies, however, new vulnerabilities built up, including highly dollarized balance sheets, overvalued exchange rates, and excessive indebtedness. As is dis-

[33]The extent of privatization has varied considerably among countries, with Bolivia, Brazil, and Argentina having undertaken the most aggressive programs. For the region, more than half the privatizations (measured by value) have taken place in the infrastructure sector, with another 10 percent in the banking sector.

cussed in detail in Section IV, the eventual breakdown of these plans—which lacked viable exit strategies—in a context of highly dollarized or indebted balance

Box 2.2. Latin America: Impediments to Business Activity and Growth

Empirical studies on cross-country growth point to the strong role of the institutional environment—and, specifically, the legal and other factors that affect private markets—in determining growth outcomes.[1] In this context, Latin America has long been known as a region with a relatively weak and inefficient legal framework for economic activity, and a burdensome regulatory environment for business. These problems have tended to stifle entrepreneurship and risk taking and discourage private investment. They have also discouraged participation in the formal, as opposed to the informal, sector of the economy, which, in turn, has reduced the fiscal revenues from taxation. Finally, the large informal sectors in Latin America indicate that a substantial share of business activity and the labor force operates with little or no legal status or regulatory oversight.[2]

The importance of impediments to business activity in Latin American relative to those in other regions is illustrated in the following figures. The indicators describe the degree of difficulty in opening a business, the inflexibility of labor market laws, and the complexity of enforcing contracts. On all of these measures, Latin America ranks worst out of the six regions shown using data for 2003. The continuing poor performance of the region underscores the failure of reform programs in the 1990s to effectively improve the institutional environment for business activity and helps to explain why strong economic growth was not sustained beyond the initial stages of such programs.

[1]Barro and Sala-ì-Martin (2004), Chapter 12. Further details are also contained in World Bank (2004).

[2]The situation in Argentina is described in detail in World Bank (2003a).

Impediments to Business Activity

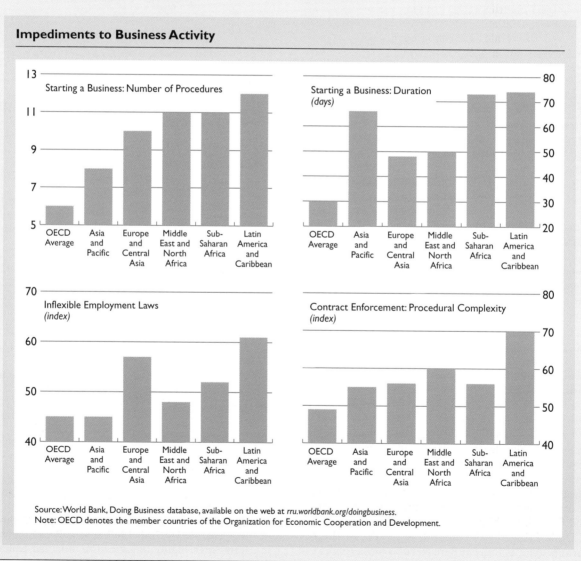

Source: World Bank, Doing Business database, available on the web at *rru.worldbank.org/doingbusiness*.
Note: OECD denotes the member countries of the Organization for Economic Cooperation and Development.

sheets created considerable economic and social instability, although the resulting inflation reductions have proved to be enduring.

Financial Reforms

Reforms in the financial sector during the first half of the 1990s focused on liberalization, as bank reserve ratios were reduced and curbs on interest rates were eliminated. Undertaking financial liberalization and capital market opening (including the growth of offshore centers, especially in Central America) without having effectively strengthened supervision and regulation (including of cross-border flows), however, resulted in undue risk taking by institutions in a deregulated environment, amplifying the impact of financial shocks. Overall, financial intermediation remained relatively limited in Latin America, especially for the small- and medium-sized enterprise sector, and contributed to growing inequality in access to financial assets. In addition, informal dollarization in several countries created balance-sheet mismatches and hidden vulnerabilities. These issues are discussed further in Sections V and VI.

External Policies

Trade liberalization was generally an area of considerable progress during the early 1990s. Average tariff rates in Latin America dropped to around 10 percent from nearly 50 percent in the mid-1980s, with Bolivia, Chile, Uruguay, and Peru having the most efficient tariff structures by the end of the 1990s. Trade openness remained quite low, however, while capital market opening proceeded much more rapidly, creating another set of imbalances. The vulnerabilities created by the surge in external capital flows in the 1990s and the lack of progress in trade opening are reviewed in Section VII.

Conclusion

The reform programs of the 1990s brought low inflation and an initial period of financial stability and economic growth. Stability and growth were both eventually undermined, however, by interrelated factors: external shocks, domestic vulnerabilities, and reform programs that did not go far enough in some key areas. The degree of fiscal prudence needed to sustain the rest of the macroeconomic policy framework was not generally realized. In combination, these factors set the stage for financial crises that had severe repercussions on growth, social indicators, and financial stability.

Underlying the disappointing results of the reform programs was a failure to build more robust in-

stitutions and governance structures that would have underpinned sustained, sound economic policies. Instead, policy credibility became excessively reliant on more fragile foundations, such as adherence to rigid exchange rate regimes. In the absence of institutional reforms that would have provided the policy flexibility needed to support these regimes, confidence faltered and the policy framework as a whole was undermined. Succeeding sections will elaborate on the experience of the 1990s in the key macroeconomic areas and explain how the region is moving ahead with absorbing and distilling the lessons from this period and developing a renewed commitment to entrenching a robust policy framework for sustained growth and reduced poverty over the medium term.

References

Barro, Robert J., and Xavier Sala-ì-Martin, 2004, *Economic Growth* (Cambridge, Massachusetts: MIT Press).

Behrman, Jere, Nancy Birdsall, and Miguel Székely, 2001, "Pobreza, Desigualdad, y Liberalización Comercial y Financiera en América Latina," in *Liberalización, Desigualdad y Pobreza: América Latina y el Caribe en los 90s,* ed. by Enrique Ganuza, Ricardo Paes de Barrois, Lance Taylor, and Rob Vos (Buenos Aires: United Nations Development Program and Universitaria de Buenos Aires).

Belaisch, Agnès, 2003, "Exchange Rate Pass-Through in Brazil," IMF Working Paper 03/141 (Washington: International Monetary Fund).

Benabou, R., 1996, "Inequality and Growth," in *NBER Macroeconomics Annual 1996,* ed. by Ben S. Bernanke and Julio J. Rotemberg (Cambridge, Massachusetts: MIT Press), pp. 11–74.

Berry, Albert, 1998, *Confronting the Income Distribution Threat in Latin America: Poverty, Economic Reforms, and Income Distribution in Latin America* (Boulder, Colorado: Lynne Rienner).

Beyer, Harald, and Rodrigo Vergara, 2002, "Productivity and Economic Growth: The Case of Chile," in *Economic Growth: Sources, Trends, and Cycles*, ed. by Norman Loayza and Raimundo Soto (Santiago, Chile: Central Bank of Chile).

Birdsall, Nancy, and Miguel Székely, 2003, "Bootstraps, not Band-Aids: Poverty, Equity and Social Policy," in *After the Washington Consensus,* ed. by Pedro-Pablo Kuczynski and John Williamson (Washington: Institute for International Economics), pp. 49–73.

Botero, Juan, and others, 2003, "The Regulation of Labor," NBER Working Paper No. 9756 (Cambridge, Massachusetts: National Bureau of Economic Research).

Brazil, Ministry of Finance, 2003, *Economic Policy and Structural Reforms* (Brasilia). Also available on the Web at *http://www.fazenda.gov.br*.

Calvo, Guillermo, Leonardo Leiderman, and Carmen Reinhart, 1992, "Capital Inflows and Real Exchange Rate Appreciation in Latin America: The Role of

External Factors," IMF Working Paper 92/62 (Washington: International Monetary Fund).

Calvo, Guillermo, and Carmen Reinhart, 1999, "Capital Flow Reversals, the Exchange Rate Debate, and Dollarization," *Finance & Development*, Vol. 36 (September), pp. 13–15.

Carstens, Agustín, and Alejandro Werner, 1999, "Mexico's Monetary Policy Framework under a Floating Exchange Rate Regime," Serie Documento de Investigación No. 9905 (Mexico City: Banco de Mexico).

de Ferranti, David, Guillermo Perry, Indermit Gill, and Luis Servén, 2000, *Securing Our Future in a Global Economy* (Washington: World Bank).

Deininger, Klaus, and Lyn Squire, 1996, "A New Data Set Measuring Income Inequality," *World Bank Economic Review*, Vol. 10, No. 3, pp. 56–91.

———, 1998, "New Ways of Looking at Old Issues: Inequality and Growth," *Journal of Development Economics*, Vol. 57 (December) pp. 259–87.

Dominguez, Jorge, 1997, "Latin America's Crisis of Representation," *Foreign Affairs*, Vol. 76 (January–February), pp. 100–13.

Easterly, William, Norman Loayza, and Peter Montiel, 1997, "Has Latin America's Post-Reform Growth Been Disappointing?" *Journal of International Economics*, Vol. 43 (November), pp. 287–311.

Economic Commission for Latin America and the Caribbean (ECLAC), 1997, *The Equity Gap: Latin America, the Caribbean, and the Social Summit* (Santiago, Chile: United Nations).

———, 2001, *Social Panorama of Latin America, 2000–2001* (Santiago, Chile: United Nations).

———, 2002, *Social Panorama of Latin America, 2001–2002* (Santiago, Chile: United Nations).

———, 2003, *Social Panorama of Latin America, 2002–2003* (Santiago, Chile: United Nations).

Escaith, Hubert, and Samuel Morley, 2000, "The Impact of Structural Reforms on Growth in Latin America and the Caribbean: An Empirical Investigation," Economic Development Division, ECLAC (Santiago, Chile: United Nations).

Fernandez-Arias, Eduardo, and Peter Montiel, 1997, "Reform and Growth in Latin America: All Pain, No Gain?" *Staff Papers*, International Monetary Fund, Vol. 48, No. 3, pp. 522–46.

Fernandez-Arias, Eduardo, and Ugo Panizza, 2001, "Capital Flows to Latin America: New Issues and Old Concerns," paper presented at the Conference on Domestic Finance and Global Capital in Latin America, Federal Reserve Bank of Atlanta, November 1–2.

Fischer, Stanley, 2001, "The International Financial System: Crises and Reform," Robbins Lecture, London School of Economics, October 29–31.

Forbes, Kristin, 2003, "A Reassessment of the Relationship Between Inequality and Growth," *American Economic Review*, Vol. 90 (November), pp. 869–87.

Foxley, Alejandro, 2003, "Development Lessons of the 1990s: Chile" (unpublished: Santiago, Chile).

Hall, Robert, and Charles Jones, 1999, "Why Do Some Countries Produce So Much More Output per Worker Than Others?" *Quarterly Journal of Economics*, Vol. 114 (February), pp. 83–116.

Inter-American Development Bank (IADB), 1997, *Latin America After a Decade of Reform* (Washington).

———, 2004, *Good Jobs Wanted: Labor Markets in Latin America* (Washington).

International Monetary Fund (IMF), 2002, "Debt Crises: What's Different About Latin America?" Chapter II in *World Economic Outlook: A Survey by the Staff of the International Monetary Fund*, April, World Economic and Financial Surveys (Washington), pp. 61–74.

———, 2003, "Growth and Institutions," Chapter III in *World Economic Outlook: A Survey by the Staff of the International Monetary Fund*, April, World Economic and Financial Surveys (Washington), pp. 95–128.

Kaufmann, Daniel, and Aart Kraay, 2002, "Growth Without Governance," Governance, Corruption and Legal Reform Working Paper No. 2928 (Cambridge, Massachusetts: Harvard University).

———, and Pablo Zoido-Lobatón, 2002, "Governance Matters II: Updated Indicators for 2000–01," World Bank Policy Research Department Working Paper No. 2772 (Washington: World Bank).

Kochhar, Kalpana, Timothy Lane, and Miguel Savastano, 2003, "Macroeconomic Consequences of a Financial Crisis," in *Managing Financial Crises: Recent Experience and Lessons for Latin America*, ed. by Charles Collyns and G. Russell Kincaid (Washington: International Monetary Fund), pp. 26–33.

Latinobarometer, 2001, *Latin American Public Opinion Survey* (Santiago, Chile: Cooperación Latinobarómetro).

Loayza, Norman, Pablo Fajnzylber, and César Calderón, 2003, "Economic Growth in Latin America and the Caribbean: Stylized Facts, Explanations, and Forecasts," IMF Research Department Paper No. 2003–13 (Washington: International Monetary Fund).

Lora, Eduardo, 2001, "Structural Reforms in Latin America: What Has Been Reformed and How to Measure It," IADB Research Department Working Paper No. 466 (Washington: Inter-American Development Bank).

———, and F. Barrera, 1997, "Una década de reformas estructurales en América Latina: El crecimiento, la productividad y la inversión, ya no son como antes," IADB Research Department Working Paper No. 350 (Washington: Inter-American Development Bank).

Lora, Eduardo, and Ugo Panizza, 2002, "Structural Reforms in Latin America Under Scrutiny," IADB Research Department Working Paper No. 470 (Washington: Inter-American Development Bank).

Lustig, Nora, 1995, *Coping with Austerity: Poverty and Inequality in Latin America* (Washington: Brookings Institution).

———, and Omar Arias, 2000, "Poverty Reduction," *Finance & Development*, Vol. 37 (March) pp. 30–33.

Mauro, Paolo, 1995, "Corruption and Growth," *Quarterly Journal of Economics*, Vol. 110 (August), pp. 681–712.

Menezes-Filho, Naércio, 2001, "Educação e Desigualdade," in *Microeconomia e Sociedade na Brasil*, ed. by M. Lisboa and N. Menezes-Filho (São Paulo: Editoria Contracapa).

Mihaljek, Dubravko, and Marc Klau, 2001, "A Note on the Pass-through from Exchange Rate and Foreign Price

Changes to Inflation in Selected Emerging Market Economies," in "Modelling Aspects of the Inflation Process and the Monetary Transmission Mechanism in Emerging Market Countries," BIS Paper No. 8 (Basel: Bank for International Settlements), pp. 69–81.

Morley, Samuel, 2001, *The Income Distribution Problem in Latin America and the Caribbean* (Santiago, Chile: United Nations).

Navia, Patricio, and Andrés Velasco, 2003, "The Politics of Second-Generation Reforms," in *After the Washington Consensus*, ed. by Pedro-Pablo Kuczynski and John Williamson (Washington: Institute for International Economics).

Ocampo, José Antonio, 2004, "Beyond the Washington Consensus: An ECLAC Perspective" (New York: United Nations, Economic Commission for Latin America and the Caribbean).

Perotti, R., 1996, "Growth, Income Distribution and Democracy," *Journal of Economic Growth*, Vol. 1 (June), pp. 149–87.

Pfeffermann, Guy, 2002, "Why Latin America Stays Trapped," *The Globalist*, November 21.

Rodrik, Dani, 1999, "Where Did All the Growth Go? External Shocks, Social Conflict, and Growth Collapses," *Journal of Economic Growth*, Vol. 4 (December), pp. 385–412.

———, Arvind Subramanian, and Francesco Trebbi, 2002, "Institutions Rule: The Primacy of Institutions over Geography and Integration in Economic Development," NBER Working Paper No. 9305 (Cambridge, Massachusetts: National Bureau of Economic Research).

Saavendra, Jaime, 2003, "Labor Markets During the 1990s," in *After the Washington Consensus*, ed. by Pedro-Pablo Kuczynski and John Williamson (Washington: Institute for International Economics).

Stallings, Barbara, and Wilson Peres, 2000, *Growth, Employment, and Equity: The Impact of Economic Reforms in Latin America and the Caribbean* (Washington: Brookings Institution).

Székely, Miguel, 2001, "The 1990s in Latin America: Another Decade of Persistent Inequality, but with Somewhat Lower Poverty," IADB Working Paper No. 454 (Washington: Inter-American Development Bank).

———, Nora Lustig, Martin Cumpa, and José Mejia-Guerra, 2000, "Do We Know How Much Poverty There Is?" IADB Working Paper No. 437 (Washington: Inter-American Development Bank).

United Nations Development Program (UNDP), 2003, *Human Development Report 2003* (New York: Oxford University Press).

World Bank, 2000, *World Development Report 2002, Building Institutions for Markets* (New York: Oxford University Press).

———, 2001, *World Development Report 2000/2001: Attacking Poverty* (Washington).

———, 2003a, "Argentina's Challenge: Growth, Social Inclusion and Governance," Policy Note (Washington).

———, 2003b, *Inequality in Latin America and the Caribbean: Breaking with History?* (Washington).

———, 2003c, *World Development Indicators* (Washington).

———, 2004, *Doing Business in 2004: Understanding Regulation* (Washington).

III Fiscal Sustainability

Difficulties in ensuring credible sustainability of fiscal policies have been central to the problems of Latin American economies.[34] Notable examples over the past decade have been the financial crises in Mexico (1994–95), Ecuador (1999), Brazil (1999 and 2002), Argentina (2001), and Uruguay (2002). Although the relative importance of domestic policy errors versus external developments is a matter of debate, it is clear in retrospect that these economies were not sufficiently "crisis-proofed" to weather the global shocks that materialized in the late 1990s.[35] Most of the region continued to experience procyclicality in fiscal policies that contributed to macroeconomic volatility and reduced resilience with respect to external shocks. In contrast, Chile is an example of a country in the region that has followed generally sound fiscal policies and avoided financial crises under similarly challenging external circumstances.

This section first discusses why fiscal policy lacked discipline in many Latin American economies in the 1990s, despite its importance in their overall policy frameworks and the common fragilities that resulted: rising debt levels combined with fragile financing structures and hidden government exposures, particularly to the financial sector. It then turns to the deeper weaknesses in fiscal structures that gave rise to these fragilities, including narrow tax bases, spending rigidities, inadequate coordination among different levels of government, hidden government liabilities, and institutional arrangements that failed to create incentives for setting sound policy. Finally, it draws some key lessons from the fiscal experiences in the 1990s and explains how countries in the region are responding to these lessons and preparing to address future challenges.

Lack of Short-Term Policy Constraints

Conceptually, government debt should be used to fund projects that have long-lived streams of benefits and to finance short-term countercyclical policies. Of course, many advanced countries have deviated from these principles by allowing debt levels to rise over extended periods to finance current spending, without triggering financing crises. Latin American economies, however, faced particularly demanding fiscal challenges in the 1990s. Fiscal slippages were not as well tolerated as in other regions owing to existing structural weaknesses, including inefficient revenue mechanisms, weak domestic financing channels, low trade shares, and macroeconomic volatility (as discussed in Section II).

In the 1990s, against the background of these long-standing weaknesses, prudent fiscal policies were particularly important to support exchange rate-based stabilization plans in an environment where underlying credibility was fragile. Fiscal discipline was crucial for several reasons: (1) to moderate expansions in aggregate demand in the initial stages of exchange rate-based stabilization plans; (2) to prevent an accumulation of public debt that would raise the risk of financing crises; (3) to provide scope for countercyclical fiscal policy, given constraints on monetary policy; and (4) to establish credibility that fiscal deficits would not eventually be monetized.[36]

Absence of Immediate Constraints on Fiscal Policy

Although these issues were widely recognized in the early 1990s, the limitations they imposed on policies were less clear. Following the Brady debt restructuring, initial public debt levels of 40–50 percent of GDP in major Latin American countries did not seem

---

[34]Of course, debt problems in the region have a long history, dating back to the Peruvian default in 1826; see Kaminsky, Reinhart, and Végh (2003).

[35]See Montiel and Reinhart (2001) for a general discussion of different views on the role of "push" versus "pull" factors in causing volatility in capital flows. On Argentina's widely analyzed experience in the late 1990s, Mussa (2002) and Perry and Servén (2003) emphasize domestic policy errors, while Calvo, Izquierdo, and Talvi (2002) place more weight on external influences.

[36]Contrary to the widespread view at the time that exchange rate-based stabilization plans would discipline fiscal policies, Tornell and Velasco (1995, 1998) and, more recently, Sun (2003) provide theoretical models of why fixed exchange rates would not have this effect. Empirically, Hamann (2001) finds no evidence that fiscal discipline has been enhanced by exchange rate-based stabilization plans.

Figure 3.1. International Comparison: Government Net Debt,[1] 1996

(In percent of GDP)

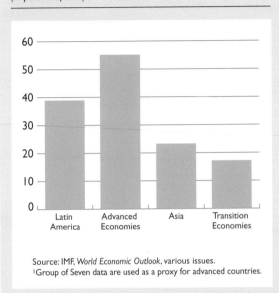

Source: IMF, *World Economic Outlook*, various issues.
[1]Group of Seven data are used as a proxy for advanced countries.

Figure 3.2. Selected Latin American Countries: Public Sector Balances

(In percent of GDP)

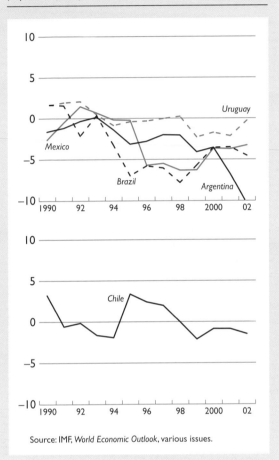

Source: IMF, *World Economic Outlook*, various issues.

high compared with those in advanced economies, although they were above debt ratios in countries of some other emerging market regions (Figure 3.1).[37] At the same time, reform programs were expected to yield substantial dividends in terms of economic growth, while financing conditions were favorable: interest rates were low in industrial countries and markets endorsed the overall change in policy strategy in the region. Furthermore, underlying fiscal positions were sometimes obscured by cyclical effects and accounting ambiguities—for instance, in dealing with privatization receipts and recognition of fiscal "skeletons." Taken together, these factors led to uncertainty about what constituted sustainable fiscal policy in the initial stages of reform programs.

Absent unambiguous criteria for assessing fiscal sustainability, and with external financing readily available, there were few immediate constraints on policy. Nevertheless, budget deficits did fall somewhat in the early 1990s, though part of the improvement was cyclical and another part reflected the impact of lower inflation on nominal interest rates and, thus, on debt-service payments (Figure 3.2).

As the cyclical impact faded later in the decade, persistent deficits contributed to gradual increases in debt-to-GDP ratios, which had previously declined from peaks reached during the debt crises of the 1980s (Figure 3.3). With economic growth slowing, underlying imbalances in fiscal positions became increasingly apparent as debt and debt-service ratios in several countries began to rise more visibly. As discussed in the subsections below, a number of other factors also contributed to rising debt levels in Latin America.[38] A large portion of

---

[37]As discussed in IMF (2003), external public debt was not notably high relative to GDP in Latin America, as ratios for countries in this region were similar to those in emerging Asian economies in the 1980s and 1990s. There was an important difference, however, in the ratio of external public debt to exports, which was much higher in Latin America than in Asia. The implications of this imbalance are discussed in more detail in Section VII.

[38]The average public debt ratio in Latin America rose by 13 percentage points during 1993–2002. Replicating the decomposition used in IMF (2003) indicates that cumulated primary balances over this period caused the ratio to fall by 10 percentage points while real growth contributed to a decline of another 9 percentage points. In contrast, "other factors"—including interest costs and off-balance-sheet and contingent liabilities, and, in many cases, the fiscal costs of bank restructuring—contributed to a 32 percentage point increase in the ratio.

Figure 3.3. Selected Latin American Countries: Public Debt
(In percent of GDP)

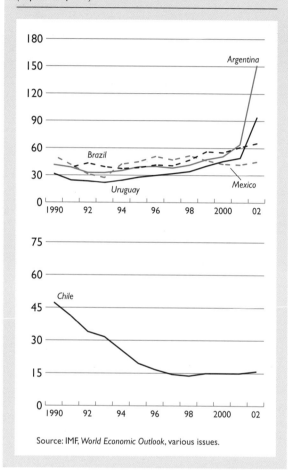

Source: IMF, *World Economic Outlook*, various issues.

Figure 3.4. International Comparison: Cyclical Sensitivity of Primary Balance[1]
(In percent of GDP, 1990–2002)

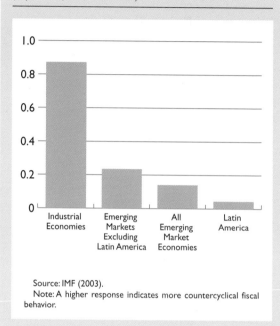

Source: IMF (2003).
Note: A higher response indicates more countercyclical fiscal behavior.

public debt was issued at short maturities, indexed to overnight interest rates or the exchange rate, or denominated in foreign currencies, leaving the stock of debt vulnerable to movements in interest rates and exchange rates. Moreover, one-time influences such as the recognition of off-balance-sheet and contingent liabilities also added to debt burdens, as did the cost of banking crises. Chile is a notable exception to the pattern of rising public debt burdens, as is shown in the lower panels of Figures 3.2 and 3.3.

Common Fragilities

Rising Debt

The absence of a decisive policy response to this upward drift in debt-to-GDP ratios led to an impor-

tant common fragility in the region.[39] Rising indebtedness and debt-service payments also contributed to a tendency toward procyclical fiscal behavior in Latin America.[40] Indeed, empirical evidence suggests that a 1 percentage point narrowing in the output gap improved the primary balance by just 0.04 percentage point of GDP in Latin America, compared with 0.87 percentage point in industrial countries (Figure 3.4).[41]

Underlying this procyclical fiscal behavior was a tendency for governments to increase spending in response to a pickup in growth, favorable terms of trade shocks, and surges in capital inflows, while cutting spending during downturns when financing dried up. As a result, debt accumulated during periods of abundant capital inflows, exacerbating the procyclicality of

---

[39]See Mussa (2002) for a discussion of the Argentina case. Reinhart, Rogoff, and Savastano (2003) show that countries with characteristics common in Latin America become vulnerable to crises at debt levels that are moderate by international standards.

[40]See IMF (2003) and Perry (2002) for an overview of this procyclical bias. See also López Murphy (1994) for Argentina; Gavin and others (1996) and Gavin and Perotti (1997) for Latin America; Talvi and Végh (2000); and Hausmann (2002a). Calderón and Schmidt-Hebbel (2003) present evidence that procyclicality was specific to countries with low credibility and larger associated risk premiums.

[41]See IMF (2003).

Box 3.1. Chile's Fiscal Consolidation in 1990s

Chile stands out among Latin American countries with its strong, crisis-free growth record since the late 1980s. Prudent public finances have played an important role in achieving this outcome. In particular, net government debt fell from more than 40 percent of GDP in 1989 to about 10 percent in 1996 (see figure). Accordingly, spreads on debt have been well below those on other sovereign credits in the region in recent years, and market access was retained during September–October 2001 amid turmoil in Argentina and a sharp drop in the terms of trade. Continued market confidence, in turn, has allowed the government to avoid forced procyclical fiscal policies, thereby reinforcing confidence in economic management.

Several elements have contributed to this record of successful fiscal management. Strong expenditure adjustment occurred in the 1980s, complemented by growth in the tax base owing to expanding activity. Losses in the state enterprise sector were reversed to yield significant profit transfers, especially during copper-boom years, without spurring higher spending. The government often ran overall, as well as primary, surpluses, allowing the nominal debt stock to fall. Net debt was also reduced through privatization, while real exchange rate appreciation lowered the ratio of external debt to GDP.

Chile did not impose specific rules requiring fiscal balance until 2000, but other long-standing institutional factors played useful roles in maintaining discipline. These included giving more power to the finance ministry than to other ministries; prohibiting the central bank from extending credit to the government; and preventing lower levels of government from borrowing, thereby eliminating subnational free-rider problems.

As net debt declined, its composition became more stable. Most debt is now denominated in local currency and inflation indexed, although unindexed instruments are being increasingly promoted. Long-term instruments pay a real return of about 3 percent, similar to the yield in industrial countries. The public sector has positive net foreign assets, since official reserves exceed foreign currency debt; short-term external debt is less than 2 percent of GDP.

Since 2000, the government has committed to an annual target for the central government structural balance, adjusted for cyclical effects and copper-price movements, thus allowing automatic stabilizers to work. This is central to the design of each year's budget. The target currently aims for a surplus of 1 percent of GDP. To further boost credibility, an expert committee determines the methodology used to calculate the structural balance.

Challenges remain, however, to sustaining a strong fiscal performance. The structural budget target has been introduced at a time of cyclical weakening in the overall budget position. Preserving sound policies will require distinguishing temporary from permanent shocks in real time, a notoriously difficult task. An important challenge will be to ensure that any errors in estimating the structural balance average out over time.

Chile: Fiscal Indicators
(In percent of GDP)

Source: Chilean authorities.

---

policies by increasing the magnitude of the adjustments that became necessary when conditions deteriorated. An important counterexample in the region is Chile, which engaged in a concerted debt-reduction effort throughout the decade (Box 3.1).

Weak Financing Structures

A second common fragility was weak financing structures for public debt. The availability of external financing, combined with limited development of domestic capital markets and incomplete policy credibility, encouraged the issuance of debt at short maturities and/or linked to foreign currencies (Table 3.1).[42] This approach to financing shifted the risks of market movements, in the first instance,

---

[42]The difficulty for emerging markets borrowing abroad in domestic currency—"original sin"—has been extensively analyzed. See Hausmann (2002a) and Eichengreen, Hausmann, and Panizza (2002) for recent discussions. Ortíz (2002) notes, however, that Chile and, more recently, Mexico are examples of countries that have overcome original sin through the promotion of domestic financial markets.

Table 3.1. Selected Latin American Countries: Composition of Public Debt, 2000

| | Public Sector Gross Debt | External Debt | Domestic Debt | |
			Exchange-rate-indexed	Other indexation mechanism
	(In percent of GDP)		(In percent of total debt)	
Argentina	51.0	58.0	37.5	...
Brazil	69.0	22	22.3	52.2
Chile	33.7	20.6	6.1	70.2
Colombia	58.0	...	6.2	23.8
Costa Rica	46.7	42.3	11.5	6.3
Ecuador	103.6	100.0	...	...
Mexico	49.0	29.9	...	63.2
Peru	45.9	73.6	7.7	...
Uruguay	45.5	66.6	33.4	...
Venezuela	33.6	77.0	...	22.9

Sources: National authorities; and IMF staff estimates.

Table 3.2. Selected Latin American Countries: Real Effective Exchange Rates and Foreign Currency Debt

	Period	Real Effective Exchange Rate Appreciation (Cumulative percentage over pre-crisis period)	Pre-Crisis Public Debt: External and Foreign Currency Linked (In percent of GDP)
Mexico	1990–94	23.1	31.3
Brazil	1993–98	30.8	18.9
Ecuador	1990–98	41.6	74.0
Argentina	1990–2001	87.7	64.1
Uruguay	1990–2001	82.6	70.3

Sources: IMF Information Notice System; and IMF staff estimates.

from lenders to governments, lowering short-run financing costs and making it easier to market the debt initially. But to the extent that governments were ill-equipped to bear the risk, this approach amplified the fragilities in the underlying policy framework and reduced the scope for corrective measures when problems arose. Weak financing structures then created room for self-reinforcing and, ultimately, self-validating market pressures.

A related issue was the effect overvalued real exchange rates had in understating the medium-term burden associated with debt denominated in foreign currency. Real exchange rates tended to appreciate sharply when monetary stabilization was achieved using exchange rate anchors, as is discussed in Sec-

tion IV. Real exchange rate appreciation, in turn, tended to reduce the value of foreign currency-denominated debt in relation to GDP (Table 3.2). Again, this contributed to a belated recognition of the true magnitude of the fiscal problem, which only became apparent when exchange rates eventually adjusted downward.[43] In Argentina, for instance, almost all of the 65 percentage point increase in the

---

[43]The view that equilibrium real exchange rates would be more appreciated as a result of structural reforms contributed to this belated recognition. For Argentina, however, Calderón and Schmidt-Hebbel (2003) calculate that even large productivity increases would have an effect of less than 1 percent on the real exchange rate over three years.

public debt/GDP ratio in 2002 was due to exchange rate depreciation.[44]

Exposure to Financial Sector

The third common fragility was a variety of hidden and contingent liabilities to the public sector. Government exposure to the financial sector was particularly important in amplifying shocks, since many financial institutions faced the same mismatches as the government in the event of sharp exchange rate or interest rate movements (as is discussed in Section V). Supervision and regulation of these exposures were often weak.[45] This strong correlation of risks meant that governments were less equipped to provide support to the financial sector when the need was greatest. Again, the result was to increase the scope for self-reinforcing financial market pressures. The cost to the financial sector of these hidden exposures added substantially to government debt burdens at the same time other factors were working in the same direction—as shares of GDP, the estimated costs amounted to 19 percent in Mexico (1995–97), 14½ percent in Argentina (1999–2002), and 8½ percent in Brazil (1996–2000).[46]

In the reverse direction, high levels of government debt posed risks for financial systems even if they appeared to be well capitalized and regulated. The experience of Argentina in 1999–2001 is a case in point. Reduced access to international capital markets, followed by a public debt restructuring, resulted in a substantial increase in the exposure of Argentina's banks to the government (to more than 20 percent of bank assets at the end of 2001, compared with around 10 percent a few years earlier), thereby linking the fate of the banking system to that of the public finances.[47] At the same time, the in-

creased government borrowing from banks crowded out credit to the private sector, which was already suffering from financing constraints. Credit constraints further depressed economic activity, which, in turn, exacerbated the fiscal problems and undermined bank asset quality. Ironically, however, one of the effects of the substitution of public debt for private credit in bank portfolios was to raise measured capital ratios, since public debt carried a much lower risk weight than private sector exposures under the Argentine prudential framework.[48]

Underlying Weaknesses

Fiscal indiscipline and procyclical policies in the 1990s were the result of deeper systemic weaknesses that made implementing corrective measures more difficult, both politically and administratively.[49] As a result, fiscal adjustments were often ad hoc and undermined the longer-term sustainability of the reform process. Cuts in infrastructure spending, for instance, reduced longer-term growth prospects and, thus, contributed to problems of fiscal sustainability, while reductions in social programs exacerbated income inequality and weakened support for market-oriented reforms.

Narrow Tax Bases

A common structural problem in achieving fiscal sustainability was narrow tax bases, combined with weak tax-collection mechanisms and frequent resort to amnesties. Little progress was made in expanding stable and predictable tax bases: general government tax revenues accounted for less than 14 percent of GDP in roughly half of the economies in the region in the mid-1990s, and this share increased only modestly in the latter part of the decade (Table 3.3). Brazil and Colombia were, however, notable exceptions. Brazil, in particular, increased general government tax revenue by more than 5 percentage points of GDP in the years following the 1998 financial crisis, largely reflecting increases in indirect taxes and the financial transaction tax (see Section V).

The most notable weakness in tax systems related to revenues from taxes on incomes and profits—as a share of GDP, these amounted to less than 5 percent in 2001 for Latin America, compared with 12½ percent for OECD countries and 6½ percent for emerg-

---

[44]Of course, part of the eventual depreciation in Argentina likely reflected an overshooting of the real exchange rate. Using a model-based estimate of the equilibrium real exchange rate, Perry and Servén (2003) calculate an overvaluation of the Argentine peso of 53 percent in 2001, implying an adjusted debt-to-GDP ratio of 95 percent, in contrast to the measured 62 percent.

[45]Carstens, Hardy, and Pazarbaşioğlu (2004) observe that these failures in supervision were generally not due to a lack of technical skill or ignorance of the true situation, but rather to political interference in oversight of the financial system. They stress the need to insulate supervision from political influences and to ensure that these institutions have the appropriate resources and legal authority to operate effectively.

[46]See Hemming and Ter-Minassian (2003). In some countries, such as Brazil, the eventual cost may decrease as guarantees are liquidated.

[47]Some authors characterized the increase in bank exposure to the government as involuntary, as described, for example, in de la Torre, Levy Yeyati, and Schmukler (2003): "in April 2001, the government used moral suasion to place some $2 billion of bonds with banks in Argentina, allowing banks to use those bonds to meet up to 18 percent of the liquidity requirement."

[48]Indeed, this was common to the prudential frameworks of all countries that subscribed to the Basel I capital-adequacy guidelines.

[49]The role of structural fiscal weaknesses in contributing to failed stabilization efforts in the region is discussed in Ter-Minassian and Schwartz (1997).

Table 3.3. Selected Latin American Countries: General Government Tax Revenues[1]
(In percent of GDP)

	1994	2001
Argentina	16.2	17.6
Bolivia	17.2	18.1
Brazil	21.1	24.3
Chile	16.0	16.7
Colombia	12.8	16.6
Ecuador	10.9	12.3
Mexico[2]	11.3	11.2
Peru	13.6	12.2
Uruguay	20.5	22.6
Venezuela	13.3	12.2
Latin America average[3]	17.6	20.4
Excluding Brazil[3]	14.9	16.1

Source: IMF staff calculations.
[1]Excluding social security contributions and taxes on state-owned oil companies.
[2]Central government only.
[3]Excluding Mexico.

ing market countries in other regions.[50] In addition, property taxes accounted for an insignificant share of revenue in Latin America, compared with about 3 percent of GDP in OECD countries.[51]

Problems of tax evasion remained severe, as weak legal enforcement and repeated amnesties undermined incentives for compliance. (Box 3.2 discusses the experience with tax amnesties in Argentina.)[52] In addition, extensive recourse to tax expenditures created an implicit drain on revenues while hiding the true extent of subsidies to various special interests.[53] The problem of exemptions and avoidance in many of these countries is illustrated by the relatively low yield from value-added taxes compared with statutory tax rates in many countries (Table 3.4). The inefficiency of tax systems in the region was also reflected in higher administrative costs than in other countries (Table 3.5).

Besides being low in relation to GDP, government revenues tended to be volatile owing to the impor-

tance of income associated with production of primary commodities. Obvious examples were the strong dependence of Ecuador, Mexico, and Venezuela on oil revenues; other countries were affected by sharp swings in agricultural prices, notably for coffee. Of the few formal attempts in the region to insulate fiscal positions from swings in commodity prices through mechanisms such as stabilization funds, only Chile's copper stabilization fund appears to have demonstrated lasting effectiveness.[54]

Government Spending Rigidities

Inflexibility in government spending was another obstacle to imposing fiscal discipline. The estimated extent of spending rigidities varies widely across countries in the region, from around 80 percent in Brazil and Colombia to virtually none in Peru (Table 3.6).[55] In Brazil, spending rigidities took several forms:

- measures to earmark revenue to specific expenditures, particularly for social purposes such as health, social security, and the Poverty Fund;

- constitutional or legislative mandates that set floors on certain types of spending (again, often aiming at protecting social spending);[56]

- automatic adjustments of expenditure items to movements in other macroeconomic variables (e.g., linking of social and pension benefits to the minimum wage);

- inflexible labor legislation and powerful unions that constrained the public sector's ability to adjust personnel costs (one of the largest components of fiscal outlays);[57] and

- mandatory revenue transfers to subnational governments.

Although these measures were intended to protect key spending categories, they impaired allocative efficiency and fiscal flexibility. With about 80 percent of Brazil's public spending being nondiscretionary by the end of the 1990s (Figure 3.5), its ability to adapt to changing macroeconomic circumstances was compromised. In addition, rigidities in these areas meant that most of the adjustment undertaken

[50]See Artana, López Murphy, and Navajas (2003).
[51]In addition to lack of institutional capacity at the local government level, this may have reflected weak incentives for local governments to raise revenues given the availability of federal transfers in several countries.
[52]See, for example, Silvani and Brondolo (1993) and Silvani and Baer (1997).
[53]In Mexico, for instance, tax expenditures are estimated to amount to about 5 percent of GDP, compared with total tax revenues of 12 percent of GDP.

[54]See Davis and others (2001).
[55]Earmarked spending is defined to include constitutionally mandated floors on certain spending items and subnational government transfers.
[56]Since 1999, for example, the Brazilian constitution has required that spending on health care rise by at least 5 percent per year.
[57]Another contributor to high and rigid wage costs was generous pension plans provided to the public sector, including public enterprises, teachers, and the military.

Box 3.2. Tax Amnesties in Argentina

Argentina has long suffered from poor revenue collection, reflecting administrative and enforcement weaknesses. Repeated tax amnesties—11 since 1990—have thwarted efforts to improve efficiency and led to the view that taxes can be avoided by waiting until the next amnesty (see table). A credible commitment to ending amnesties is likely to be a prerequisite for a turnaround in tax compliance.

• Amnesties appeal to cash-constrained governments because they tend to raise revenue in the short run. An amnesty today raises expectations of future amnesties, however, undermining future tax compliance and producing a long-run drain on the budget.

• Indicators of the cost of amnesties are difficult to collect. After adjusting Argentina's revenue-to-GDP ratio for changes in tax policy, however, we observe that tax yields fell significantly over the 1990s. For instance, revenue would have fallen by 2½ percent of GDP during 1996–2000 if new taxes had not been introduced. (This includes the revenue losses from the crisis as well as from weaker compliance.) Sectoral compliance rates are also down: the tax administration estimates that the construction industry now pays only one-third of its value-added tax (VAT) obligations and only

40 percent of its social-security obligations; for agriculture, the corresponding ratios are one-half and two-thirds, respectively. Compared with other countries in the region that have used amnesties infrequently, Argentina's compliance rates are low. In Chile, for instance, the overall compliance rate is around 80 percent.

• Tax amnesties create other administrative problems besides deterring compliance. These include an additional workload (to manage the amnesty), diversion of resources from other taxpayer services, and an undermining of existing court cases (since all delinquent taxpayers have access to the amnesty). These inefficiencies are seen as contributing to tax-collection difficulties. Staff estimates suggest that in 2000, tax collection in Argentina cost 2 percent of total tax revenue, compared with 1½ percent in Mexico, around 1 percent in Bolivia and Ecuador, three-fourths of 1 percent in Chile, and less than ½ of 1 percent in the United States.

• Given the high costs of amnesties, legislation to preclude the granting of further amnesties without congressional support would be an important first step toward reestablishing the credibility of tax enforcement.

Argentina: Recent History of Tax Amnesties

Date	Minister	Terms and Conditions
August 1990	E. Gonzales	2 percent, 40 installments
May 1993	D. Cavallo	1 percent, 50 installments
March 1995	D. Cavallo	1.15 percent, 48 installments
February 1997	R. Fernandez	2 percent, special payment regime
September 1997	R. Fernandez	3 percent, 50 installments
January 1999	R. Fernandez	2 percent, 60 installments
May 2000	J. L. Machinea	1–3 percent, 60 installments
October 2000	J. L. Machinea	1.5 percent, 60 installments
July 2001	D. Cavallo	Payment of tax debt with public bonds
November 2001	D. Cavallo	0.5 percent, 120 installments
April 2002	J. Remes-Lenicov	0.5 percent, 8 installments

in the late 1990s was disproportionately carried out by reducing capital spending, to which there was less political opposition.

Deterioration in Spending Quality

Narrow tax bases and spending rigidities heightened pressures on unprotected expenditure areas—such as infrastructure investment and social safety

nets—during periods of fiscal adjustment. Since the 1980s, public infrastructure investment as a share of GDP has fallen throughout Latin America without being offset by higher private investment, including that which might have been associated with privatization of public enterprises (Box 3.3). Calderón, Easterly, and Servén (2002a and 2002b) estimate that more than half of the total fiscal adjustment in Argentina, Bolivia, Brazil, Chile, and Peru during

Table 3.4. Selected Latin American Countries: Value-Added-Tax (VAT) Revenue Productivity

	Total VAT Revenue (In percent of consumption)	Revenue Productivity (Ratio of effective tax rate to statutory tax rate)	Applicable Year
Argentina	7.9	0.38	2000
Bolivia	5.1	0.34	2001
Brazil	10.5	0.52	1999
Chile	10.5	0.58	2000
Colombia	5.1	0.32	1999
Dominican Republic	3.1	0.31	1999
Mexico	4.5	0.30	2000
Peru	7.8	0.43	2000
Uruguay	7.6	0.35	2001
Venezuela	4.5	0.31	2000
Average of above countries	6.7	0.38	...
OECD average	9.3	0.54	2000

Sources: IMF, *Government Financial Statistics,* various issues; *International Financial Statistics,* various issues; and World Economic Outlook database; International Bureau of Fiscal Documentation, *Taxation in Latin America* and *Taxation and Investment in the Caribbean,* various issues; and PriceWaterhouse Coopers, *Corporate Taxes 2001–02, Worldwide.*

Note: OECD refers to the member countries of the Organization for Economic Cooperation and Development.

Table 3.5. Selected Latin American Countries: Cost of Tax Collection, 1998[1]

	Percent of Total Tax Revenue
Argentina	2.2
Bolivia[2]	1.3
Brazil	1.6
Chile[3]	0.7
Ecuador[2]	2.0
Mexico	1.5
Peru[2]	2.0
Canada	1.1
Spain	0.9
United States[4]	0.4

Source: IMF staff calculations.

[1]Primary sources are annual reports and statistical tabulations of the national tax authorities. Tax authorities generally do not reveal the approach used to derive their cost computations; and, in turn, their reported ratios may not be fully comparable.

[2]National tax authorities in these countries receive a fixed proportion of revenue collected.

[3]Does not include customs administration.

[4]U.S. authorities compute their ratio using "gross" revenue—use of net revenue would increase the reported ratio by about 10 percent.

Table 3.6. Selected Latin American Countries: Earmarked Spending, 2002
(In percent of primary spending)

Argentina	60
Brazil	80
Colombia	81
Peru	1
Guatemala	55
Costa Rica	45
El Salvador	12
Honduras	11

Sources: National authorities; and IMF staff estimates.

the 1990s reflected infrastructure compression. As a result, long-run growth may have been lowered by 1 percentage point per year. Similarly, during the Mexican crisis in 1995, capital spending was cut sharply.[58] At the same time, the share of public wages in GDP steadily increased through the 1990s, with Chile again being an exception (Figure 3.6).

Concerns about the low level of public infrastructure spending have led several countries in the region to question the treatment of public investment and the operations of public enterprises in fiscal accounts. In particular, a public sector "net worth" calculation would subtract the stock of productive capital from the financial debt. On a net worth basis, then, the measured deficit should exclude borrowing to finance in-

[58]See World Bank (2001).

Figure 3.5. Brazil: Composition of Spending
(In percent of total spending)

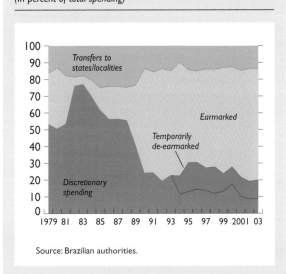

Source: Brazilian authorities.

vestment in new productive capital. It is also argued that commercially run public enterprises should be excluded from the fiscal data and treated similarly to private-sector firms. This would allow them to undertake profitable investment projects, free from deficit target constraints. Similarly, investment carried out through public-private partnerships (PPPs) should be treated as private-sector investment.

Although these points have conceptual merit, there are also important, offsetting practical issues to consider. Financial debt, whether used for capital or current expenditures, creates financing vulnerabilities, which have proven problematic for these countries. Furthermore, there are questions of how to measure the quality and productivity of public investment, and depreciation on the existing capital stock, which should be treated as a current expense. Finally, the operations of public enterprises and PPPs are likely to expose the government to significant implicit risks of the type discussed earlier.

Although it is needed most during economic downturns, social spending on the poor has tended to be procyclical in the region.[59] Wodon and others (2000) estimate that each percentage point decrease in GDP per capita reduces targeted public spending per poor person by about 2 percent. In Argentina and Mexico, targeted spending per poor person decreased by 28 and 24 percent, respectively, between 1994 and 1996—the reductions were driven both by reductions in social spending and an increase in

poverty rates.[60] Moreover, the bulk of social spending in Latin America was used to subsidize social security systems, which exclude the neediest segments of society, while only a relatively small share of it went toward primary education or basic and preventive health care, which are of most benefit to the poor.[61]

Intergovernmental Relations

Fiscal activities by subnational governments also created an underlying weakness in some countries.[62] Local governments may have been better able to identify where budgetary resources should be used, but they also often had limited institutional capacity to effectively implement spending; in addition, they had less incentive to observe macroeconomic budget constraints. Local autonomy was particularly strong in Argentina, where provinces received automatic shares of tax revenues and the federal government was constitutionally prohibited from infringing upon provincial autonomy.[63]

In Brazil, chronic inflation in the early 1990s artificially boosted the finances of state governments, with deficits being financed at low real interest rates through borrowing from state banks. The drastic reduction of inflation under the *real* plan revealed the weaknesses in local finances (Figure 3.7). Agreements covering the debts of local governments to federal banks were first reached in 1993. In 1997, agreements were reached with states and municipalities to restructure outstanding liabilities incurred before 1996. The federal government assumed state liabilities and, in return, states entered contracts that placed limits on new borrowing and set schedules for paying off restructured debt. States were required to pledge their federal transfers and their own revenues as collateral, which could be withheld in the event of noncompliance. In addition, agreements were reached for the federal government to intervene and subsequently liquidate or privatize many state banks. This was followed, in 2000, by further institutional changes to establish a cooperative, rules-based framework for decentralized fiscal policymaking.

---

[59]See Hicks and Wodon (2001), Wodon and others (2000), and Braun and di Gresia (2003).

[60]See Hicks and Wodon (2001).

[61]See Lloyd-Sherlock (2000) and Chu, Davoodi, and Gupta (2000). A study by the World Bank (1994) reveals that social insurance programs in Latin America rarely cover more than half of the labor force, versus an estimated 94 percent in OECD member countries.

[62]See Fukasaku and Hausmann, eds. (1998); Ter-Minassian, ed. (1997); and Dillinger and Webb (1999).

[63]In Colombia, by contrast, although public expenditure has been decentralized, the central government has retained considerable control (for example, in setting wages and earmarking intergovernmental transfers for specific functions). Mexico is another example of limited decentralization, with the central government maintaining control over the majority of expenditures.

Box 3.3. Infrastructure Spending and Growth in Latin America[1]

Weak fiscal institutions and spending rigidities have complicated the task of budget consolidation in Latin America. As a result, adjustment measures have tended to focus on a narrow spending base—frequently public infrastructure spending. Although cuts in this area narrow the fiscal deficit in the near term, public sector capital formation is neglected. This, in turn, lowers longer-term output growth and government debt-servicing capacity.

Since the mid-1980s, infrastructure spending as a share of GDP has fallen in most Latin American countries (see figure). Empirical evidence suggests that fiscal consolidation has played a small but significant role; negative time trends indicate that other factors have been important as well. One explanation is that privatization—and thus private investment—simply displaced public infrastructure spending. Statistical tests reveal, however, that lower infrastructure spending was not matched by higher private investment.

Owing to persistently weak infrastructure spending in Latin America, the quality and quantity of its public assets have decreased relative to those of other developing regions. Compared with the fast-growing East Asian economies, for instance, Latin America's infra-

structure shortfall—that is, East Asia's infrastructure stock per worker minus that in Latin America—has widened dramatically since the early 1980s.

Empirical studies confirm that infrastructure compression has negatively affected overall economic growth:

- On average, reduced infrastructure spending has lowered long-run GDP growth by 1 percentage point per year. Results vary from 3 percentage points in Argentina, Bolivia, and Brazil; to 1½–2 percentage points in Mexico, Chile, and Peru; and to very little in Colombia and Venezuela, where investment cuts were modest.

- The gap in GDP per worker between East Asia and Latin America increased by about 90 percent during 1980–97. About one-third of this appears to be linked to Latin America's relatively weak public infrastructure spending.

These results do not imply that infrastructure spending should never be cut, but rather that such compression may be inefficient in achieving fiscal adjustment over the longer term. Improvements in fiscal systems that would allow better-balanced adjustments would be less harmful to sustained growth. Hence, revenue mobilization efforts; de-earmarking of budget expenditures; and rationalization of wages, entitlements, and other current outlays should be seen as important elements in a strategy for supporting growth through investment. Moreover, fiscal targets should be consistent with investment priorities. The IMF is currently reexamining the coverage of its targets to ensure that high-priority investments—notably, those by fully commercial public enterprises—are not inadvertently crowded out.

Public-private partnerships (PPPs) may permit more resources to be channeled to infrastructure investment than is desirable to include in the country's budget and may enhance efficiency. PPPs have begun to account for significant shares of public investment in some Latin American countries (Mexico, Chile) and in Europe. It is, however, important that government commitments under PPPs be transparent and consistent with medium-term budget priorities; that PPPs involve clear transfers of risk to the private sector; and that independent assessments are made to ensure that PPPs have appropriately high rates of return.

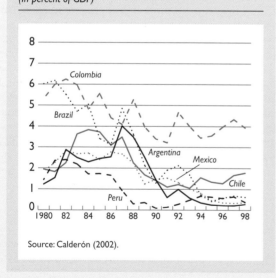

Selected Latin American Countries: Public Infrastructure Investment
(In percent of GDP)

Source: Calderón (2002).

---

[1]This box draws on Calderón, Easterly, and Servén (2002a, 2002b); and Calderón and Schmidt-Hebbel (2003).

Off-Balance-Sheet Operations and Fiscal Skeletons

Published fiscal balances often failed to measure the full extent of fiscal operations owing to nontransparent accounting practices and reliance on off-

balance-sheet spending. In some countries, the recognition of off-balance-sheet liabilities led to increases in debt that were much larger than the cumulative sum of headline budget deficits. These liabilities were generally linked to losses from central bank operations, support to the financial system (in-

Figure 3.6. Selected Latin American Countries: General Government Expenditure on Wages and Infrastructure
(In percent of GDP)

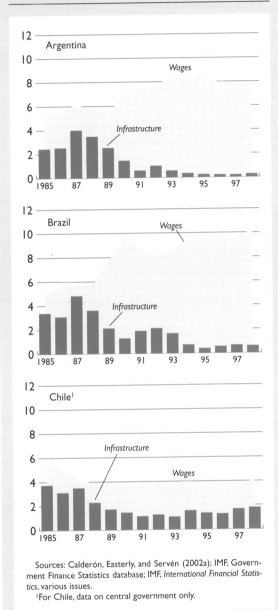

Sources: Calderón, Easterly, and Servén (2002a); IMF, Government Finance Statistics database; IMF, *International Financial Statistics*, various issues.
¹For Chile, data on central government only.

cluding development banks), and compensation payments to pensioners and suppliers. Although such hidden liabilities pose problems for many countries, their significance for Latin America in the 1990s was particularly great, since many shocks were experienced when the credibility of sustained prudent policies was central to the policy framework.

Figure 3.7. Brazil: Public Sector Primary Balance
(In percent of GDP)

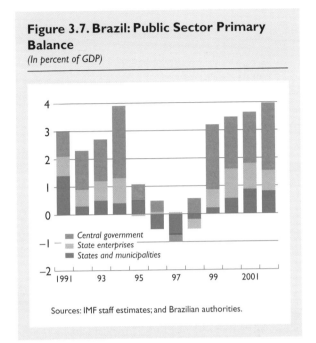

Sources: IMF staff estimates; and Brazilian authorities.

In Argentina, for instance, the recognition of fiscal skeletons—that is, the making explicit of government liabilities that had previously been implicit—is estimated to have added about 1½ percent of GDP to public debt yearly during 1992–2001—compared with a headline consolidated primary balance that averaged close to zero (Figure 3.8). During this period, more than half of the observed doubling of the debt-to-GDP ratio was accounted for by the recognition of off-balance-sheet liabilities (Figure 3.9). These mainly reflected bond-financed expenditures mandated by the judiciary, including compensation payments to beneficiaries after the social security reform of the early 1990s, payments to suppliers, refunds of tax credit arrears, and the assumption of liabilities of state enterprises prior to their privatization.[64] In Brazil, the recognition of fiscal skeletons—many arising from legal claims asserting inadequate compensation during the period of high inflation—is estimated to have led to an increase in the debt ratio of about 2½ percent of GDP between 2000 and 2002.

In other countries, lack of transparency in fiscal accounts and narrow coverage of official fiscal statistics tended to delay recognition of the true extent of government indebtedness.[65] In Mexico, until recently, headline fiscal figures failed to recognize government liabilities from bank-restructuring operations and public-investment projects with a de-

[64]See Marx (2003), Teijeiro and Espert (1996), Teijeiro (2001), and Dal Din and López Isnardi (1998).
[65]See IMF (2003).

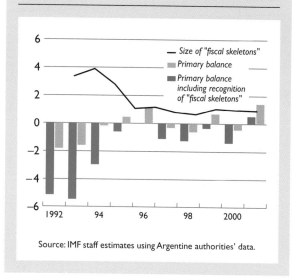

**Figure 3.8. Argentina: "Fiscal Skeletons"
and Primary Balance**
(In percent of GDP)

Source: IMF staff estimates using Argentine authorities' data.

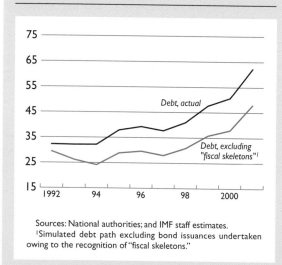

**Figure 3.9. Argentina: "Fiscal Skeletons"
and Public Debt Paths**
(In percent of GDP)

Debt, actual

Debt, excluding
"fiscal skeletons"[1]

Sources: National authorities; and IMF staff estimates.
[1]Simulated debt path excluding bond issuances undertaken
owing to the recognition of "fiscal skeletons."

ferred fiscal impact (the so-called PIDIREGAS).[66] In many countries, fiscal accounts were clouded by a nontransparent accounting treatment of certain financial operations—including exchanges of physical

assets for financial assets, central bank transfers, debt buybacks—and by underrecording of interest costs for indexed debt and zero-coupon bonds.

Pension reforms in the 1990s revealed another form of fiscal skeleton. Public pay-as-you-go (PAYGO) pension systems in Latin America had run into serious financial problems in the 1970s and 1980s.[67] Cash deficits emerged in a number of countries—including Argentina, Brazil, and Uruguay—as adverse demographic trends and inflation indexation of benefits proved costly. To improve the longer-term fiscal outlook, reforms were common in the 1990s as countries moved toward funded, private pension systems.[68] Although holding out the promise of higher national savings and enhanced fiscal sustainability in the long term, such moves made explicit the liabilities of PAYGO systems—that is, the present value of accrued payments to current and future retirees. Attempts had been made to quantify these implicit liabilities (prior to reform) in Latin America (Table 3.7). Although the estimates reflect differing methodologies, are inherently imprecise, and tend to vary widely, the potentially large scale of these liabilities is apparent.

These liabilities often led to initial increases in government payments to satisfy the claims on public pension systems of past contributors.[69] Although these initial payments would eventually be more than offset, in present-value terms, by savings, the need to make them increased short-term financing pressures on governments. In addition, permanent fiscal costs arose in some countries where pension reform included government contributions to individual retirement accounts or minimum pension guarantees.

Fiscal Institutions

At a more fundamental level, weak institutional structures for setting policy contributed to lax fiscal discipline in the 1990s. A growing literature has analyzed ways in which institutions fail to align the in-

---

[66]PIDIREGAS stands for Proyectos de Infraestructura Productiva de Largo Plazo.

[67]Mackenzie (1995) surveys the problems of public pension systems in Latin America.

[68]Chile was the first Latin American country to radically reform its pension system by introducing a private, defined-contribution scheme in 1981. See, for example, Diamond (1994) and Edwards (1996). In the 1990s, Chile's reform formed the basis for reforms in other Latin American countries. For example, in Bolivia and Mexico, the public system was replaced with a privatized one, whereas Argentina, Uruguay, Colombia, and Peru added a new private tier and modified the public system. In contrast, Brazil offered supplementary pensions. For a detailed comparison, see Kay and Kritzer (2001) and Mitchell and Barreto (1997).

[69]For example, in Chile, Colombia, and Peru, active labor force participants at the time of reform were given "recognition bonds" that would mature at retirement. In contrast, Argentina and Bolivia simply pay compensatory pensions. See Schmidt-Hebbel (1999).

Table 3.7. Selected Latin American Countries: Estimates of Implicit Pension Debt in 1990s

Country	Ratio of Debt to GDP (in percent)
Argentina	55–305
Bolivia	40
Brazil	188–213
Chile	130
Colombia	59–88
Mexico	37–188
Peru	37–45
Uruguay	187–289
Venezuela	30–37

Sources: Kane and Palacios (1996), Bravo and Uthoff (1999), FIEL (1998), Grandolini and Cerda (1998), and Kuczynski and Williamson (2003).

centives of politicians and policymakers with the long-term public interest, focusing on[70]

- *electoral institutions* that promote polarization and fractionalization, implying government instability and, thus, policy "myopia"; and

- *budgetary institutions* that allow narrow interests to prevail or that suffer from "common pool" problems—for example, the absence of incentives for provincial governments in Argentina to internalize the costs of expenditures.[71]

The evidence suggests that institutional weaknesses in these areas have played an important role in influencing fiscal outcomes, both globally and in Latin America.[72] Countries in the region have lacked institutions that can promote sound fiscal policies, including (1) laws that establish ex ante constraints on deficits;[73] (2) "hierarchical" budget procedures that give relatively more power to the executive than to congress, and to the finance minister than to spending ministries; (3) transparency, including controls on subnational government and public enterprise budgets; and (4) judicial systems that control tax evasion and ensure prompt resolution of disputes between federal and local governments.

Chile is a notable example of a country where institutional strengths promoted sound policies. The following factors have been at play:[74]

- *Centralization of budgetary powers.* The constitution favors the executive over the legislature, and the ministry of finance over spending ministries. Only the executive can initiate budgetary proposals; and in the event of congressional opposition, the government's initial proposal becomes law after 60 days.

- *Central government budget constraint.* The central bank (which is independent) is constitutionally prohibited from lending to the government, and other government borrowing is subject to congressional approval.

- *Constraints on subnational governments.* Subnational governments are essentially prohibited from borrowing.

- *Electoral rules that encourage political stability.* Chile's president is elected at fixed intervals of six years and does not require congressional backing to remain in office. Congressional representation is determined in a majoritarian, rather than a proportional, manner. Finally, electoral rules create incentives for parties to join stable coalitions, causing political parties to moderate their demands to find common ground.[75]

It is worth noting that Chile's record of fiscal discipline was established without the support of "rules" or targets and absent a high degree of trans-

---

[70]Reviews of the literature include Alesina and Perotti (1996) and Annett (2002).

[71]See, for example, Jones, Sanguinetti, and Tommasi (2000).

[72]See Alesina and others (1999).

[73]As discussed in Kopits (2001), however, fiscal rules are not a panacea. Governments with strong fiscal records, for instance, may find explicit rules to be overly restrictive; conversely, in cases where the underlying political commitment to prudence is lacking, rules may not effectively constrain actual policy implementation.

[74]See Espinosa and Phillips (2004).

[75]See Foxley and Sapelli (1999).

parency. Nevertheless, the current government has made both of these areas high priorities, committing itself to a steady structural-balance target and improving transparency on many fronts.

Fiscal Lessons, Policy Responses, and Challenges

Following the region's experience since the early 1990s, there has generally been a renewed commitment in Latin America to learn from the lessons of this period, address fiscal vulnerabilities, and tackle the fiscal deficit and public debt problems. Recognizing that inflexible exchange rate regimes generally failed in instilling necessary fiscal discipline, countries have increasingly adopted explicit fiscal rules and budget procedures that promote sound policies, combined with more transparent, comprehensive, and frequent disclosure of their fiscal positions. Such institutional strengthening responds well to the main lessons of the last decade that have been reviewed in this section, notably the need to reform fiscal institutions; provide adequate incentives for the fiscal activities of subnational governments; focus on a broad view of the exposure of the public sector; and keep a watchful eye on implicit liabilities from pension systems, the financial sector, and other quasi-fiscal sources in comprehensive debt-sustainability assessments.

The experience of Brazil is a good example of a Latin American country's response to the fiscal lessons of the 1990s. Progressively, the Brazilian authorities have undertaken reforms to improve fiscal institutions significantly. Legislation was approved in 1995 that introduced ceilings on personnel expenditures (including retirement benefits for former civil servants) as a percentage of each jurisdiction's net revenues.[76] The law was modified in 1999 to include certain fringe benefits. In addition, as noted above, in 1997 the federal government entered into debt-restructuring agreements with subnational governments that strengthened local fiscal adjustment by prohibiting new borrowing until the ratio of existing debt to net revenues equaled one to one. Perhaps most significantly, in May 2000, the Brazilian congress approved a fiscal responsibility law to improve fiscal transparency and encourage continued fiscal consolidation at all levels of government.

- The law requires the annual submission of budget guidelines laws (Lei de Diretrizes Orçamentárias, or LDO) for each level of government, in-

cluding a target for the current-year primary balance and projections for revenues, expenditures, the primary balance, and the public debt stock for the following three years.

- The law also requires that the annual budget approved by congress later in the year abide by the primary-surplus target in the LDO and include a reserve against unspent commitments from the previous year.

- In addition, the law prohibits primary deficits and the creation of unfunded permanent spending mandates, bans new spending commitments that cannot be executed before the end of the incumbent government's tenure in office, sets limits on personnel spending (as a share of revenues) for all levels of government, and contains "golden-rule" provisions that limit annual credit disbursements to the level of capital expenditure. It also bans the issuance of public debt by the central bank with effect from May 2002.

- Finally, the law provides for more transparent fiscal recording, with bimonthly reports on budget execution and more comprehensive reports every four months on fiscal performance.

Brazil's experience with the fiscal responsibility law illustrates the potential advantages associated with improving fiscal institutions. It has contributed to much stronger fiscal outturns at all levels of government and has substantially increased fiscal transparency, helping maintain continuity through the political transition in 2002–2003. Financial markets have welcomed these developments.

Other countries in the region have been taking steps in the same direction, although in some of them the process still needs to be carried to completion or be fully tested. Thus, Peru introduced a fiscal law in 1999 that, although it needed refinements in 2003, likely helped reduce Peru's fiscal deficit from 3.2 percent of GDP in 2000 to 1.7 percent in 2003. Ecuador and Colombia have also recently introduced fiscal responsibility laws in 2002 and 2003, respectively. A track record needs to be built to assess implementation. Argentina's fiscal responsibility law, approved in 1999, has not effectively disciplined policy as discussed in Gadano (2003). A law on public finances was introduced in Venezuela in 2000, with provisions to be phased in over several years. During this transition period, it is difficult to clearly judge the performance of the framework, but continuing large actual and projected fiscal deficits suggest its effectiveness has been limited. Generally speaking, the experience in the region (and elsewhere) suggests that fiscal responsibility laws can play a useful role in complementing sound policy intentions but may not effectively restrain policies when

---

[76]Net revenues were defined as total current revenues, *less* constitutionally mandated transfers from the federal government and social security contributions from current civil servants.

the design is flawed or the constraints conflict with the underlying intentions of policymakers.

Another important policy response in the region has been ongoing efforts to take a broader view of the fiscal situation. Mexico, for instance, has published augmented fiscal measures that reflect the overall fiscal position of the public sector since the mid-1990s, including the operations of development banks and public investment projects initially financed through the private sector. More generally, the treatment of public/private investment partnerships in the region is receiving close scrutiny, with pilot projects under way in Peru, Chile, Colombia, and Brazil to systematically assess the appropriate treatment of such activities in the fiscal accounts. Another area in which the accounting treatment has improved is in public pension liabilities, with several countries undertaking reforms that reduce the longer-term fiscal burden of maturing pension systems and aging populations. Pension reform will, in many cases, require constitutional change. For example, Colombia is discussing a constitutional amendment that would eliminate special pension regimes and implement other measures to reduce further the actuarial deficit of the country's pension system.

Owing to the experience of the imprudent financing of fiscal deficits in many cases during the 1990s, there is clear recognition of the need to strengthen public debt structures. Chile has actively moved toward longer-term, fixed-rate domestic debt instruments; and Mexico is taking similar steps to reduce vulnerabilities to exchange rate risk and short-term interest rate fluctuations. Brazil has done very well in reducing significantly the exchange rate sensitivity of its public debt. Separately, the widespread adoption of collective-action clauses in debt instruments promises to significantly enhance private sector involvement in debt-workout activities.

In a number of countries, important efforts are under way to increase the flexibility of budget structures. This is being done through progressive fiscal reforms that seek to strengthen revenue administration and tax policy, reduce revenue earmarking, and curtail the use of minimum spending floors, thereby creating room for the government to better address priority needs and reduce the procyclicality of fiscal policy. Making further progress in this direction is a major priority and challenge for the region, especially since it might entail—in some cases—constitutional change. Brazil, for example, has undertaken an important study in 2004 on the implications of budget rigidities for the management of fiscal policy, with a view to making the budget more flexible and improving the quality of public spending.

Thus, although countries have progressed at different speeds in responding to the lessons of the 1990s, considerable and welcome changes in the manage-ment of fiscal policy—and the role of the state—are in the pipeline. These efforts are already bearing fruit. In the region, primary public sector balances have generally improved since 2002, with many countries taking advantage of cyclical improvements to strengthen their policies. Latin America is by no means alone among emerging market and developing countries in confronting the consequences of past lax fiscal control and rising debt, and the manner in which Latin America deals with these challenges will be of considerable interest to countries in other regions. In this context, recent experience in Latin America has already demonstrated that fiscal discipline and reform are not inimical to growth. Indeed, growth has generally picked up in Latin America as fiscal positions have improved, thereby creating opportunities to provide benefits to the poor.

References

Alesina, Alberto, Ricardo Hausmann, Rudolf Hommes, and Ernesto Stein, 1999, "Budget Institutions and Fiscal Performance in Latin America," NBER Working Paper No. 5586 (Cambridge, Massachusetts: National Bureau of Economic Research).

Alesina, Alberto, and Roberto Perotti, 1996, "Budget Deficits and Budget Institutions," NBER Working Paper No. 5556 (Cambridge, Massachusetts: National Bureau of Economic Research).

Annett, Anthony, 2002, "Politics, Government Size, and Fiscal Adjustment in Industrial Countries," IMF Working Paper 02/162 (Washington: International Monetary Fund).

Artana, Daniel, Ricardo López Murphy, and Fernando Navajas, 2003, "A Fiscal Policy Agenda," Chapter 4 in *After the Washington Consensus,* ed. by Pedro-Pablo Kuczynski and John Williamson (Washington: Institute for International Economics), pp. 75–101.

Bauer, Andreas, 2002, "The Financial Soundness of Mexico's Pension System," in *Mexico: Selected Issues,* IMF Country Report No. 02/238 (Washington: International Monetary Fund).

Braun, Miguel, and Luciano di Gresia, 2003, "Towards Effective Social Insurance in Latin America: The Importance of Countercyclical Fiscal Policy," paper presented at the Annual Meetings of the Board of Governors, Inter-American Development Bank and Inter-American Investment Corporation, Milan, Italy, March 23.

Bravo, Jorge, and Andras Uthoff, 1999, "Transitional Fiscal Costs and Demographic Factors in Shifting from Unfunded to Funded Pensions in Latin America," Serie Financiamiento del Desarrollo, No. 88 (Santiago, Chile: Economic Commission for Latin America and the Caribbean).

Calderón, César, William Easterly, and Luis Servén, 2002a, "How Did Latin America's Infrastructure Fare in the Era of Macroeconomic Crises?" Central Bank of Chile Working Paper No. 185 (Santiago, Chile: Central Bank of Chile).

————, 2002b, "Infrastructure Compression and Public Sector Solvency in Latin America," Central Bank of Chile Working Paper No. 187 (Santiago, Chile: Central Bank of Chile).

Calderón, César, and Klaus Schmidt-Hebbel, 2003, "Learning the Hard Way: Ten Lessons for Latin America's Turmoil" (unpublished; Santiago, Chile: Central Bank of Chile).

Calvo, Guillermo, Alejandro Izquierdo, and Ernesto Talvi, 2002, "Sudden Stops, the Exchange Rate and Fiscal Sustainability: Argentina's Lessons" (unpublished; Washington: Inter-American Development Bank).

Carstens, Agustín, Daniel Hardy, and Ceyla Pazarbaşioğlu, 2004, "Banking Crises in Latin America and the Political Economy of Financial Sector Policy," paper presented at the IADB-IIC Annual Meetings, Lima, Peru, March 28.

Catão, Luis, 2002, "Debt Crises: What's Different About Latin America?" Chapter II in *World Economic Outlook: A Survey by the Staff of the International Monetary Fund, April* (Washington: International Monetary Fund), pp. 61–74.

Chu, Ke-Young, Hamid Davoodi, and Sanjeev Gupta, 2000, "Income Distribution and Tax, and Government Social Spending Policies in Developing Countries," WIDER Working Paper No. 214 (Helsinki: World Institute for Development Economics Research).

Dal Din, Claudio, and Norberto López Isnardi, 1998, "La Deuda Pública Argentina 1990–1997," FIEL Documento de Trabajo No. 56 (Buenos Aires, Argentina: Fundación de Investigaciones Económicas Latinoamericanas). Available on the Web at *http://200.80.42.118/fiel.org/docu/DOC56.pdf.*

Davis, Jeffrey, Rolando Ossowski, James Daniel, and Steven Barnett, 2001, *Stabilization and Savings Funds for Nonrenewable Resources: Experience and Fiscal Policy Implications*, IMF Occasional Paper No. 205 (Washington: International Monetary Fund).

de Ferranti, David, Danny Leipziger, and P.S. Srinivas, 2002, "The Future of Pension Reform in Latin America," *Finance & Development*, Vol. 39 (September), pp. 39–43.

de la Torre, Augusto, Eduardo Levy Yeyati, and Sergio Schmukler, 2003, "Living and Dying with Hard Pegs: The Rise and Fall of Argentina's Currency Board," World Bank Domestic Finance Policy Research Working Paper No. 2980 (Washington: World Bank).

Diamond, Peter, 1994, "Privatization of Social Security: Lessons from Chile," *Revista de Analisis Económico*, Vol. 9 (June), pp. 21–23.

Dillinger, William, and Steven B. Webb, 1999, "Fiscal Management in Federal Democracies: Argentina and Brazil," World Bank Policy Research Working Paper No. 2121 (Washington: World Bank).

Edwards, Sebastian, 1996, "The Chilean Pension Reform: A Pioneering Program," paper presented at the conference on Privatizing Social Security, National Bureau of Economic Research, Cambridge, Massachusetts, August. Also published as NBER Working Paper No. 5811.

Eichengreen, Barry, Ricardo Hausmann, and Ugo Panizza, 2002, "Original Sin: The Pain, the Mystery, and the Road to Redemption," paper presented at the Conference on Currency and Maturity Mismatching: Redeeming Debt from Original Sin, Inter-American Development Bank, Washington, November.

Espinosa-Vega, Marco A., and Steven Phillips, 2004, "The Role of Institutions in Chile," in *Chile: Institutions and Policies Underpinning Stability and Growth*, ed. by Eliot Kalter, Steven Phillips, Marco A. Espinosa-Vega, Rodolfo Luzio, Mauricio Villafuerte, and Manmohan Singh, IMF Occasional Paper No. 231 (Washington: International Monetary Fund), pp. 6–20.

Foxley, Alejandro, and Claudio Sapelli, 1999, "Chile's Political Economy in the 1990s: Some Governance Issues," in *Chile: Recent Policy Lessons and Emerging Challenges*, ed. by Guillermo Perry and Danny M. Leipziger (Washington: World Bank).

Fukasaku, Kiichiro, and Ricardo Hausmann, eds., 1998, *Democracy, Decentralization, and Deficits in Latin America* (Paris: Inter-American Development Bank and Development Center of the Organization for Economic Cooperation and Development).

Fundación de Investigaciones Económicas Latinoamericanas (FIEL), 1998, *La Reforma Provisional en la Argentina* (Buenos Aires).

Gadano, Nicolas, 2003, "Rompiendo las Reglas: Argentina y la Ley de Responsabilidad Fiscal," *Desarrollo Económico*, Vol. 43 (July–September), pp. 231–63.

Gavin, Michael, Ricardo Hausmann, Roberto Perotti, and Ernesto Talvi, 1996, "Managing Fiscal Policy in Latin America and the Caribbean: Volatility, Procyclicality, and Limited Creditworthiness," IADB Working Paper No. 326 (Washington: Inter-American Development Bank).

Gavin, Michael, and Roberto Perotti, 1997, "Fiscal Policy in Latin America," *NBER Macroeconomics Annual 1997*, ed. by Ben S. Bernanke and Julio Rotemberg (Cambridge, Massachusetts: MIT Press).

Goldfajn, Ilan, 2002, "Are There Reasons to Doubt Fiscal Sustainability in Brazil?" Technical Note No. 25 (Brasilia: Banco Central do Brasil).

Grandolini, Gloria, and Luis Cerda, 1998, "The 1997 Mexican Pension Reform: Genesis and Design Features," Financial Markets and Pension Reform Project, Policy Research Working Paper No. 1733 (Washington: World Bank).

Hamann, A. Javier, 2001, "Exchange-Rate-Based Stabilization: A Critical Look at the Stylized Facts," *Staff Papers*, International Monetary Fund, Vol. 48, No. 1, pp. 111–38.

Hausmann, Ricardo, 2002a, "The Elusive Quest for Macro Stability: The Role of Debt Denomination," paper presented at the Inter-American Development Bank meetings, Fortaleza, Brazil, March 10.

————, 2002b, "Unrewarded Good Fiscal Behavior: The Role of Debt Structure" (unpublished; Cambridge, Massachusetts: Harvard University, Department of Economics).

Hemming, Richard, and Teresa Ter-Minassian, 2003, "Public Debt Dynamics and Fiscal Adjustment," in *Managing Financial Crises: Recent Experience and Lessons for Latin America*, ed. by Charles Collyns and G. Russell Kincaid, IMF Occasional Paper No. 217 (Washington: International Monetary Fund).

Hicks, Norman, and Quentin Wodon, 2001, "Social Protection for the Poor in Latin America," *CEPAL Review*, Comisión Económica para América Latina, Vol. 73 (April), pp. 93–113.

International Monetary Fund (IMF), 2003, *World Economic Outlook: A Survey by the Staff of the International Monetary Fund, October* (Washington: International Monetary Fund).

Jones, Mark P., Pablo Sanguinetti, and Mariano Tommasi, 2000, "Politics, Institutions, and Fiscal Performance in a Federal System: An Analysis of the Argentine Provinces," *Journal of Development Economics*, Vol. 61 (April), pp. 305–33.

Kaminsky, Graciela L., Carmen M. Reinhart, and Carlos A. Végh, 2003, "The Unholy Trinity of Financial Contagion," NBER Working Paper No. 10061 (Cambridge, Massachusetts: National Bureau of Economic Research).

Kane, Cheikh, and Robert Palacios, 1996, "The Implicit Pension Debt," *Finance & Development*, Vol. 33 (June), pp. 36–38.

Kay, Stephen, and Barbara Kritzer, 2001, "Social Security in Latin America: Recent Reforms and Challenges," *Federal Reserve Bank of Atlanta Economic Review*, First Quarter, Vol. 86, No. 1, pp. 41–52.

Kopits, George, 2001, "Fiscal Rules: Useful Policy Framework or Unnecessary Ornament?" IMF Working Paper 01/145 (Washington: International Monetary Fund).

Kuczynski, Pedro-Pablo, and John Williamson, eds., 2003, *After the Washington Consensus: Restarting Growth and Reform in Latin America* (Washington: Institute for International Economics).

Lloyd-Sherlock, Peter, 2000, "Failing the Needy: Public Social Spending in Latin America," *Journal of International Development*, Vol. 12 (January), pp. 101–19.

López Murphy, R., 1994, "Los Programas de Estabilización: Algunas Experiencias Recientes en Latinoamérica," Serie Seminarios No. 19/1994 (Buenos Aires: Instituto Torcuato di Tella).

Mackenzie, George, 1995, "Reforming Latin America's Old-Age Pension Systems," *Finance & Development*, Vol. 32 (March), pp. 10–13.

———, Peter Heller, Phillip Gerson, and Alfredo Cuevas, 2003, "Pension Reform and the Fiscal Policy Stance," *Public Budgeting & Finance*, Vol. 23 (March), pp. 113–27.

Marx, Daniel, 2003, "Sovereign Debt Restructuring: The Upcoming Case of Argentina," paper presented at the Inter-American Development Bank conference on "Debt Restructuring in Argentina: The Road Ahead and Lesson for Emerging Markets," Washington, March 31.

Mesa-Lago, Carmelo, 2002, "Myth and Reality of Pension Reform: The Latin American Evidence," *World Development*, Vol. 30, No. 8, pp. 1309–21.

Mitchell, Olivia, and Flávio Barreto, 1997, "After Chile, What? Second-Round Social Security Reforms in Latin America," Pension Research Council Working Paper No. 97-4 (Philadelphia: University of Pennsylvania, Wharton School).

Montiel, Peter, and Carmen M. Reinhart, 2001, "The Dynamics of Capital Movements to Emerging Economies During the 1990s," in *Short-Term Capital Flows and Economic Crises*, ed. by Stephany Griffith-Jones, Manuel Montes, and Anwar Nasution (Oxford, United Kingdom: Oxford University Press), pp. 3–28.

Mussa, Michael, 2002, "Argentina and the Fund: From Triumph to Tragedy," Policy Analyses in International Economics No. 67 (Washington: Institute for International Economics).

Ortíz, Guillermo, 2002, "Monetary Policy in a Changing Economic Environment: The Latin American Experience," paper presented at the Federal Reserve Bank of Kansas City's symposium on Rethinking Stabilization Policy, Jackson Hole, Wyoming, August 29–31.

Perry, Guillermo, 2002, "Can Fiscal Rules Help Reduce Macroeconomic Volatility in LAC?" paper presented at the IMF/World Bank conference on "Fiscal Rules and Institutions," Oaxaca, Mexico, February.

———, and Luis Servén, 2003, "The Anatomy of a Multiple Crisis: Why Was Argentina Special and What Can We Learn From It?" World Bank Working Paper No. 3081 (Washington: World Bank).

Reinhart, Carmen M., Kenneth S. Rogoff, and Miguel A. Savastano, 2003, "Debt Intolerance," NBER Working Paper No. 9908 (Cambridge, Massachusetts: National Bureau of Economic Research).

Schmidt-Hebbel, Klaus, 1999, "Latin America's Pension Revolution: A Review of Approaches and Experience," paper presented at the World Bank's Annual Bank Conference on Development Economics (ABCDE), Washington, April 28–30.

Silvani, Carlos, and Katherine Baer, 1997, "Designing a Tax Administration Reform Strategy: Experience and Guideline," IMF Working Paper 97/30 (Washington: International Monetary Fund).

Silvani, Carlos, and John Brondolo, 1993, "Analysis of VAT Compliance" (unpublished; Washington: International Monetary Fund, Fiscal Affairs Department).

Sun, Yan, 2003, "Do Fixed Exchange Rates Induce More Fiscal Discipline?" IMF Working Paper 03/78 (Washington: International Monetary Fund).

Talvi, Ernesto, and Carlos Végh, 2000, "Tax Base Variability and Procyclical Fiscal Policy," NBER Working Paper No. 7499 (Cambridge, Massachusetts: National Bureau of Economic Research).

Teijeiro, Mario, 2001, "Una Vez Mas, La Política Fiscal . . ." (unpublished: Centro de Estudios Públicos). Available on the Web at *http://www.cep.org.ar/articulo.php?ids= 156.*

———, and J.L. Espert, 1996, "Una Estilización de la Política Fiscal Durante la Convertibilidad" (unpublished; Santiago, Chile: Centro de Estudios Públicos).

Ter-Minassian, Teresa, ed., 1997, *Fiscal Federalism in Theory and Practice* (Washington: International Monetary Fund).

———, and Gerd Schwartz, 1997, "The Role of Fiscal Policy in Sustainable Stabilization: Evidence from Latin America," IMF Working Paper 97/94 (Washington: International Monetary Fund).

Tornell, Aaron, and Andrés Velasco, 1995, "Fiscal Discipline and the Choice of Exchange Rate Regime," *European Economic Review*, Vol. 39 (April), pp. 759–70.

———, 1998, "Fiscal Discipline and the Choice of a Nominal Anchor in Stabilization," *Journal of International Economics*, Vol. 46 (October), pp. 1–30.

Walker, Eduardo, and Fernando Le Fort, 2002, "Pension Reform and Capital Markets: Are There Any (Hard) Links?" Social Protection Discussion Paper No. 201 (Washington: World Bank).

Wodon, Quentin, Norman Hicks, Bernadette Ryan, and Gabriel Gonzalez, 2000, "Are Governments Pro-Poor but Short-Sighted? Targeted and Social Spending for the Poor during Booms and Busts" (unpublished; Washington: World Bank).

World Bank, 1994, *Averting the Old-Age Crisis: Policies to Protect the Old and Promote Growth* (Oxford, United Kingdom: Oxford University Press for the World Bank).

———, 2001, "Mexico: Fiscal Sustainability, Volume II: Background Papers" (unpublished; Washington: World Bank).

IV Monetary and Exchange Rate Regimes

Overview

Inflation control was an essential element of reform programs in Latin America and also the one in which achievements were most notable and enduring. Yet the means used to achieve rapid, up-front reductions in inflation—generally exchange rate-based anchors for monetary policy—led to imbalances over the longer term that increased countries' vulnerability to financial crises. Such regimes would have been sustainable only if a highly prudent approach had been taken to fiscal policy, combined with aggressive measures to increase the flexibility of prices and wages and raise the share of external trade in overall activity. In the event, reform programs in these areas were inadequate, and the "hard" exchange rate regimes eventually failed in the midst of financial turmoil. At the same time, these stabilization plans may have been necessary to arrest very high initial rates of inflation. They also left a legacy of broad popular support for low inflation that likely contributed to the successful implementation of subsequent approaches to monetary management, notably the inflation-targeting frameworks adopted in Mexico and Brazil.

This section reviews the experience with monetary stabilization in the region that began in the late 1980s and early 1990s, with a focus on the implications of exchange rate-based regimes for the results of reform programs. It first discusses the background to the introduction of monetary reforms and the influence this subsequently had on the exchange rate strategies that were taken in various countries, ranging from hard exchange rate anchors to pursuit of informal inflation objectives with a variety of intermediate targets. The macroeconomic effects of exchange rate-based stabilization plans are then described; in particular, we examine why cyclical expansions were observed in the initial stages of the plans, while the costs were borne later. The section then turns to the impact of inflexible exchange rate regimes on the implementation of other aspects of policy, including fiscal consolidation and trade opening. The eventual exit from inflexible exchange rates and the transition to alternative arrangements are then described. The section concludes with a brief assessment of the increasing experience in the region with an inflation-targeting approach that responds to the lessons of the 1990s and reviews the challenges that lie ahead in ensuring that such an approach becomes entrenched.

Alternative Approaches to Monetary Stabilization

Background

Most Latin American economies experienced chronic monetary instability during the 1980s, resulting in high and volatile inflation and plunging currencies.[77] Of the larger countries, none had an average annual inflation rate of less than 20 percent during the decade. Several experienced bouts of very high inflation, defined as annual rates of over 100 percent (Fischer, Sahay, and Végh (2002)), including Argentina, Bolivia, Brazil, Mexico, and Peru; Argentina, Brazil, and Bolivia experienced brief periods of hyperinflation.[78] Argentina had the most extreme experience in the region, with an average inflation rate of 350 percent during the decade, leading to consumer prices increasing by a factor of more than 100 million. At the other end of the spectrum, Chile, Paraguay, and Colombia witnessed relatively moderate and stable inflation rates, which averaged 20–25 percent. In addition to the negative effect on overall economic performance of high and volatile inflation, wealth disparities were exacerbated, as the costs of inflation fell disproportionately on the poor.[79]

Generally speaking, high inflation reflected rapid monetary expansion, which, in turn, was caused by central bank financing of large fiscal deficits. As discussed in Fischer, Sahay, and Végh (2002), although

---

[77]See Pazos (1972) for a review of the longer history of monetary instability in the region.

[78]Based on Cagan's (1956) definition of hyperinflation "as beginning in the month in which the rise in prices exceeds 50 percent and ending in the month before the monthly rise in prices drops below that amount."

[79]See Mishkin and Savastano (2000).

Figure 4.1. Latin America: Fiscal Deficits and Inflation, 1980–2001

(Inflation in percent, vertical scale; fiscal deficit in percent of GDP, horizontal scale)

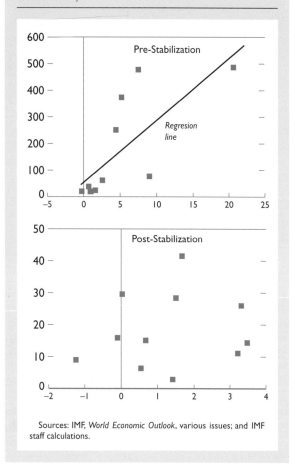

Sources: IMF, *World Economic Outlook*, various issues; and IMF staff calculations.

international evidence on the link between deficits and inflation is weak during periods of low inflation, it becomes much more robust under high inflation.[80] Figure 4.1 illustrates the relationship between cross-country averages for fiscal deficits and inflation for the major Latin American countries since 1980, divided into periods before and after monetary stabilization plans were introduced. (The timing of these plans is indicated below.) There is a positive and statistically significant relationship in the pre-stabilization period, when inflation rates were high, consistent with "fiscal dominance" of monetary policy.[81] In contrast, the pattern is less clear in the post-stabilization period, when

[80]See also Catão and Terrones (2003) and Corbo (2000).

[81]The classic reference to long-run fiscal dominance is Sargent and Wallace (1981).

inflation was much lower.[82] The change in the relationship reflects both reductions in fiscal deficits themselves and increased scope for financing deficits through debt, as opposed to money creation—at least in the near term.

Monetary Regimes and Institutions

There was a need, as a part of overall economic reform programs launched in the late 1980s and early 1990s, to establish monetary frameworks that would prevent fiscal dominance and underpin financial stability. Different approaches were taken to achieving this goal, ranging from hard pegs to the U.S. dollar to informal inflation targeting. Table 4.1 provides a categorization of monetary frameworks used for stabilization that reflects an assessment of the relative importance of exchange rates, inflation, and other criteria in policymaking.[83] Examples of stabilization programs that were centered on an objective for the exchange rate include Mexico's *pacto* (1988), Argentina's currency board (1991), Uruguay's *tablita* (1990), and Brazil's *real* plan (1994).[84] The top panels in Figure 4.2 indicate that, except for Uruguay, the introduction of exchange rate-based plans was associated with an abrupt halt in currency depreciation, while Uruguay's *tablita* involved a more gradual stabilization. In all cases, short-term volatility in currency movements dropped sharply following the introduction of exchange rate-based stabilization plans (Table 4.2).

[82]The regression in the pre-stabilization period yields a slope coefficient of 23.5 with a *t*-statistic of 3.01, while the post-stabilization coefficient is 0.014 with a *t*-statistic of 0.004. Excluding the extreme case of Bolivia in the pre-stabilization period, which had a particularly large fiscal deficit of about 20 percent of GDP, the slope coefficient is 35.2 with a *t*-statistic of 2.40.

[83]For countries with hard exchange rate targets, the classifications and timing in Table 4.1 generally correspond to the official implementation of explicit regime changes. The classification of countries with informal inflation objectives is based on Corbo (2000). Countries were defined as having "soft" exchange rate objectives when the volatility of nominal exchange rate movements was significantly greater than under hard exchange rate targeting (Table 4.2).

Looking more narrowly at exchange rate regimes, as opposed to the overall monetary policy framework, the literature on de facto classifications includes Ghosh and others (1997), Calvo and Reinhart (2000), Reinhart and Rogoff (2002), Levy Yeyati and Sturzenegger (2002a), and Bubula and Ötker-Robe (2002). For the purposes of this study, one drawback to these classifications is that they look only at exchange rate regimes as opposed to overall monetary framework. Frenkel (2003) also notes that the conclusions of these studies are often contradictory and depend on the criteria chosen.

[84]Bolivia is excluded from this classification because stabilization was initially achieved in 1985–86 without an explicit exchange rate anchor. The crawling-peg system was introduced in late 1986 after inflation had fallen sharply.

Countries that opted for exchange rate-based stabilization plans were generally those with the highest inflation rates and most volatile exchange rates in the pre-stabilization period, although Peru is an exception (Table 4.2).[85] The experience in Central America was also quite different, as discussed in Box 4.1. The high-inflation countries stood to benefit even more than the others in the region from the credibility afforded by a visible and easily monitored link to an external anchor in the form of U.S. monetary policy. At the same time, hard exchange rate targets were often not accompanied, at least in the first instance, by explicit measures to limit fiscal deficits or increase central bank independence (Table 4.3), thereby jeopardizing the longer-term insulation of monetary policy from fiscal dominance.[86]

The exception was Argentina, which introduced constitutional reforms to increase the independence of the central bank in early 1992, shortly after the currency board was introduced.[87] In the other countries that adopted exchange rate-based stabilization plans, central bank reforms were introduced much later (e.g., in Mexico) and/or they left central banks with relatively low degrees of effective independence.

Other countries adopted approaches that assigned a less important role to the exchange rate and instead focused on an inflation objective. Examples are the monetary regimes introduced in Chile (1989), Colombia (1991), and Peru (1993).[88] These arrangements could not be characterized as full inflation targeting as it is currently understood, partly because they involved monitoring other variables—notably monetary aggregates and/or the exchange rate—at least in the short run. Yet an analysis of the way policy was implemented suggests that inflation developments were the primary determinant of policy actions.[89] Interestingly, these countries, unlike most of

---

Table 4.1. Monetary Stabilization Plans: Objectives and Timing

"Hard" Exchange Rate Objective	
Argentina	Apr. 1991–Dec. 2001
Brazil	Jul. 1994–Dec. 1998
Mexico	Apr. 1988–Dec. 1994
Uruguay	Nov. 1990–Dec. 2001
"Soft" Exchange Rate Objective	
Ecuador	Oct. 1992–Sep. 1998
Paraguay	Apr. 1989–Dec. 2001
Venezuela	Apr. 1989–Feb. 2002
Inflation Objective	
Chile	Oct. 1989–present
Colombia	Jan. 1991–present
Peru	Jan. 1993–present

Sources: For countries with hard exchange rate targets, the classifications and timing generally correspond to the official implementation of explicit regime changes. The classification of countries with informal inflation objectives is based on Corbo (2000). Countries were defined as having "soft" exchange rate objectives when the volatility of nominal exchange rate movements was significantly greater than under hard exchange rate targeting (Table 4.2).

---

the countries that adopted explicit exchange rate objectives, also introduced measures to increase central bank independence in conjunction with stabilization plans.

For the other countries shown in Table 4.1—specifically Ecuador, Paraguay, and Venezuela—the timing of the introduction of stabilization plans and the characterization of the exchange rate regime are more ambiguous. Nevertheless, the evidence suggests that these countries focused on the exchange rate in setting policy, although control was less tight than in countries that explicitly adopted exchange rate-based stabilization, as reflected in greater short-term volatility in exchange rates (see Table 4.2 and Figure 4.2). Venezuela, in particular, experienced episodes of discrete, sharp depreciations in the exchange rate that were not subsequently reversed.

Broadly speaking, then, countries with the highest pre-stabilization inflation rates tended to opt for exchange rate-based stabilization plans, while those with more moderate rates adopted inflation objectives. Bolivia and Peru, however, stand out as countries that successfully reduced inflation from high levels without using an exchange rate anchor, at least initially. In any case, the frequent recourse to exchange rate-based stabilization may have reflected the difficulty in credibly implementing inflation targeting starting from triple-digit inflation rates, especially given that inflation targeting was not, at the

---

[85]The choice of exchange rate regime in stabilization plans is discussed in Edwards (1998) and Gould (1996). Interestingly, these studies generally argue that a history of high inflation is associated with the choice of money-based stabilization as opposed to exchange rate-based stabilization, which seems to be at odds with the experience in Latin America in the late 1980s and early 1990s.

[86]In terms of fiscal measures, Brazil is an exception, since its primary surplus in 1994 reached 5.1 percent of GDP. Both Jácome (2001) and Gutiérrez (2003) find evidence that greater central bank independence is associated with better inflation performance in Latin America.

[87]Of course, subsequent developments underscore the fact that institutional arrangements of this nature do not offer complete protection against the failure of monetary regimes.

[88]For Peru, the beginning of the stabilization effort could also be dated from mid-1990, with the election of Alberto Fujimori's government; specific inflation objectives were not introduced until the beginning of 1993.

[89]See Mishkin and Savastano (2000) for a discussion of this issue. Corbo (2000) analyzes econometrically the response of these countries' policies to various factors, supporting the view that they behaved as inflation targeters.

Figure 4.2. Latin America: Exchange Rate Developments
(In logarithms; January 1990 = 0)

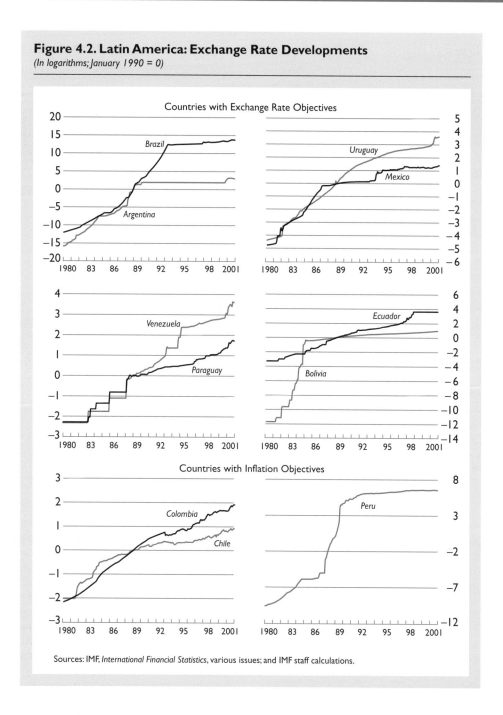

Sources: IMF, *International Financial Statistics*, various issues; and IMF staff calculations.

time, well established internationally as a monetary policy regime. Exchange rate anchors yielded rapid, up-front reductions in inflation. They also tended to produce initial cyclical upswings in activity, reinforcing the immediate attractiveness of the approach. Absent viable exit strategies over the longer term, however, and without clear frameworks to prevent eventual fiscal dominance, the durability of these exchange rate-based stabilization plans was jeopardized.

Macroeconomic Impact of Exchange Rate-Based Stabilization Plans

Inflation

Inflation tended to come down much more quickly under explicit exchange rate-based stabilization plans than under inflation targeting (Figure 4.3). In Argentina, inflation was reduced from more than 700 percent at the beginning of 1991 to

Table 4.2. Pre- and Post-Stabilization Inflation and Exchange Rate Developments

	Pre-Stabilization[1]			Stabilization Period[2]		
	Inflation	Growth in REER	Exchange Rate Volatility[3]	Inflation	Growth in REER	Exchange Rate Volatility[3]
	"Hard" Exchange Rate Objective					
Argentina	374.0	−1.7	20.8	2.9	2.7	0.1
Brazil	478.3	0.8	10.4	11.1	4.2	1.9
Mexico	76.7	−4.4	7.5	15.9	3.3	0.9
Uruguay	61.8	−4.1	7.1	28.4	5.1	1.4
Unweighted average	241.0	−2.4	11.5	14.6	3.8	1.1
	"Soft" Exchange Rate Objective					
Ecuador	38.3	−6.8	5.6	29.6	4.3	2.9
Paraguay	19.5	−7.9	7.7	15.1	0.0	5.1
Venezuela	19.6	−6.4	7.9	41.5	2.5	8.6
Unweighted average	25.8	7.0	7.1	28.7	2.3	5.5
	Inflation Objective					
Chile	20.5	−5.8	3.1	9.0	−0.1	2.0
Colombia	24.2	−3.3	0.7	14.4	−2.1	2.5
Peru	251.4	7.8	22.5	6.4	0.2	1.1
Unweighted average	98.7	−0.4	8.8	8.9	−0.7	1.9
	Not Classified[4]					
Bolivia	487.0	−2.2	43.2	26.0	−7.6	0.6

Sources: IMF, *International Financial Statistics*; and IMF staff calculations.
Note: REER denotes the real effective exchange rate.
[1]Defined as 1980M1 until the last month before stabilization plans began (see Table 4.1).
[2]Defined as the period extending from when the stabilization plans were introduced until they ended (see Table 4.1).
[3]Standard deviation of monthly log changes in the exchange rate vis-à-vis the U.S. dollar.
[4]See discussion in the text.

less than 10 percent by mid-1993, less than two years after the currency board was introduced. In Mexico, inflation fell from 180 percent at the beginning of 1988 to less than 20 percent by April 1989, one year after the *pacto* came into effect. And Brazil's inflation rate plunged from more than 3,000 percent in 1994 to single digits by the end of 1996, less than two years after the *real* plan was introduced. These rapid declines in inflation are consistent with international evidence that the inflationary process lacks inertia when inflation reaches very high levels (Fischer, Sahay, and Végh, 2002).[90]

In Chile and Colombia, in contrast, inflation started from much lower levels. In Chile, inflation

stood at about 25 percent in 1990 but did not decline to single digits until late 1994, five years after stabilization began. In Colombia, as noted previously, progress in inflation reduction was modest through much of the 1990s; and it was not until mid-1999, or nine years after the plan was introduced, that inflation fell below 10 percent.[91] In Peru, the initial stabilization process without an inflation target was quite rapid, as inflation fell from more than 10,000 percent in mid-1990 to 56 percent by the end of 2002. It did not, however, reach single digits until early 1997.

The evidence, then, suggests that the exchange rate-based stabilization plans likely had a significant and rapid effect on near-term inflation expectations, in spite of past failures in the region. In countries

[90]At the same time, it may be surprising that the plans enjoyed sufficient credibility to bring down inflation quickly, given the extensive and unsuccessful track record of exchange rate-based stabilization plans in the region. See Edwards (2000) for a discussion of the experience in the 1970s and Pazos (1972) for a longer historical perspective. The difference may have been that these plans were introduced in the context of more comprehensive efforts to correct deficiencies in fiscal and monetary policies.

[91]As discussed below, Mexico had a similar experience of slow disinflation after adopting an informal inflation objective following the 1994–95 crisis; Brazil, in contrast, made the transition to formal inflation targeting in 1999 without a sustained period of double-digit inflation.

Box 4.1. Exchange Rate Experience in Central America

During the 1990s, most of Central America pursued some form of fixed exchange rate regime. Costa Rica, Honduras, and Nicaragua adopted crawling pegs, while El Salvador relied on a fixed peg, which, in 2001, culminated in formal dollarization, making it the second country in Central America—along with Panama—in which the U.S. dollar is legal tender. Guatemala relied on a managed float, but one with relatively limited exchange rate volatility. Despite the adoption of exchange rate-based anchors, Central America's monetary regimes managed to withstand a number of adverse external shocks—including devastating hurricanes, earthquakes, and a sustained fall in the price of one of the region's most important commodities (coffee)—without major disruptions. (See figure.) This raises the question of whether the initial conditions in Central America differed from those in other Latin American countries and whether the reliance on fixed exchange rate systems was complemented by positive institutional developments and increased flexibility in factor markets, especially labor markets.

In contrast with much of Latin America, initial annual inflation rates in Central America were more modest, ranging from about 8 percent in Honduras to 27 percent in Costa Rica during the 1980s.[1] Consequently, the use of U.S. dollar-based exchange rate anchors in Central America was primarily a reflection of the relatively small size of the countries and their strong dependence on the U.S. economy, rather than an instrument to bring inflation down quickly. In addition to being their most important trading partner, the United States was a major source of income owing to remittances received from workers. For example, during the 1990s, remittances reached, on average, 12 percent of GDP in El Salvador and 3 percent of GDP in Honduras. These close links to the United States also contributed, at least partly, to the high degree of dollarization of their banking systems.

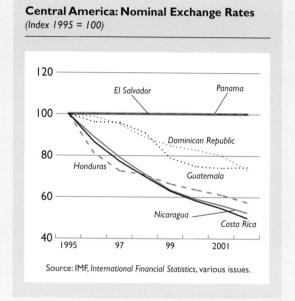

Central America: Nominal Exchange Rates
(Index 1995 = 100)

Source: IMF, *International Financial Statistics*, various issues.

During the 1990s, the reliance on exchange rate pegs in Central America was supported by a strengthening of institutions, including increased central bank independence and the curtailment of central bank financing of government activities. Also, Central America made progress in reducing fiscal deficits and public sector debt, although reconstruction efforts in the aftermath of natural disasters resulted in setbacks.[2] Although labor markets in El Salvador were quite flexible, overall improvements in labor market flexibility lagged; the region profited substantially, however, from its proximity to the United States, and, in many respects, the U.S. labor market acted as a shock absorber.

[1]The only exception was Nicaragua, which experienced substantially higher inflation rates during both the 1980s and the first half of the 1990s.

[2]At the end of 2002, Central America's average debt-to-GDP ratio amounted to about 55 percent, compared with an average of about 60 percent of GDP in South America.

that adopted inflation objectives, in contrast, there was little indication of significant, front-loaded credibility gains. This is consistent with the wider experience with inflation targeting, which indicates that monetary policy credibility has to be earned by good observed performance after inflation-targeting regimes are introduced.[92]

Exchange Rates and Interest Rates

Although inflation came down quickly in countries that adopted exchange rate-based stabilization, it did not decelerate rapidly enough to avoid appreciation of the real exchange rate. As shown in Figure 4.4, countries that adopted exchange rate-based stabilization generally experienced significant real

[92]See, for example, Almeida and Goodhart (1998) and Bernanke and others (1999). Brazil's experience in 1999 is somewhat unique, in that the initial level of inflation was very low (1.7 percent through 1998). The challenge for the inflation-

targeting framework, then, was to contain inflation in the face of a large exchange rate depreciation as opposed to engineering a disinflation process.

Table 4.3. Latin America: Increases in Central Bank Independence

	Monetary Stabilization Introduced	Central Bank Law or Constitution Changed	Index of Central Bank Independence[1]
	"Hard" Exchange Rate Objective		
Argentina	April 1991	September 1992	18.5
Brazil	July 1994	June 1999	12.0
Mexico	April 1988	April 1994	16.0
Uruguay	November 1990	March 1995	12.5
	"Soft" Exchange Rate Objective		
Paraguay	April 1989	June 1995	10.5
Venezuela	April 1989	December 1992	9.5
	Inflation Objective		
Chile	October 1989	October 1989	16.5
Colombia[2]	January 1991	August 1991	15.0
Peru	January 1993	January 1993	17.0

Source: Jácome (2001).
[1]Following changes in the law; the higher the index, the more independent is the central bank.
[2]Corresponds to the date when the new, independent central bank board was appointed.

exchange rate appreciation in the starting years of the plans, in contrast to what occurred in countries that adopted inflation objectives.[93] In some countries, such as Mexico and Uruguay, the initial level of the real exchange rate was relatively depreciated from a historical perspective; thus, a component of this appreciation reflected a return to more typical levels. Brazil's stabilization began with a real exchange rate that was similar to the historical average, while Argentina introduced the currency board at a real exchange rate level that was significantly appreciated compared with those prevailing in the 1980s.[94] By the time of the collapse of its currency board, Argentina's real effective exchange rate had appreciated by some 60 percent relative to the 1980s, seriously undermining the country's competitiveness. Countries that had informal inflation objectives tended to avoid substantial real appreciations through the use of crawling exchange rate bands that were adjusted in response to inflation developments. For Chile, the imposition of controls on capital inflows may also have played a role.

Nominal interest rates also came down quickly in countries that adopted exchange rate-based stabilization. A dramatic example was Argentina, where money market rates fell from about 250 percent at the beginning of 1991 to 20 percent by the end of the year; in Brazil, rates fell from 7,000 percent in early 1994 to 56 percent by the end of the year.[95] Access to foreign capital also expanded rapidly with the stabilization of the exchange rate and improved investor confidence in the overall direction of the government's reform programs.

Business-Cycle Dynamics

Low domestic interest rates, the availability of foreign capital, and the apparent lack of risk of borrowing in foreign currency created a favorable environment for debt-financed spending. Cycles resulted that were typical of those observed in other countries, inside and outside the region, under exchange rate-based stabilization.[96] Box 4.2 summarizes the experience with such programs in Latin America and discusses alternative explanations for the stylized

[93]If the starting point of monetary stabilization for Peru is instead dated at August 1990, when the "Fujishock" program was introduced, the real effective exchange rate would have depreciated about 20 percent during the period shown in Figure 4.4.
[94]The consumer price index (CPI)-based real effective exchange rates of Mexico and Uruguay were, respectively, about 20 percent and 25 percent below the average of the 10 years preceding stabilization, while Argentina's exchange rate was about 30 percent above the comparable level.

[95]Although it would also be desirable to look at the evolution of real interest rates, it is difficult, in practice, to construct reliable estimates of inflation expectations given the high degree of financial volatility during the transition to stabilization.
[96]References to the typical cycle associated with exchange rate-based stabilization include Végh (1992), Calvo and Végh (1999), and Kiguel and Liviatan (1992).

Figure 4.3. Inflation Under Alternative Stabilization Plans
(In percent)

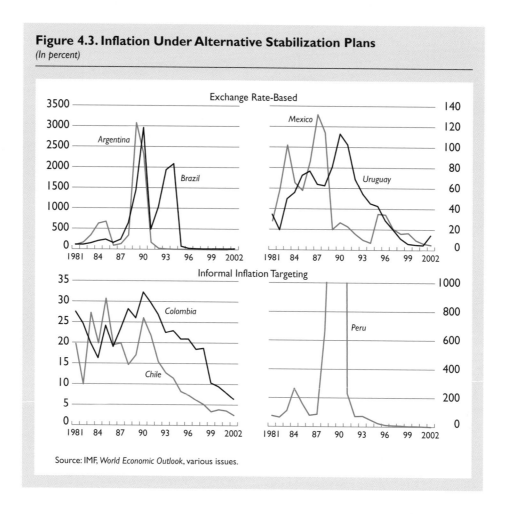

Source: IMF, *World Economic Outlook*, various issues.

facts. In particular, growth in output initially increased, fueled by higher private consumption spending.[97] The trade balance tended to deteriorate as the real exchange rate appreciated, and capital inflows surged.

These developments were unsustainable, as reflected in a rising ratio of external debt-servicing payments to exports.[98] But reversing these trends without changing the nominal exchange rate would have required a sharp contraction in domestic spending and an associated decline in the domestic price level to restore competitiveness. Few countries have managed this transition successfully, especially in an environment of high international capital mobility. Instead,

Latin American countries displayed the more typical pattern of persistent external deficits combined with domestic recession, notably in Argentina from 1999 through 2001. In the absence of either a viable strategy for a controlled exit from these regimes or any scope for fiscal policy to actively support demand, the outcome was a self-reinforcing loss of confidence in financial markets and eventual crisis.[99] It is striking that all of the countries that adopted exchange rate-based stabilization ended up abandoning the policy framework during financial turmoil, while none of the countries that adopted informal inflation targeting experienced similar outcomes.

When crises hit, they were particularly damaging, given high levels of informal dollarization, particularly in Argentina and Uruguay. Although the emer-

---

[97]It is notable that business investment was typically not a driving force, perhaps reflecting underlying weaknesses in reform plans that failed to instill longer-term confidence.

[98]This assessment, of course, is easier to make in hindsight. As discussed in Section II, there was a view at the time that higher potential owing to the reforms would allow countries to service debt more easily over the longer term. There was also an expectation that trade liberalization would lead to more rapid export growth than actually occurred, as is discussed in Section VII.

[99]Designing a viable exit strategy would have presented its own challenges. The relevant issues are discussed in Eichengreen and Masson (1998), who observe that exit from a fixed exchange rate is easier when financial conditions are stable. Yet this is also the environment in which the motivation for abandoning the exchange rate anchor is least compelling.

gence of informal dollarization had initially been associated with financial volatility prior to stabilization, it continued even after stabilization had been achieved. Indeed, further informal dollarization of liabilities was often encouraged by an environment of exchange rate stability, which obscured the risk that exchange rate movements posed for balance sheets (see Section VI).[100] When exchange rate targets were eventually abandoned, borrowers in foreign currency (including governments) experienced sharp increases in the domestic currency value of debt and debt-servicing payments. As creditworthiness worsened and financing dried up, pressures on the exchange rate were exacerbated, leading to a self-reinforcing plunge in currencies.

Role of Capital Controls

Given the absence of flexibility to conduct countercyclical monetary policy, avoiding this typical cycle under exchange rate-based stabilization would have required a combination of firm fiscal discipline from the outset, significant increases in wage and price flexibility, and concerted trade opening—none of which were observed in practice. Another supporting measure could have been controls on capital inflows to limit the buildup in external debt and the appreciation of the real exchange rate. Chile and Colombia both adopted "price-based" capital controls in the form of unremunerated reserve requirements on short-term inflows.[101]

There is an extensive but inconclusive literature on the success of Chile's strategy in insulating the economy from swings in foreign financing, as critically surveyed in Nadal-De Simone and Sorsa (1999). In any event, it is clear that attempts to evade controls created problems that had to be addressed by tightening their application over time. Although there is disagreement on whether controls sheltered Chilean monetary policy from external influences, most observers agree that they lengthened the maturity of foreign inflows (De Gregorio, Edwards, and Valdes, 2000).[102] Given that the level of short-term

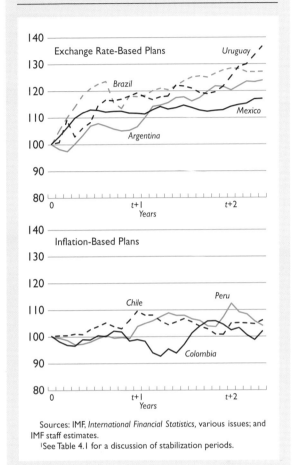

Figure 4.4. Latin America: Real Effective Exchange Rates[1]
(Index = 100 at start of stabilization)

Sources: IMF, *International Financial Statistics,* various issues; and IMF staff estimates.
[1]See Table 4.1 for a discussion of stabilization periods.

external debt is one of the most robust predictors of financial crises, the controls likely helped to "crisis proof" the Chilean economy, even if they did not facilitate an independent monetary policy.[103] There has been less formal analysis of the Colombian experience, but, again, the results are conflicting. Ocampo and Tovar (2003) conclude that controls both reduced the volume of inflows and increased their maturity, while Cárdenas and Barrera (1997) and Cárdenas and Steiner (2000) arrive at the opposite conclusion.

Whether controls on capital inflows would have similarly helped to crisis proof other countries in the

---

[100]Martinez and Werner (2002) provide firm-level evidence for Mexico that the foreign exchange exposure of corporations increased during the period of exchange rate-based stabilization.

[101]Agosín and Ffrench-Davis (2001) discuss Chile's experience. Controls were instituted in 1991 with a reserve requirement of 20 percent. The rate was raised to 30 percent a year later, reduced to 10 percent during the Asian crisis, and eventually eliminated in 1998. Ocampo and Tovar (2003) analyze the Colombian case. Controls in the form of compulsory deposits were in place from 1993 to 2000, with deposit rates that varied over time from 10 percent to almost 100 percent and also depended on the maturity of the inflow.

[102]Le Fort and Budnevich (1996) and Le Fort and Lehmann (2003) argue that more scope was provided for policy independence, while De Gregorio, Edwards, and Valdes (2000) find little

evidence of such an effect. Espinosa, Smith, and Yip (2000) provide a theoretical framework for how capital controls can reduce economic volatility and raise growth.

[103]On the role of short-term external debt in predicting financial crises, see Radelet and Sachs (1998); Berg and Patillo (1999); and Berg, Borensztein, and Pattillo (1999).

Box 4.2. Cyclical Impact of Exchange Rate-Based Stabilization Plans

The boom-bust cycle associated with several exchange rate-based stabilization programs in Latin America is illustrated in the panels in the accompanying figure. Strong initial output growth is led by a consumption boom, particularly in durable goods. Inflation falls quickly, but not by enough to avoid appreciation of the real exchange rate. The trade balance deteriorates and capital inflows increase, leading to a rising ratio of external debt-servicing payments to exports. As the initial boom in consumption wanes, GDP growth falls sharply in the third and fourth years after stabilization. Reversing this cycle without making adjustments in the nominal exchange rate would require substantial flexibility of domestic wages and prices to bring the real exchange rate back to its original level—or possibly even lower to compensate for higher debt-servicing payments.

This pattern of effects under exchange-rate based stabilization is not unique to Latin America. Cross-country analysis—including Israel (1986) and Turkey

(1995)—indicates similar behavior.[1] What accounts for the boom-bust cycle under exchange rate-based stabilization? Alternative hypotheses have been proposed:[2]

- *Wealth effects:* The decline in inflation reduces the inflation tax on households and firms, increasing wealth and thus boosting spending (Kimbrough, 1986). The problem with this explanation is that it

---

[1]In contrast, Gould (1996) argues that money-based and exchange rate-based stabilizations have similar output effects after controlling for past inflation and reserve levels. His results are sensitive to the choice of timing of stabilization, however. More generally, his model is based on the view that countries with high past inflation choose money-based stabilization, contrary to the stylized facts in Latin America since the mid-1980s.

[2]For reviews of this literature, see Rebelo and Végh (1995) and Fischer, Sahay, and Végh (2002).

Experience with Exchange Rate-Stabilization Plans in Latin America
(Centered on year of program introduction)

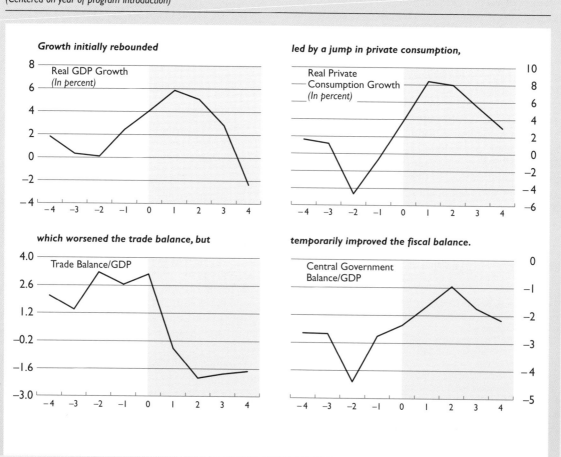

is difficult to obtain effects as large as those observed in the data, especially if it is assumed that the government "rebates" the inflation tax to the public in the pre-stabilization period.

- *Imperfect credibility and intertemporal substitution:* If stabilization plans are not fully credible, households may shift consumption from the future to the period when the plan is in place, thus reducing transaction costs associated with the inflation tax (Calvo, 1986; Calvo and Végh, 1993; and Mendoza and Uribe, 1999). As for wealth effects, however, it is difficult to generate a significant impact unless the intertemporal elasticity of substitution is well above typical estimates (Reinhart and Végh, 1995).

- *Inflation stickiness:* Introducing inflation stickiness helps to explain why real interest rates may be quite low at the beginning of these plans, as well as why the real exchange rate tends to appreciate (Rod-

riguez, 1982; Celasun, 2003)). The difficulty here is how to motivate inflation stickiness when inflation is actually often observed to drop very sharply when stabilization plans are introduced.

In short, there are drawbacks to each of these explanations considered individually. More recently, however, Burstein and others (2003) have shown that the presence of distribution costs in the traded-goods sector can substantially increase the predicted impact of exchange rate-based stabilization arising from these factors, especially for the real exchange rate. This feature allows them to closely mimic the effects of the 1991 stabilization plan in Argentina, even in a model in which stabilization is perfectly credible. In practice, a combination of the above factors has probably played a role in most experiences with exchange rate-based stabilization, and collectively they appear capable of explaining the main stylized facts.

Experience with Exchange Rate-Stabilization Plans in Latin America (concluded)
(Centered on year of program introduction)

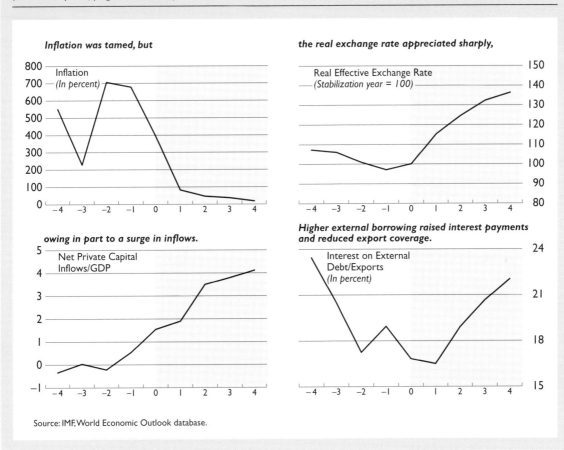

Source: IMF, World Economic Outlook database.

region during the 1990s is difficult to assess. Chile's controls, for instance, were implemented in the context of a robust, preexisting institutional structure for monitoring financial flows that was not available in some other countries. Continuing efforts were also needed to ensure broad coverage of the controls to maintain their macroeconomic effectiveness and minimize microeconomic distortions. Finally, Chile's controls were viewed as a supporting measure for sound monetary, exchange rate, and fiscal policies; and even their proponents agree they would not have been effective absent sound policies in these areas. Beyond implementation issues, there is the more general question of whether short-term capital inflows were perceived as a problem by other countries in the region. Indeed, many governments were themselves actively issuing short-term external debt, since they viewed strong foreign demand for these instruments as an indication of confidence in their policy regimes. In the event, it seems that both weak implementation capacity and absence of will presented obstacles to the introduction of controls on capital inflows elsewhere in the region.

Effects on Other Elements of Reform Programs

As discussed above, exchange rate-based stabilization plans had immediate benefits in terms of reducing inflation and stimulating demand. Medium-term sustainability, however, was more difficult to achieve in an environment of decreasing competitiveness and rising external debt. These plans also tended to affect policy implementation in other areas, including fiscal consolidation and trade opening.

Regarding fiscal consolidation, it was generally understood from the outset of stabilization plans that budgetary restraint would be necessary to sustain inflexible exchange rate regimes. Yet immediate, tangible incentives to consolidate fiscal positions were absent, or even perverse, under exchange rate-based stabilization. As discussed in Section III, expanded access to external finance lowered borrowing costs, especially in foreign currencies, which, in turn, encouraged greater debt issuance along with a shift to riskier short-term external financing. Given uncertainties about the willingness of governments to take further consolidation measures, it was difficult to assess whether "fiscal dominance" had, indeed, been avoided. In any case, the immediate financing environment under exchange rate-based stabilization did not encourage prudence.[104]

The second feature that undermined fiscal discipline was the lack of scope for countercyclical monetary policy implied by inflexible exchange rate regimes to offset the contractionary effects of fiscal consolidation on activity. This was not a major problem in the initial stages of stabilization, when output growth tended to be robust owing to strong growth in private domestic demand. It became more problematic later, however, when the initial boost to private demand faded and markets began to question the sustainability of fiscal policy, causing sovereign yield spreads to rise. Opportunities to take credible fiscal policy initiatives to address these doubts became very limited, since fiscal contraction would have undermined activity further.

As is discussed in Section VII, trade opening may also have been hindered by inflexible exchange rates. Without scope for adjustments in nominal exchange rates, the relative price changes needed to adapt to trade liberalization had to come about through movements in domestic prices and wages.[105] Since these markets remained inflexible, the adjustment process was slow and export growth was suppressed. With exports stagnating relative to overall activity and falling relative to interest payments on external debt, the ability of these economies to adapt to shocks was undermined.

Another area in which inflexible exchange rates may have had indirect spillovers was the financial sector. Specifically, there was a tendency during the 1990s for informal dollarization to rise in Latin American economies that had inflexible exchange rate regimes. As is discussed in Section VI, low observed exchange rate volatility may have suppressed the risks arising from the associated currency mismatches, encouraging the informal dollarization of liabilities.[106] The result was to increase vulnerabilities in the financial sector, which exacerbated crises when these exchange rate regimes were eventually abandoned.

Exit and Regime Change

Almost all of the exchange rate-based stabilization plans culminated in financial crises and forced exits to more flexible regimes. Mexico was first, with its tequila crisis of 1994–95, followed by Brazil (1999), Argentina (2001), and Uruguay (2002).[107] Ecuador,

---

[104]On the general issue of why fiscal prudence may not be promoted by exchange rate-based stabilization, see Tornell and Velasco (1995, 1998).

[105]In particular, a decline in domestic prices was needed to offset the decline in the domestic prices of imported goods associated with a reduction in trade barriers.

[106]See Cuevas and Werner (2003) for evidence on liability dollarization in the Mexican corporate sector.

[107]In this context, Hamann and Prati (2002) find that exchange rate anchors enhance the probability of a successful disinflation

although classified here as having a "soft" exchange rate objective, also experienced a financial crisis in 1999, but it exited instead to a more rigid relationship by adopting formal dollarization. In contrast to these crisis-driven exits, the countries that pursued informal inflation targeting during the 1990s—Chile, Colombia, and Peru—managed to achieve gradual transitions to more formal inflation-targeting regimes without experiencing sharp volatility in exchange rates or inflation.

These financial crises were generally associated with sharp declines in activity, with the impact often being exacerbated by belated attempts to counteract market pressures made in the period immediately before the crisis. Examples are Mexico's issuance of *Tesobonos* in 1994 and Argentina's forced debt restructuring in 2000–2001. What is perhaps more surprising is that the financial volatility accompanying these crises did not presage a quick return to the triple-digit inflation rates of the 1980s. In Mexico, for instance, inflation averaged 50 percent in the 12 months following the collapse of the exchange rate at the end of 1994 and then decelerated steadily back to single-digit levels in the context of a floating exchange rate regime and an announced objective for inflation.[108] Formal inflation targeting was introduced in 2000, with the target gradually being lowered to 3 percent in 2003.

Brazil's experience with abandoning an inflexible exchange rate anchor in 1999 is another striking break from the region's past experience of a return to hyperinflation. Despite depreciation in the *real* of almost 60 percent through 1999, inflation averaged under 10 percent that year and remained in single digits until late 2002.[109] In Argentina, in spite of a plunge in the exchange rate to about one-third of its pre-crisis value in 2002, inflation peaked at only about 40 percent.

Lessons, Policy Responses, and Challenges

It seems, then, that the underlying dynamics of inflation in the region were altered by the experience of

the 1990s. Inflation expectations appear to have become better anchored; and, in a related development, the pass-through of exchange rate changes to inflation has declined. These developments provide support for the view that exchange rate-based stabilization plans, while not in themselves sustainable in the context of the structures of these economies and other policies, set the stage for establishing the credibility of sustained low inflation in the region. Much credit goes to the progressive introduction of more flexible policy responses in the region that have sustained low inflation despite the market pressures and financial crises of recent years. In many countries, the inflation-targeting approach has provided the basic framework underlying these responses and, in most cases, the greater constitutional or de facto autonomy of central banks has been fundamental in providing credibility for the commitment to low inflation.

The recent experience with inflation targeting in Latin American countries—including Brazil, Chile, Colombia, Mexico, and Peru—has been promising.[110] As shown in Figure 4.5, inflation has generally been kept in line with targets in these countries:

- Mexico's experience with a flexible exchange rate and inflation targeting is discussed in detail in Cuevas and Werner (2003). They conclude that growth in trade and foreign investment has not been undermined by exchange rate flexibility, although it has had the desirable effect of reducing informal dollarization of corporate liabilities. At the same time, movements in the nominal exchange rate have been important in allowing adjustments to changing competitiveness without abrupt internal adjustments. Monetary policy has been used flexibly to provide countercyclical support for activity in times of internal and external weakness.

- In Brazil, the relatively new inflation-targeting regime (adopted in 1999) was severely tested in the context of the political transition in 2002–2003, and associated market pressures and shocks. The regime has worked well to guide expectations, minimize slippages from original targets, and bring inflation rapidly down by the end of 2003, thereby enabling policy-determined interest rates in Brazil to return relatively quickly to levels below those prevailing before the crisis in market pressures occurred in 2002.

- These generally favorable experiences under inflation targeting point to the viability of monetary policy strategies that focus on the ultimate objec-

strategy. Their evaluation period, however, extends only three years after the beginning of the disinflation. Thus, the stabilizations in Argentina (1991), Mexico (1989), Uruguay (1992), and Ecuador (1994) are judged to have been successful, even though they eventually ended in crisis.

[108]See Berg and others (2003) for a review of monetary regimes following financial crises, including Mexico (1994), Brazil (1999), and Ecuador (1999). The Mexican experience is described in more detail in Carstens and Werner (1999).

[109]See Belaisch (2003) for a discussion of why inflation pass-through may have been low in Brazil during this episode.

[110]About twenty countries worldwide have adopted inflation-targeting regimes, demonstrating a trend that is likely to continue. Argentina is also preparing to implement inflation targeting.

Figure 4.5. Inflation Targeting in Latin America
(12-month percentage change in CPI)

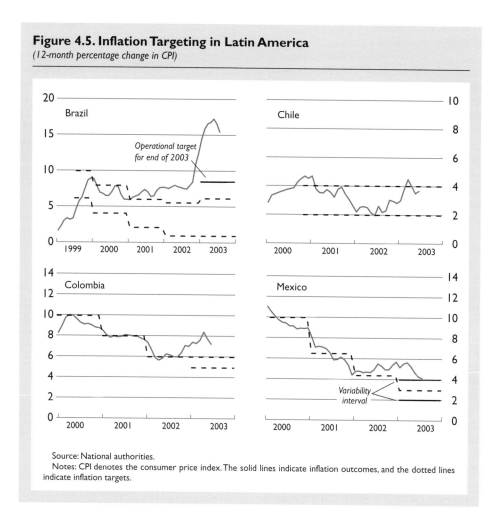

Source: National authorities.
Notes: CPI denotes the consumer price index. The solid lines indicate inflation outcomes, and the dotted lines indicate inflation targets.

tive of keeping inflation low while allowing exchange rates to be determined by market forces—an outcome that was not evident when the initial stabilization plans were introduced in the late 1980s and early 1990s.[111] These approaches, supported by growing policy credibility, have also allowed monetary policy to play a more active countercyclical role in recent years.[112]

It is important to recognize that the inflation-targeting approach is still evolving in Latin America, even in countries where it has operated for some time, and that lessons are still being learned from its implementation. Thus, there are still challenges to

ensuring that the approach becomes entrenched. Meeting these will require efforts extending well beyond countries' central banks. As is well known, full-fledged inflation targeting is based on several important pillars, many of which are more challenging for emerging market countries—including those in Latin America—to construct than for the industrial countries in which the approach originated. Among the enabling conditions for the approach are the absence of fiscal dominance and the presence of a well-established macroeconomic framework, policy instrument independence, and a sound and developed financial system. In addition, countries in Latin America are generally more vulnerable to shocks than their industrial country counterparts and may face more difficult trade-offs between output and inflation—especially in deciding upon the time frame within which to adjust to shocks—both of which add to the challenges they face in implementing inflation targeting. Although inflation targeting has generally been conceived in the context of a flexible exchange rate regime, recent thinking suggests that it can still

[111]Ho and McCauley (2003) analyze how exchange rate movements have been incorporated in inflation-targeting frameworks in emerging market economies. Other recent analyses of inflation targeting and exchange rate policy in emerging markets include Schaecter, Stone, and Zelmer (2000); Williamson (2000); Rojas-Suarez (2003); and Goldstein (2002).

[112]Ortíz (2002) discusses the recent experiences with countercyclical monetary policy in Mexico and Chile.

play a role in countries that are unwilling to let the exchange rate float freely.[113]

Despite these concerns, it is important to note that most countries that have adopted inflation targeting have been able to phase in—sometimes over an extended period—the conditions needed for effective, full-fledged inflation targeting.[114] For example, among industrial countries, the Bank of England adopted inflation targeting well before gaining instrument independence. Most central banks have gradually improved their policy transparency and the sophistication and dissemination of their inflation forecasts. Indeed, a country is more likely to put in place the enabling conditions—which are needed in any case for sound monetary policy—once it has adopted inflation targeting, so there seems to be an important, mutually reinforcing process involved.

Thus, countries in Latin America are making steady progress in creating the conditions necessary for full-fledged inflation targeting. Given their countries' history of higher and more variable rates of inflation, and concern about their greater vulnerability to monetization of government debt, policymakers in Latin America have been working toward formal institutional frameworks that extend central bank autonomy and restrict or prohibit central bank financing of government deficits. Many central banks are also enhancing their analytical capacities and making their operations and decision-making processes more transparent. For example, some central bank inflation reports now feature greater emphasis on forward-looking analyses of inflation (in Colombia and Argentina, among others). Carrying these efforts to completion is an important challenge for the region, especially in ensuring that central bank laws clearly assign monetary responsibility to senior bank officials, and provide central banks with appropriate objectives, incentives for good performance, and operational independence.

Nevertheless, conditions in emerging market countries—including those in Latin America—continue to pose special challenges for ensuring that full-fledged inflation targeting becomes entrenched. First, there may be considerable pressure to suspend inflation targets and resist bringing inflation down, particularly when growth is weak. Second, continued fiscal dominance still creates a risk, although, as explained in Section III, countries in the region have renewed

their commitment to establishing stronger fiscal institutions that would keep fiscal policy in check. Third, a high degree of informal dollarization is also potentially a problem, notably because it might induce central banks to try to prevent sharp exchange rate fluctuations that could undermine adherence to the inflation objective. Fourth, even in countries without high dollarization, central banks may be sensitive to movements in the exchange rate, making it more difficult to establish and maintain the credibility of the approach. To some extent, these dilemmas can be addressed by recognizing that inflation targeting still allows policymakers some room to consider short-term trade-offs with other objectives and deciding upon the extent of flexibility to accommodate within the approach (i.e., to avoid being "inflation nutters" as described by Mervyn King).

In concluding this section, there is much reason for optimism about the recent transition in Latin America to more robust approaches to sustaining low inflation. The experience already gained has shown that inflation targeting, combined with exchange rate flexibility, presents a viable and robust monetary regime for countries in the region. The durability of the "constrained discretion" implied by these inflation-targeting regimes remains to be fully tested, however, given their relatively short histories. Successful implementation also requires strong institutional autonomy and capacities of the sort that the region's many central banks are striving to put in place. The IMF is closely engaged in helping its member countries with the development of these new institutional structures.

References

Agosín, Manuel R., and Ricardo Ffrench-Davis, 2001, "Managing Capital Flows in Chile," in *Short-Term Capital Flows and Economic Crises*, ed. by Stephany Griffith-Jones, Manuel F. Montes, and Anwar Nasution (New York: Oxford University Press).

Almeida, Alvaro, and Charles Goodhart, 1998, "Does the Adoption of Inflation Targets Affect Central Bank Behaviour?" *Banca Nazionale del Lavoro Quarterly Review*, Vol. 51 (March), pp. 9–107.

Belaisch, Agnès, 2003, "Exchange Rate Pass-Through in Brazil," IMF Working Paper 03/141 (Washington: International Monetary Fund).

Berg, Andrew, Eduardo Borensztein, and Catherine Pattillo, 1999, *Anticipating Balance of Payments Crises: The Role of Early Warning Systems*, IMF Occasional Paper No. 186 (Washington: International Monetary Fund).

Berg, Andrew, Christopher J. Jarvis, Mark R. Stone, and Alessandro Zanello, 2003, "Reestablishing Credible Nominal Anchors After a Financial Crisis: A Review of Recent Experience," IMF Working Paper 03/76 (Washington: International Monetary Fund).

---

[113]Truman (2003).

[114]See Mishkin (2000); Mishkin and Schmidt-Hebbel (2001); and Fraga, Goldfajn, and Minella (2003) for comprehensive assessments of the conditions and unresolved issues regarding the implementation of inflation targeting, especially of the implications for emerging market countries. Corbo and Schmidt-Hebbel (2001) and Corbo (2002) present additional material on the Latin American experience.

Berg, Andrew, and Catherine Pattillo, 1999, "Predicting Currency Crises: The Indicators Approach and an Alternative," *Journal of International Money and Finance*, Vol. 18 (August), pp. 561–86.

Bernanke, Ben S., Thomas Laubach, Frederic S. Mishkin, and Adam Posen, 1999, *Inflation Targeting: Lessons From the International Experience* (Princeton, New Jersey: Princeton University Press).

Bubula, Andrea, and Inci Ötker-Robe, 2002, "The Evolution of Exchange Rate Regimes Since 1990: Evidence from De Facto Policies," IMF Working Paper 02/155 (Washington: International Monetary Fund).

Burstein, Ariel T., João C. Neves, and Sergio Rebelo, 2003, "Distribution Costs and Real Exchange Rate Dynamics During Exchange Rate-Based Stabilizations," *Journal of Monetary Economics*, Vol. 50, No. 6, pp. 1189–214.

Cagan, Philip, 1956, "The Monetary Dynamics of Hyperinflation," in *Studies in the Quantity Theory of Money*, ed. by Milton Friedman (Chicago: University of Chicago Press), pp. 25–117.

Calderón, César, and Klaus Schmidt-Hebbel, 2003, "Learning the Hard Way: Ten Lessons for Latin America's Turmoil" (unpublished; Santiago, Chile: Central Bank of Chile).

Calvo, Guillermo A., 1986, "Temporary Stabilization: Predetermined Exchange Rates," *Journal of Political Economy*, Vol. 94 (December), pp. 1319–29.

———, and Carmen Reinhart, 2000, "Fear of Floating," NBER Working Paper No. 7993 (Cambridge, Massachusetts: National Bureau of Economic Research).

Calvo, Guillermo A., and Carlos Végh, 1993, "Exchange Rate-Based Stabilization Under Imperfect Credibility," in *Open Economy Macroeconomics*, ed. by Helmut Frisch and Andreas Wörgötter (London: Macmillan), pp. 3–28.

———, 1999, "Inflation Stabilization and Balance of Payments Crises in Developing Countries," in *Handbook of Macroeconomics*, ed. by John Taylor and Michael Woodford (Amsterdam: North-Holland), pp. 1531–614.

Cárdenas, Mauricio, and Felipe Barrera, 1997, "On the Effectiveness of Capital Controls: The Experience of Colombia During the 1990s," *Journal of Development Economics*, Vol. 54 (October), pp. 27–57.

Cárdenas, Mauricio, and Roberto Steiner, 2000, "Private Capital Flows in Colombia," in *Capital Flows, Capital Controls and Currency Crises: Latin America in the 1990s*, ed. by Felipe Larraín (Ann Arbor, Michigan: University of Michigan Press).

Carstens, Agustín, and Alejandro Werner, 1999, "Mexico's Monetary Policy Framework under a Floating Exchange Rate Regime," Serie Documento de Investigación No. 9905 (Mexico City: Banco de México).

Catão, Luis, and Marco E. Terrones, 2003, "Fiscal Deficits and Inflation," IMF Working Paper 03/65 (Washington: International Monetary Fund).

Celasun, Oya, 2003, "Sticky Inflation and the Real Effects of Exchange Rate-Based Stabilization," IMF Working Paper 03/151 (Washington: International Monetary Fund).

Corbo, Vittorio, 2000, "Monetary Policy in Latin America in the 90s," Central Bank of Chile Working Paper No. 78 (Santiago, Chile: Central Bank of Chile).

———, 2002, "Monetary Policy in Latin America in the 90s," in *Monetary Policy and Transmissions Mechanisms*, ed. by Norman Loayza and Klaus Schmidt-Hebbel (Santiago, Chile: Central Bank of Chile).

———, and Klaus Schmidt-Hebbel, 2001, "Inflation Targeting in Latin America," Central Bank of Chile Working Paper No. 105 (Santiago, Chile: Central Bank of Chile).

Cuevas, Alfredo, and Alejandro Werner, 2003, "Mexico's Experience with a Flexible Exchange Rate Regime," *Management International*, Vol. 8 (Autumn), pp. 29–49.

De Gregorio, José, Sebastian Edwards, and Rodrigo O. Valdés, 2000, "Controls on Capital Inflows: Do They Work?" *Journal of Development Economics*, Vol. 63 (October), pp. 59–83.

Edwards, Sebastian, 1998, "Exchange Rate Anchors and Inflation: A Political Economy Approach," in *Positive Political Economy: Theory and Evidence*, ed. by Sylvester Eijffinger and Harry Huizinga (New York: Cambridge University Press).

———, 2000, "Twenty-Five Years of Stabilization Programs in Latin America: The Exchange Rate Connection" paper presented at the conference celebrating the Banco de México's seventy-fifth anniversary, Mexico City, November 14–15.

———, and Miguel Savastano, 1999, "Exchange Rates in Emerging Economies: What Do We Know and What Do We Need to Know?" NBER Working Paper No. 7228 (Cambridge, Massachusetts: National Bureau of Economic Research).

Eichengreen, Barry, and Paul R. Masson, 1998, *Exit Strategies: Policy Options for Countries Seeking Greater Exchange Rate Flexibility*, IMF Occasional Paper No. 168 (Washington: International Monetary Fund).

Espinosa-Vega, Marco A., Bruce Smith, and Chong K. Yip, 2000, "Barriers to International Capital Flows: When, Why, How Big, and for Whom?" Federal Reserve Bank of Atlanta Working Paper No. 2000-16 (Atlanta).

Fischer, Stanley, Ratna Sahay, and Carlos Végh, 2002, "Modern Hyper- and High Inflations," IMF Working Paper No. 02/197 (Washington: International Monetary Fund).

Fraga, Arminio, Ilan Goldfajn, and Andre Minella, 2003, "Inflation Targeting in Emerging Market Economies," NBER Working Paper No. 10019 (Cambridge, Massachusetts: National Bureau of Economic Research).

Frenkel, J.A., 2003, "Experience of and Lessons from Exchange Rate Regimes in Emerging Economies," background paper for *Study on Monetary and Financial Cooperation in East Asia* (McMillan Press).

Ghosh, Atish, Anne-Marie Gulde, Jonathan Ostry, and Holger Wolf, 1997, "Does the Nominal Exchange Rate Regime Matter?" NBER Working Paper No. 5874 (Cambridge, Massachusetts: National Bureau of Economic Research).

Goldstein, Morris, 2002, "Managed Floating Plus," Policy Analyses in International Economics No. 66 (Washington: Institute for International Economics).

Gould, D., 1996, "Exchange Rate- vs. Monetary-Based Stabilization: Recession Now vs. Recession Later?" (unpublished; Dallas: Federal Reserve Bank of Dallas).

Gutiérrez, Eva, 2003, "Inflation Performance and Constitutional Central Bank Independence: Evidence From Latin America and the Caribbean," IMF Working Paper 03/53 (Washington: International Monetary Fund, March).

Hamann, A. Javier, 2001, "Exchange Rate-Based Stabilization: A Critical Look at the Stylized Facts," *Staff Papers*, International Monetary Fund, Vol. 48, No. 1, pp. 111–37.

———, and Alessandro Prati, 2002, "Why Do Many Disinflations Fail? The Importance of Luck, Timing, and Political Institutions," IMF Working Paper 02/228 (Washington: International Monetary Fund).

Ho, Corinne, and Robert McCauley, 2003, "Living with Flexible Exchange Rates: Issues and Recent Experience in Inflation Targeting Emerging Market Economies," BIS Working Paper No. 130 (Basel: Bank for International Settlements).

Jácome, Luis I., 2001, "Legal Central Bank Independence and Inflation in Latin America During the 1990s," IMF Working Paper 01/212 (Washington: International Monetary Fund).

Kiguel, Miguel, and Nissan Liviatan, 1992, "The Business Cycle Associated with Exchange Rate-Based Stabilization," *World Bank Economic Review*, Vol. 6 (May), pp. 279–305.

Kimbrough, K.P., 1986, "The Optimum Quantity of Money Rule in the Theory of Public Finance," *Journal of Monetary Economics*, Vol. 18 (November), pp. 277–84.

Le Fort, Guillermo R., and Carlos Budnevich, 1996, "Capital Account Regulation and Macroeconomic Policy: Two Latin Experiences," Jerome Levy Economics Institute Working Paper No. 162 (Annandale-on-Hudson, New York: Bard College).

Le Fort, Guillermo R., and Sergio Lehmann, 2003, "The Unremunerated Reserve Requirement and Net Capital Flows: Chile in the 1990s," *ECLAC Review*, Economic Commission for Latin America and the Caribbean, Vol. 81 (December).

Levy Yeyati, Eduardo, and Federico Sturzenegger, 2002a, "Classifying Exchange Rate Regimes: Deeds vs. Words" (unpublished; Buenos Aires: Universidad Torcuato Di Tella).

———, 2002b, "To Float or to Trail: Evidence on the Impact of Exchange Rate Regimes" (unpublished; Buenos Aires: Universidad Torcuato di Tella). Also available on the Web at *http://www.utdt.edu/~ely/Marzo2002.pdf.*

Martinez, Lorenzo, and Alejandro Werner, 2002, "The Exchange Rate Regime and the Currency Composition of Corporate Debt: The Mexican Experience," *Journal of Development Economics*, Vol. 69, No. 2, pp. 315–34.

Mendoza, Enrique G., and Martín Uribe, 1999, "Devaluation Risk and the Syndrome of Exchange Rate-Based Stabilizations," NBER Working Paper No. 7014 (Cambridge, Massachusetts: National Bureau of Economic Research).

Mishkin, Frederic, 2000, "Inflation Targeting in Emerging Market Countries," NBER Working Paper No. 7618 (Cambridge, Massachusetts: National Bureau of Economic Research).

———, and Miguel Savastano, 2000, "Monetary Policy Strategies for Latin America," NBER Working Paper No. 7617 (Cambridge, Massachusetts: National Bureau of Economic Research).

Mishkin, Frederic, and Klaus Schmidt-Hebbel, 2001, "One Decade of Inflation Targeting in the World: What Do We Know and What Do We Need to Know?" NBER Working Paper No. 8397 (Cambridge, Massachusetts: National Bureau of Economic Research).

Nadal-De Simone, Francisco, and Piritta Sorsa, 1999, "A Review of Capital Account Restrictions in Chile in the 1990s," IMF Working Paper 99/52 (Washington: International Monetary Fund).

Ocampo, José A., and Camilo Tovar, 2003, "Managing the Capital Account: Colombia's Experience with Price-Based Controls on Capital Inflows," *ECLAC Review (Revista de la CEPAL)*, No. 81 (December), pp. 47–75.

Ortíz, Guillermo, 2002, "Monetary Policy in a Changing Economic Environment: The Latin American Experience," paper presented at the Federal Reserve Bank of Kansas City's symposium on Rethinking Stabilization Policy, Jackson Hole, Wyoming, August 29–31.

Pazos, Felipe, 1972, *Chronic Inflation in Latin America* (New York: Praeger).

Radelet, Steven, and Jeffrey Sachs, 1998, "The Onset of the East Asian Financial Crisis," NBER Working Paper No. 6680 (Cambridge, Massachusetts: National Bureau of Economic Research).

Rebelo, Sergio, and Carlos A. Végh, 1995, "Real Effects of Exchange Rate-Based Stabilization: An Analysis of Competing Theories," in *Macroeconomic Annual,* ed. by Ben S. Bernanke and Julio Rotemberg (Cambridge, Massachusetts: National Bureau of Economic Research), pp. 125–74.

Reinhart, Carmen, and Kenneth Rogoff, 2002, "The Modern History of Exchange Rate Arrangements: A Reinterpretation," NBER Working Paper No. 8963 (Cambridge, Massachusetts: National Bureau of Economic Research).

Reinhart, Carmen, and Carlos A. Végh, 1995, "Nominal Interest Rates, Consumption Booms, and Lack of Credibility: A Quantitative Investigation," *Journal of Development Economics*, Vol. 46 (April), pp. 357–78.

Rodriguez, Carlos A., 1982, "The Argentine Stabilization Plan of December 20th," *World Development*, Vol. 10 (September), pp. 801–11.

Rojas-Suarez, Liliana, 2003, "Monetary Policy and Exchange Rates: Guiding Principles for a Sustainable Regime," in *After the Washington Consensus*, ed. by Pedro-Pablo Kuczynski and John Williamson (Washington: Institute for International Economics), pp. 123–56.

Sargent, Thomas J., and Neil Wallace, 1981, "Some Unpleasant Monetarist Arithmetic," *Federal Reserve Bank of Minneapolis Quarterly Review*, Vol. 5 (Fall), pp. 1–17.

Schaecter, Andrea, Mark R. Stone, and Mark Zelmer, 2000, *Adopting Inflation Targeting: Practical Issues for Emerging Market Countries*, IMF Occasional Paper No. 202 (Washington: International Monetary Fund).

Tornell, Aaron, and Andrés Velasco, 1995, "Fiscal Discipline and the Choice of Exchange Rate Regime," *European Economic Review*, Vol. 39 (April), pp. 759–70.

———, 1998, "Fiscal Discipline and the Choice of a Nominal Anchor in Stabilization," *Journal of International Economics*, Vol. 46 (October), pp. 1–30.

Truman, Edwin, 2003, *Inflation Targeting in the World Economy* (Washington: Institute for International Economics).

Végh, Carlos A., 1992, "Stopping High Inflation: An Analytical Overview," *Staff Papers*, International Monetary Fund, Vol. 39 (September), pp. 626–95.

Williamson, John, 2000, "Exchange Rate Regimes for Emerging Markets: Reviving the Intermediate Option," Policy Analyses in International Economics No. 60 (Washington: Institute for International Economics).

V Latin American Financial Systems: Crises and Reforms

Limited access to bank credit and uncertainty about financial system stability have been serious constraints on Latin America's growth and have contributed to volatility during the past decade. Financial liberalization and the promise of reforms spurred credit growth during the early part of the 1990s, but bank lending slowed after a series of banking crises in the mid-1990s (Figure 5.1). Subsequently, bank restructuring and regulatory reforms were successful in strengthening banking systems in a number of countries. Reforms were less successful in others, however, particularly in addressing the specific vulnerabilities associated with dollarization of banks' assets and liabilities. Another round of pressures hit many Latin American banking systems in the late 1990s and early in the present decade.

This section seeks to explain how these financial sector developments have been related to the structural characteristics of Latin American economies, and to highlight the channels through which financial sector shortcomings may have affected Latin America's macroeconomic performance. The economic literature has long recognized the existence of a close connection between financial development and economic growth, although the long-running debate about the direction of causality of this linkage has yet to be fully resolved.[115] The analysis presented here does not attempt a formal econometric investigation of this relationship, but it provides further evidence that financial systems do matter for economic performance. Hence, a critical element of a strategy to strengthen Latin America's growth going forward must be continued efforts to ensure financial system soundness and promote deeper financial intermediation.

This section opens by presenting the key features of financial intermediation in Latin America today. Banking systems are highly concentrated, intermediation margins are high, and the scale of bank lending is low relative to economic activity. It then discusses how the shape of banking systems in Latin America today is the result of a number of underlying, often

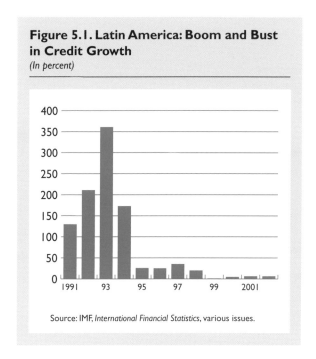

Figure 5.1. Latin America: Boom and Bust in Credit Growth
(In percent)

Source: IMF, *International Financial Statistics*, various issues.

structural weaknesses that affected most countries in the region during the 1990s. The following subsection explains how many of these weaknesses were at the source of the banking crises in the 1990s. The section finally draws some lessons from Latin America's experience about the best way to promote financial system stability and intermediation, which are key ingredients for sustained growth.

Key Characteristics of Latin American Financial Systems

Market Structure

Latin American financial systems are still largely bank-based, with security markets mostly small and illiquid. In an environment of uncertainty and economic instability, banks have retained a comparative advantage in the costly collection and processing of

---

[115]See the recent discussion in Fischer (2003).

Table 5.1. International Comparison: Financial Systems, 2003
(In percent of GDP)

| | Banking System[1] | | | Outstanding Domestic Debt Securities, by Issuer[2] | | | | Stock Market Capitalization | Money (M2) |
	Deposits	Loans	Assets	Total	Corporate	Financial institutions	Public sector		
Argentina	25.3	14.2	44.8	25.2	8.4	4.6	12.2	144.4	30.1
Brazil	30.6	21.5	74.6	47.2	0.4	8.8	38.0	41.0	29.7
Chile	38.1	68.5	79.8	52.9	9.9	14.0	29.0	100.0	38.4
Colombia	19.7	19.7	37.9	...	...	...	...	12.5	29.1
Ecuador[3]	16.8	15.1	22.0	24.8	2.5	...	22.4	15.7	23.4
Mexico	25.5	16.1	52.3	13.9	1.3	0.6	12.0	23.9	29.1
Paraguay	24.6	17.6	31.7	...	...	...	...	5.5	31.4
Peru	14.5	13.7	19.2	7.1	2.3	1.6	3.0	23.9	29.6
Uruguay	36.4	64.3	82.6	...	...	...	...	1.6	67.7
Venezuela[3]	20.0	8.1	23.9	1.3	...	...	1.3	9.2	22.1
Memorandum items:									
Advanced economies									
United States	31.7	60.8	67.7	155.3	23.1	89.0	43.2	123.0	66.7
Japan	121.2	122.9	146.5	169.8	18.9	29.1	121.7	67.9	133.5
Euro area	85.4	140.6	303.9	97.1	7.4	32.4	57.3	50.8	92.2
Emerging markets									
Malaysia	96.0	117.7	129.6	86.9	39.9	11.1	35.7	157.0	102.6
Thailand	90.5	90.9	106.2	37.4	5.1	9.4	22.9	76.8	96.7
Korea, Republic of	76.6	98.9	114.0	82.5	29.0	32.8	20.7	53.5	76.7

Sources: National bank supervisory agencies and central banks; Bankscope (industrial countries' banking systems); Bank for International Settlements (outstanding domestic debt securities, except for Chile and Ecuador); Federación Iberoamericana de Bolsas de Valores.

[1]Only deposit-taking commercial banks are considered.

[2]At book value, except for Chile and Ecuador, for which market values are provided. (For these two countries, the corporate figures include financial institutions.)

[3]Domestic debt securities data are as of 2000.

information that is central to financial intermediation. International experience suggests that market-based finance typically develops only after banking systems have matured, information has become more easily available, and financial operations and services have turned more complex.[116] In most Latin American countries, the private sector's use of bond and equity markets to raise finance remains limited, relative to its recourse to banks, although, in some countries, pension reforms have begun to encourage broader capital market development.

Despite their prominence, banking systems remain relatively small compared with GDP, and the depth of intermediation is particularly low (Table 5.1). Deposit-to-GDP ratios are less than 50 percent, compared with typical ratios of 90 percent in East Asian emerging markets. Moreover, bank credit represents only a fraction of bank assets. In most countries, excepting Chile and Ecuador, lending represents no more than a third of bank assets. Again excepting Chile, the ratio of bank credit to economic activity remains much smaller than in the bank-based financial systems of the advanced economies of the euro area and Japan, or of the emerging market economies of Asia.

The pattern of credit growth in Latin America has been marked by boom-bust cycles. Credit growth was particularly rapid in the early 1990s in most countries, but collapsed in many cases after banking crises in the mid-1990s and has since remained subdued (see Figure 5.1). Argentina, Brazil, and Mexico all follow this pattern, although in Mexico the growth of other sources of financial intermediation has partly compensated for the lack of bank activity (Box 5.1). Chile has managed to achieve a more even pattern of credit growth, because of its longer track record of macroeconomic stability and earlier financial sector reform.

Over this period, a rising share of bank balance sheets has been absorbed by government securities. During the second half of the 1990s, many banks in

---

[116]See, for example, Rojas-Suarez and Weisbrod (1994).

Box 5.1. Finance for Growth: Experiences in Chile and Mexico

Chile and Mexico, the fastest-growing Latin American economies in the 1990s, provide useful case studies of the role of banks in the financing of the economy. The large, developed Chilean banking system has assets about the size of the country's GDP. The rapid adoption of a strong institutional framework following a banking crisis in the early 1980s helped credit to recover quickly and expand by more than a third during the 1990s, to reach 70 percent of GDP in 2000, while financial liberalization and innovation continued. In Mexico, the banking crisis of the mid-1990s cut the size of the banking system by more than half. Credit to the private sector declined drastically, from 45 percent to 14 percent of GDP during 1994–2002, and is only now beginning to recover in the wake of continued financial sector reforms.

In both countries, weak regulatory structures were at the root of banking crises. In Chile (in the mid-1970s) and in Mexico (in the late 1980s and early 1990s), interest rates were liberalized, entry barriers removed, the banking system privatized, and restrictions on capital flows reduced. In each country, financial liberalization was followed by a large jump in bank credit to the private sector. This credit boom, however, occurred in the context of a weak regulatory and supervisory framework, leading to banking crises, in the early 1980s in Chile (at a cost now estimated at 30 percent of GDP) and in the mid-1990s in Mexico (at a cost now estimated at 20 percent of GDP). In both cases, the crises contributed to a decline in bank credit and spurred restructuring and consolidation in the sector, with increasing participation by foreign banks.

Banking crises required an overhaul of banking regulation. Drawing on the lessons learned from mistakes that led to the crisis, Chile adopted a stringent banking law in 1986 that seriously limits risk taking by banks by restricting related lending, requiring banks to rate the quality of their investments, and strengthening capital-adequacy requirements. The law also sets clear workout procedures for the resolution of bank insolvencies and stipulates that lender-of-last-resort facilities will not be used to bail out distressed banks. Market discipline is also encouraged through strong disclosure requirements for banks and a limited deposit-insurance system. In Mexico, the regulatory regime initially focused on measures aimed at averting a collapse of the banking system, including provision of financial assistance to distressed banks and debtor-support programs. Since 1999, Mexico has embarked on a new round of structural reforms, accelerating the resolution of troubled banks and bringing the regulatory framework closer to best international practices.

Structural impediments have delayed the resumption of bank lending in Mexico. The lack of liquidity of the notes issued by the government to banks in exchange for nonperforming loans following the crisis restricted the pool of loanable funds and, thus, credit and economic activity. In addition, the sizable demand for resources from the public sector and the perception of a dearth of creditworthy private clients made it easier and more cost-effective for banks to concentrate on a few clients (the government and large corporations) than to take on additional credit risk via broad-based lending. This has not been the case in Chile, where the low level of public debt ensures that private borrowers do not have to compete with the public sector for bank finance. Finally, institutional factors and judicial procedures have in the past complicated loan recovery in Mexico, hampering lending, especially to lesser-known small and medium-sized enterprises (SMEs). Legislation enacted in early 2003 aims at providing creditors with greater legal certainty by improving their ability to recover collateral. In addition, the resolution of issues related to banks' restructuring of debt in mid-2004 has removed an important source of uncertainty in the financial system.

Strong and tightly regulated Chilean banks are engaged in financing across the corporate sector. In Chile, SMEs have as much access to banks for finance as large firms (see table). This has not been the case in Mexico, where bank credit has so far remained principally reserved for large firms. In Mexico, access to credit is available mainly to high-grade borrowers, with most of the financing short term and, thus, not available for the financing of investment. In Chile as well, short-term lending represents a large share of banks' credit portfolios, mostly as a result of tight prudential regulation to limit maturity mismatches. Banks' high degree of risk aversion limits the access of other segments of the economy to credit in both countries. The availability of mortgage credit from banks in Mexico has fallen short of what is needed to satisfy its acute housing needs. However, mortgage lending (including through specialized institutions) has recently begun to grow rapidly.

Sources of financing other than bank credit have come to play a significant role in the expansion of activity in both countries (see figure). In Mexico, in particular, nonbank institutions—including mutual funds, pension

Chile and Mexico: Beneficiaries of Bank Credit
(In percent of total)

	Chile	Mexico
Large firms	34	44
SMEs	31	13
Consumers	8	15
Mortgage	17	22
Other	10	6

Sources: Central banks of Chile and Mexico.
Note: SMEs denotes small and medium-sized enterprises.

Box 5.1 (concluded)

funds, leasing and factoring firms, and savings and loan cooperatives—have grown rapidly in recent years, significantly increasing their shares of credit to the consumer sector and for mortgages. Large exporters rely heavily on foreign financing, including from parent companies. Not surprisingly, the sectors that led growth in the second half of the 1990s were those with access to credit—the export and consumer sectors. In other sectors, suppliers remain the main source of financing for most firms. More than 80 percent of firms granted some type of financing to clients at the start of 2003. In Chile as well, nonbank financial institutions participate significantly in financing activity. Private pension funds are major collectors of savings and now hold assets in excess of 50 percent of GDP. Although large shares of this portfolio are invested in the banking system and in public debt, a small but increasing share is going into bonds issued by Chilean companies. Again, finance remains reserved for large firms in the tradable sectors, leaving whole segments of the economy with limited access to finance for growth. Equity markets represent a larger source of funding for Chilean than for Mexican companies. In both countries, retained earnings still play a major part in the funding of investment.

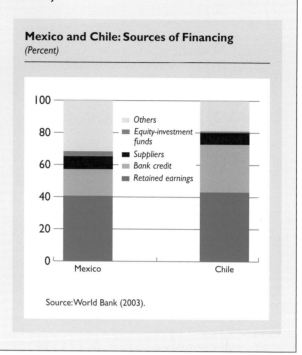

Mexico and Chile: Sources of Financing
(Percent)

Source: World Bank (2003).

Latin America replaced nonperforming loans with sizable portfolios of government bonds. For public banks, this typically occurred through restructuring, with bad credits being replaced by government securities—for example, in Mexico after the 1994 banking crisis. In the private sector, this shift was often a reaction to experience with high default rates on lending to households and corporations and to a tightening of supervisory standards after setbacks to stabilization and reforms in the mid-1990s. As banks shared in the costs of these crises, they sought to hold significant amounts of high-yielding, apparently safer government bonds. For example, Argentine banks' holdings of such bonds more than doubled in 1995; and in Brazil, about a third of banks' assets were invested in government bonds by 2000.[117]

The process of bank restructuring that occurred during the 1990s led to rising foreign ownership of Latin American banking systems. During this process, legal and regulatory limitations on the activities of foreign banks were relaxed or eliminated in most countries. Foreign banks gained market shares, mostly by taking control of domestic banks in need

of fresh capital and new management rather than opening new institutions. In Brazil, for example, foreign banks grew from an insignificant presence in the mid-1990s to hold one-fifth of deposits and provide one-fourth of credit by the end of 2000. In Argentina, Chile, Mexico, Paraguay, Peru, and Venezuela, foreign banks owned more than half of banking-system assets by 2000 (Table 5.2).

A few large banks typically account for the lion's share of the system's assets. Bank restructuring that occurred during the course of the 1990s also led to increasing concentration. Typically, more than two-thirds of bank assets are concentrated in the 10 largest institutions, which hold about 70 percent of deposits and provide 75 percent of credit.

The largest institutions often remain in government hands, however. This is particularly true of Brazil and Argentina, where a few public banks still account for a significant share of banking-system assets and credit, notwithstanding privatization during the 1990s (Table 5.3). As in many banking systems around the world, a long history of government intervention has left traces that are still pervasive today. Many Latin American public banks were endowed with the role of providing credit to targeted segments of the economy, often poorer regions and sectors that had been left outside conventional channels of financing (e.g., housing, regional development, agriculture). Such operations remain impor-

---

[117]See Catão (1997) for a detailed discussion of the Argentine experience.

Table 5.2. Selected Latin American Countries: Structure of Banking Systems

	Argentina	Brazil	Chile	Colombia	Ecuador	Mexico	Paraguay	Peru	Uruguay	Venezuela
Institutions										
Number of banks	71	135	28	32	40	35	22	15	23	39
					(In percent)					
Concentration—Top 10 banks										
Share of total assets	62	70	76	67	82	95	79	95	87	81
Share of total deposits	71	77	78	68	79	90	79	96	85	36
Share of total credit	66	70	80	65	78	93	59	94	88	64
Foreign bank participation										
Number of banks[1]	28	27	18	11	...	20	17	12	16	21
					(In percent)					
Share of total assets	54	28	60	21	...	82	81	64	35	68
Share of total deposits	48	21	47	20	...	82	86	62	34	67
Share of total credit	46	25	45	21	...	77	74	62	35	72

Sources: National central banks and bank supervisory agencies; and IMF staff calculations.
Note: This table considers only deposit-taking universal banks. Data are for 2000, except for Uruguay and Mexico, for which 2002 data are used.
[1]Domestic banks with foreign participation or control. Offshore banks are not included.

tant, although questions have been raised about the cost-effectiveness and governance of such activities, and alternative mechanisms—including community-based microfinance—are being developed to deliver credit to such sectors.

The high degree of concentration suggests that lack of competition among banks may be a concern (Box 5.2). It is generally agreed in the economics literature that banks need to enjoy some degree of market power to earn rents that compensate them for risk taking in the financing of projects on which they have only imperfect information, and that economies of scale are important in containing costs and taking full advantage of new information technologies. A lack of competition, however, may also result in excessively high prices or quantity rationing for customers. In small, advanced economies, too, the banking system is often highly concentrated, but banks typically face strong competition from securities markets and nonbank financial intermediaries, as well as offshore markets. In Latin America, however, financing from securities markets is usually available to only a limited range of top-quality corporate borrowers.

Reforms to introduce private pension systems provided an important impetus to financial system development in Latin America during the 1990s. Chile was the first to replace a state-run, pay-as-you-go pension system with a privately managed, individually funded system in 1981. Its lead was subsequently followed in Argentina, Bolivia, Brazil, Colombia, Ecuador, Mexico, and elsewhere. As

Table 5.3. Selected Latin American Countries: Assets and Loans of Public Banks
(In percent of total banking system)

	Assets	Loans
Costa Rica	66	66
Brazil	33	38
Argentina	23	23
Colombia	21	16
Chile	16	12
Mexico	7	9

Source: National bank supervisory agencies.

Chile's experience has demonstrated, such reforms can accelerate the development of domestic equity and corporate bond markets by providing a substantial and growing local investor base. These pension funds can, however, also be highly vulnerable targets for governments looking for financing. For example, Argentina's pension funds have suffered heavy losses after being forced to invest sizable shares of their portfolios in government paper.

Bank Profitability

Latin American banks' profitability improved during the 1990s, but their returns on assets and equity

---

Box 5.2. Do Brazilian Banks Compete?

The Brazilian banking system is large, with the share of its assets in GDP comparable to that in the United States, but it provides less than half the loans in proportion to GDP (see table). Brazilian banks are significant players in capital markets and invest about 30 percent of their assets in securities, which is about the same as the share of loans in their portfolio. Security financing is mainly directed to the public sector, since most of these securities are government debt issues bearing attractively high yields. The number of

banks has gradually declined in Brazil, by a quarter since 1995, and market concentration in the provision of credit is high. The 10 largest institutions account for about two-thirds of bank assets and provide three-quarters of all loans, and foreign banks account for about one-fifth of deposits.

Despite the relatively small size of their loan portfolio, banks rely on interest-earning activities as a major source of income. Bank margins relative to assets are high compared with those in other Latin American economies. They are much higher than those in the United States and the euro area, where heightened competition triggered by the globalization of banking services has driven spreads down.

Concentration and the high interest margins in the Brazilian banking sector suggest the possibility that noncompetitive forces are at work. Using panel data, Belaisch (2003) finds that banks' revenues are not particularly sensitive to their costs, suggesting that banks are under limited pressure from competition. Size is found to be an important determinant of bank revenues, a finding that is consistent with the presence of market power. This would make it difficult for small banks to compete and be profitable. There is also evidence of noncompetitive behavior by the system's largest, state-owned banks.

Elements of a noncompetitive market structure in the Brazilian banking system could contribute to explaining why intermediation is relatively low and costly. When banks enjoy market power, their incentives to offer lower interest spreads are small, thus discouraging higher lending volumes.

Bank Profitability, 2000
(In percent of assets)

	Brazil	Latin America[1]	United States	EU-11
Loans	30.00	68.00	68.00	52.00
Net interest margin	5.20	4.20	3.10	1.90
Pretax profit	1.12	1.08	1.83	0.70

Source: Belaisch (2003).

Note: EU-11 denotes the following 11 countries that were members of the European Union in 2000: Austria, Belgium, Finland, France, Germany, Ireland, Italy, Luxembourg, the Netherlands, Portugal, and Spain.

[1]Argentina, Chile, Colombia, Mexico, and Peru.

---

remain below those in industrial countries (Table 5.4). This has occurred despite high interest margins on private lending. Interest spreads on lending to the private sector have declined somewhat during the past decade but remain high by international standards. Intermediation margins—the difference between banks' revenues from lending and the remuneration of deposits—averaged more than 50 percentage points in Brazil, Peru, and Uruguay during the 1990s (Figure 5.2).

In part, the weak profitability performance reflects a continued reliance on interest earnings, both from lending and from large holdings of government bonds as the main source of revenue (see Table 5.4). In industrial countries, heightened competition triggered by the opening of financial systems and the globalization of banking services has driven spreads down on most traditional income-generating activities. Interest margins have also declined relative to other sources of revenue in emerging Asia. To offset the impact of lower intermediation margins on profitability, banks diversified into other sources of income, such as commissions from asset management and fees from securities trading. In most of Latin America, these lines of business remain limited.

Cost inefficiencies have also depressed profitability. In times of high inflation, buoyant bank revenues from holdings of government bonds indexed to the overnight interest rate far exceeded the less frequently adjusted interest rate paid on deposits, providing banks with an easy source of profits. Although incentives for cost reduction have increased since inflation was brought down across the region, banks' operating costs remain high, amounting to more than 90 percent of operating income, about a third higher than in banks in advanced countries. Part of the explanation for higher costs is that banking is labor intensive and labor productivity has been low: in Brazilian banks, for example, productivity was estimated at only about 40 percent of that in U.S. banks.[118] Labor costs absorb a large part of banks' revenues, even compared with

---

[118]McKinsey and Company (1998).

Table 5.4. International Comparison: Bank Performance Indicators[1]

	Argentina	Brazil	Chile	Colombia	Mexico	Paraguay	Peru	Venezuela	United States	Japan	Europe[2]
				(In percent of operating income)							
Source of revenue[3]											
Net interest margin	110	87	92	97	90	...	100	97	82	86	67
Other net income[4]	−10	13	8	3	2	...	0	3	18	14	33
Efficiency											
Operating costs	74	76	53	78	92	89	94	99	61	61	67
Personnel costs	68	42	32	36	43	44	42	42	24	7	33
Provisions	26	23	29	43	27	63	66	9	...	...	...
				(In percent of total loans)							
Asset quality											
Nonperforming loans	...	9.5	7.8	11.9	5.8	16.2	7.6	2.8	0.9	6.1	1.2
				(In percent)							
Profitability											
Return on assets	0.4	0.0	0.5	−1.4	0.3	1.4	0.4	1.4	1.8	0.1	0.7
Return on equity	3.2	−0.4	...	...	...	12.4	2.8	...	22	−30.4	16.8

Sources: National central banks and bank supervisory agencies for Latin American countries; Belaisch and others (2001) for industrial countries; and IMF staff calculations. Data are for 2000.

Note: Selected sample includes only deposit-taking universal banks.

[1]Performance indicators may differ from traditional definitions to improve cross-country comparability. Operating income usually includes extraordinary income, but the latter is not included here to provide a more accurate assessment of bank performance. Operating costs exclude provisions, which are year and bank specific.

[2]The 11 European Union countries included are Austria, Belgium, Finland, France, Germany, Ireland, Italy, Luxembourg, the Netherlands, Portugal, and Spain. Aggregate data are for 1998.

[3]Operating income is defined as the sum of the two items below.

[4]Sum of net commission income (from asset management and other services) and net fee income (from foreign exchange trading and underwriting).

the euro area, where banks have traditionally suffered from high labor costs.

In the uncertain economic environment, nonperforming loans have been an additional burden on bank costs. Although restructuring since the mid-1990s—including by the government swapping bad loans for public securities—improved the quality of bank lending, nonperforming loans continue to represent a much larger share of loan portfolios than is standard in advanced economies. This has required high rates of loan-loss provisioning and the setup of large collection and legal departments to recover collateral, adding to banks' costs.

Dollarization[119]

In a number of countries, a large and rising share of both bank deposits and credits have been denominated in U.S. dollars. Most of these countries have been subject to a market-driven process of currency substitution. For example, in Bolivia, dollar deposits

---

[119]Section VI addresses issues associated with dollarization in Latin America.

Figure 5.2. Interest Spread in Latin America[1]
(Standard deviation band around mean, in percent)

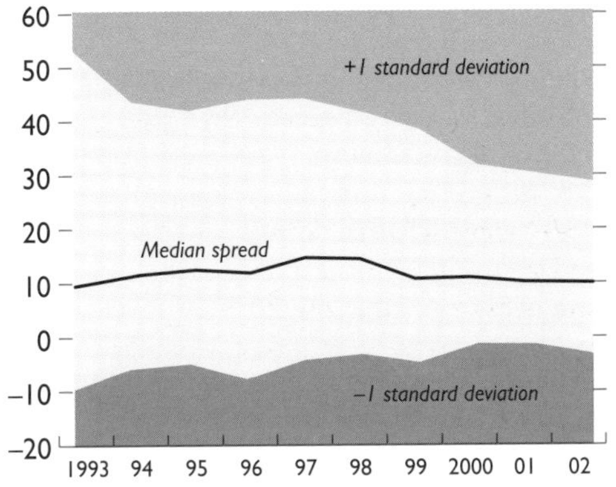

Source: IMF, *International Financial Statistics*, various issues.
[1]Difference between lending and deposit rates.

ratcheted up from 65 percent of total deposits in 1990 to 74 percent in 2001 and to about 95 percent in 2003. In some countries, formal dollarization was deliberately used to provide a nominal anchor for the economy. In 1991, Argentina adopted a currency board guaranteeing full convertibility between dollars and pesos, and the bulk of intermediation was increasingly denominated in dollars until the collapse of the regime in 2002. Ecuador in 1999 and El Salvador in 2001 chose full dollarization to bolster monetary policy credibility and price stability.

Some countries avoided dollarization altogether or were able to reduce it. Brazil and, to some extent, Mexico have prohibited most holdings of foreign currency deposits for nontransactions purposes, while Chile and Colombia have used strict prudential guidelines to reduce the incentives to hold foreign currency deposits. Placing a ban on foreign currency deposits or discouraging their use, however, also served to encourage the shifting of financial assets offshore. For example, deposits held by Venezuelans in the United States now amount to more than 200 percent of Venezuela's broad money.

Underlying Weaknesses

These key features of the Latin American financial systems today reflect a series of underlying weaknesses common to most countries in the region.

Low Savings

Low saving rates hindered the deepening of domestic financial markets in Latin America in the 1990s. Cross-country data clearly show that in the second half of the last decade, countries with higher saving rates also had larger loan-to-GDP ratios (Figure 5.3). At the same time, however, low bank intermediation coexisted with a wide range of saving rates; and, similarly, loan ratios and saving rates did not seem to be consistently determined by per capita GDP.

This observation suggests that other variables, both at the macroeconomic and microeconomic levels, have played an important role in determining the depth of bank intermediation.

Macroeconomic Instability

In most Latin American countries, an unstable macroeconomic environment has been a critical factor holding back financial system development. Throughout much of the postwar period, chronic inflation, periodic external crises, and intermittent deposit freezes have imposed heavy losses on holders of financial assets. Even after success in bringing down inflation across Latin America in the early

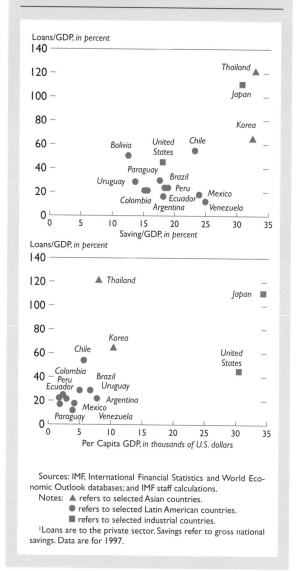

Figure 5.3. Comparative Savings and Loan Ratios in Mid-1990s[1]

Sources: IMF, International Financial Statistics and World Economic Outlook databases; and IMF staff calculations.
Notes: ▲ refers to selected Asian countries.
● refers to selected Latin American countries.
■ refers to selected industrial countries.
[1]Loans are to the private sector. Savings refer to gross national savings. Data are for 1997.

1990s, strains and vulnerabilities persisted: inflexible exchange rate regimes and excessive fiscal deficits continued to undermine confidence and contributed to the persistence of instability.

Informal dollarization has developed, particularly in countries with histories of hyperinflation. In such countries, confidence in the value of the local currency is severely undermined, and long periods of improved monetary management will be required before it can begin to recover. Indeed, allowing informal dollarization was sometimes seen as a convenient way to remonetize the economy and restore intermediation, which had often contracted sharply

---

Box 5.3. Taxation of Financial Transactions in Latin America[1]

Financial transactions taxes (FTTs) are currently in place in several Latin American countries: Argentina, Bolivia, Brazil, Colombia, Peru, and Venezuela. The tax has generally been introduced in the context of serious fiscal stress where short-run considerations related to the need for a quick source of revenue and ease of collection outweighed concerns about the efficiency of the tax. Typically, the tax is levied on bank debits at rates below 1 percent (see table).

FTTs are likely to be highly inefficient, inequitable, and subject to diminishing returns, although tax authorities see some advantages in using them to strengthen tax administration.

- *Efficiency.* The cascading nature of the tax can distort the chain of production. It is likely to stimulate inefficient behavior to evade the tax, including interenterprise netting arrangements, increased use of cash, and recourse to offshore transactions. The tax may also lead to disintermediation if the nonbank financial sector is exempted from the tax. Also, if applied to capital and exchange market transactions, the tax can severely reduce trading volumes.

- *Equity.* The tax cascades through the commercial structure, and, therefore, the impact on prices can exceed that suggested by the "low" rate, adversely affecting the poor. Moreover, the tax is relatively easily evaded by larger, more sophisticated firms, owing to their access to offshore operations or complex derivative transactions.

- *Yield.* The yield of FTTs tends to fall over time as tax evasion takes hold. When this occurs, the temptation is to raise rates, which could temporarily recoup revenue collections but, in time, create even more evasion. Eventually, this evasion spills over to the administration of other taxes. For example, value-added-tax (VAT) collections can be affected as transactions move offshore or into the informal sector.

[1]Further information is provided in Coelho, Ebrill, and Summers (2001).

Bank Debit Taxes, 2004
(In percent)

	Tax Rate
Argentina	0.60[1]
Bolivia	0.30[1]
Brazil	0.38
Colombia	0.40
Peru	0.10[1]
Venezuela[2]	0.50[1]

Source: Coelho, Ebrill, and Summers (2001).
[1]On each side of a transaction.
[2]Data for Venezuela are for 1999–2000.

- *Tax administration.* In some countries, however, the authorities have found the financial transactions tax to be a useful tool for the administration of other taxes, in particular income taxes, since it provides information on individual bank account transactions.

Empirical Evidence

- In Colombia, in the two years following the introduction of the FTT in 1999, the yield of the tax fell 28 percent, and the share of M3 in GDP fell from 36 percent to 31 percent. Moreover, the volume of transactions in the interbank and treasury bill markets also fell substantially following introduction of the tax.

- In Brazil, where an FTT is considered by the authorities to have helped tax administration, the ratio of revenues to GDP has increased since the tax was introduced in 1997. However, such gains have come at a cost of bank disintermediation, as bank deposits as a share of GDP fell from 25.6 percent to 24.1 percent during 1998–2001, as investors likely redirected resources toward the tax-exempt mutual fund industry.

---

after a full-blown crisis. Heavily managed or pegged exchange rate regimes, which obscured the risks of borrowing in foreign currency, also encouraged the development of dollarized financial systems.

The policies required to deal with this macroeconomic instability also affected the efficiency of bank intermediation. High short-term interest rates—reflecting fiscal crowding out and efforts to combat inflation or defend the exchange rate—added to banks' funding costs and increased loan-default rates. Moreover, high unremunerated reserve requirements (amounting, for example, in Brazil to 75 percent on

demand deposits during 1997–99) reduced banks' resources available to supply credit, curtailed incentives to mobilize deposits, and added to banks' intermediation margins. Similarly, a number of countries have resorted to financial transaction taxes, which have tended to discourage intermediation through the banking system (Box 5.3).

Risk Perceptions

Latin American banks have also had to cope with a range of structural factors, mostly microeconomic

Table 5.5. Three Latin American Countries: Bankruptcy Frameworks

	Original	Recent Reforms
Argentina	1972	1995, 2002
Brazil	1945	...[1]
Mexico	1943	2000

[1] A new bankruptcy law is currently being considered in congress.

and institutional, that increased perceptions of project and country risk, and deterred banks from engaging in lending to the private sector:

- The repeated sequence of crises followed by deep restructuring has resulted in a lack of adequate information on potential borrowers. Many longtime bank customers disappeared; and the new ones who emerged did not have long credit histories, were not able to present sound business plans, or did not have good collateral.[120]

- Inadequate auditing and accounting standards and practices hampered banks' ability to monitor both financial and nonfinancial companies. For example, credit assessment was too often based on valuation of collateral or personal relationships, rather than forward-looking project evaluations. The development of sound accounting practices has been hampered by periods of high inflation, the prevalence of family-owned firms, and the low level of development of securities markets.

- Legislative frameworks typically did not support the enforceability of creditors' rights once loans became overdue. Outmoded bankruptcy laws made the recovery of collateral long and costly (Table 5.5). In some countries, even after laws were reformed, inefficient judiciaries undermined the legal certainties needed to foster financial intermediation.

These structural risk factors increased banks' aversion to lending throughout the region. Although credit demand may have been high, the associated risks have been high, too, so that the supply of loans could not fully satisfy demand. Catão (1997) finds that in Argentina, even though banks restored their deposit bases soon after the Mexican crisis, more cautious lending practices resulted in a credit contraction. Banks' decisions to move away from risky corporate assets into the apparently safer assets of public sector debt is documented in Braun and Levy Yeyati (2000). Berróspide and Dorich (2001) found that, in Peru, credit slowdowns in the second part of the 1990s were supply determined and associated with an increase in banks' risk perceptions. Similar reactions were observed from Asian banks in the aftermath of the 1997–98 crisis (Kim, 1999; Agénor, Aizenman, and Hoffmaister, 2000).

Volatile Capital Flows

Latin American financial systems have had to cope with highly volatile capital inflows. The implementation of exchange rate-based stabilization programs, the introduction of structural reforms, and often high domestic interest rates triggered a rapid buildup of short-term capital inflows to Latin America during the early 1990s.[121] Investors' overshooting optimism drove an increase in private inflows to Latin America up from a yearly average of US$10 billion during 1983–90 to US$22 billion in 1991 and to US$62 billion by 1996 (Burki and Perry, 1997). Increasingly, foreign capital substituted for domestic savings to finance the upsurge in demand associated with exchange rate-based stabilization and the reform process.

Capital inflows were accompanied by rapid expansions of bank credit and consumption booms—and strong contractions and busts when they reversed. The availability of short-term external funding stimulated Latin American financial systems to lend excessive amounts during the first half of the 1990s, inflating the prices of financial assets.[122] Initially, the performance of the region's banks improved, contributing to even higher lending. This process helped, however, to inflate bubbles in the stock and real estate markets, which eventually collapsed in the face of shifts in investor sentiment, with sell-offs triggered by setbacks in domestic policies or external shocks (including fluctuations in international interest rates and contagion from events in other major emerging markets).[123]

---

[120]Carrasquilla, Galindo, and Vásquez (2000) find that the severe credit contraction observed in Colombia after 1998 was mainly due to banks' inability, rather than their unwillingness, to lend.

[121]Attractive domestic factors were reinforced by the slowdown in industrial countries in the early 1990s and the decline in their interest rates.

[122]Forty percent of all inflows during 1993–96 were in the form of short-term foreign currency lending to banks and equity portfolio flows.

[123]Herrera and Perry (2003) discuss the interaction between excessive credit creation and bubble formation in Latin America.

Banking Crises and Reforms

Over the past ten years, banking-system fragilities have contributed to a series of crises that spurred restructuring and reform efforts. A first wave of crises hit several Latin American countries during the mid-1990s, starting in 1994 with Bolivia, Brazil, Mexico, and Venezuela, followed by Argentina and Paraguay in 1995, and Ecuador in 1996. Banks were restructured and/or recapitalized, often at great fiscal cost, while regulatory systems were overhauled. In many cases, these reforms were successful in strengthening banking systems and averting banking crises when domestic or external shocks hit again. In others, however, reforms were less successful, and a second wave of crises hit several banking systems, including those in Ecuador in 1999, Argentina in 2001, Uruguay in 2002, and the Dominican Republic in 2003. Bolivia has experienced banking-system stress more recently, in 2003–2004, in the context of wider social and political pressures.

The wave of bank failures in Mexico in December 1994 followed a period of financial liberalization and rapidly expanding bank credit in the absence of proper bank regulation and supervision. The situation was further exacerbated by expansionary fiscal policy and an overvalued exchange rate. When the poor quality of Mexican banks' loan portfolios became evident, currency, stock, and real estate prices fell sharply, reducing collateral values and imposing large losses on banks. These losses were exacerbated by the substantial portion of corporate borrowing in foreign currency, both onshore and offshore.

In other countries, too, an unbalanced policy mix of lax fiscal policy and tight monetary policy contributed to banking booms and busts. In Brazil, the sharp reduction in inflation associated with the 1994 *real* plan deprived banks of the inflation tax that had allowed them to support cost inefficiencies, thereby reducing the banking sector's contribution to GDP from 12 percent in 1994 to 7 percent in 1995 (IBGE, 1997). It also accentuated state governments' arrears to public banks. To maintain their profits, banks responded by pumping up credit operations in the context of the fast growth resulting from exchange rate-based stabilization. The slowdown in the pace of economic growth in the second quarter of 1995, following the adoption of a highly restrictive monetary and credit policy after the Mexican crisis, led, however, to a collapse of asset prices and widespread banking distress.

The experience of the mid-1990s clearly demonstrated the potential for rapid contagion across borders. In the wake of the 1994 Mexico crisis, Argentine banks were seen as particularly exposed because of continuing questions about the government's ability to defend the currency board, given technical limits on the central bank's ability to provide emergency credit to illiquid banks under the Convertibility Law, and the political sustainability of tight policies in the face of a systemic bank run. Thus, following the sharp depreciation of the Mexican peso, 18 percent of deposits were withdrawn from Argentine banks in the first three months of 1995. In the end, the authorities tightened fiscal and monetary policies aggressively, and confidence was restored, but at the cost of a sharp recession.

Microeconomic influences, such as poor bank management and weak prudential regulation and bank supervision, were also responsible for bank problems in a number of countries. Banking crises in Venezuela and Bolivia in 1994, Paraguay in 1996, and the Dominican Republic in 2003 can be directly related to such influences. Typical features of poorly managed banks included overextension of credit, poor loan evaluation, excessive loan concentration, cronyism (i.e., connected lending and political interference), maturity and currency mismatches, poor loan recovery, weak internal control, and outright fraud.

Notwithstanding the heavy costs involved, Latin American crises were typically not as expensive to resolve as those that afflicted Asia in 1997–98 (Table 5.6).[124] The most costly crises in Latin America during the 1990s (in Ecuador, Mexico, and Venezuela) cost around 20 percent of GDP to resolve, large amounts to be sure, but still significantly less than the costs of dealing with the crises in Indonesia, Korea, and Thailand.[125] In East Asian emerging markets, the long period of sustained growth and the perception of implicit government guarantees implied by the close relations between the corporate and government sectors encouraged the region's banks to lend excessively (Krugman, 1998). The costs of resolution in the Asian countries were exacerbated by the very high leverage of Asian banks compared with their counterparts in Latin America.[126]

To deal with these banking crises, governments across Latin America implemented a series of banking-system reforms aimed at resolving weak banks and strengthening regulation and supervision (Figure 5.4).

---

[124]For comprehensive discussions of the costs of banking crises, see Caprio and Klingebiel (2003) and Hoelscher and Quintyn (2003).

[125]The total cost of the Argentina crisis of 2001–2002 has yet to be determined, but it is unlikely to exceed 20 percent of GDP.

[126]Pimintel Puga (1999) estimates that in the year before the Asian crisis, loans made by Korea's largest banks amounted to more than 800 percent of net equity; those in Indonesia averaged more than 900 percent; and in Thailand, they averaged 1,400 percent. In comparison, the average credit-to-equity ratio for the top five banks in the year before their banking crisis was 480 percent in Brazil and 550 percent in Argentina.

Table 5.6. Latin America: Fiscal Costs of Banking Crises in 1990s
(In percent of GDP)

	Years	Cost
Bolivia	1994	4.2
Brazil	1995	9.3
Venezuela	1994–95	18.0
Mexico	1995	20.0
Argentina	1995	0.3
Paraguay	1996–99	13.0
Ecuador	1998	20.0
Peru	1998	1.6
Memorandum items:		
Indonesia	1997–present	40.0
Korea, Republic of	1997–present	28.0
Thailand	1997–present	34.8

Sources: Caprio and Klingebiel (2003); and IMF staff estimates.

Figure 5.4. Strength of Financial Regulatory Environment in Selected Countries
(Index from 0 to 1)[1]

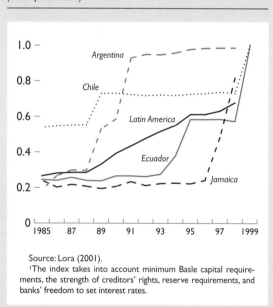

Source: Lora (2001).
[1]The index takes into account minimum Basle capital requirements, the strength of creditors' rights, reserve requirements, and banks' freedom to set interest rates.

- Many private banks were closed or merged; others were restructured and/or recapitalized at high costs; and state-owned banks were liquidated or privatized.

- The power of central banks and supervisors to deal with problem banks was increased, includ-ing by raising significant external credit to provide emergency liquidity if needed (Argentina) or providing them with authority to demand new injections of funds from shareholders or restructuring through incorporation, merger, or split-up (Brazil).

- Prudential regulation was reinforced by raising initial capital requirements for the opening of new banks (Brazil); setting prudential capital ratios above minimum Basel requirements (Argentina, Brazil, and Venezuela); introducing limits on insider lending (Venezuela and Mexico); and requiring banks to implement internal risk-control systems (Brazil and Mexico).

- Bank supervision was strengthened and made more independent (Argentina, Brazil, Mexico, and Venezuela).

- Controls were tightened over offshore operations (Brazil and others; see Box 5.4).

- Deposit-insurance schemes were introduced to protect small depositors (Argentina and Brazil) or enhanced (Mexico).

- The broader institutional framework was strengthened, including by improving accounting standards (Mexico and Venezuela); establishing disclosure requirements (Mexico); imposing strict rotation rules on external auditors (Brazil and Mexico); reforming the legal and regulatory framework for bankruptcy (Argentina and Mexico); and establishing a market for the securitization of credit, facilitating the recovery of nonperforming loans (Brazil).

These reforms played an important role in the consolidation of banking systems. Restructuring was most successful when it included broader measures aimed at improving the profitability of viable banks. In Brazil, for example, the banking business was also reformed: banks were allowed to collect fees for the traditional account-management services they provided, as well as for more sophisticated services. Banks became involved in the trading of currency-derivatives contracts, which were hedged by their holdings of indexed government securities, thereby protecting their customers against oscillations in interest and exchange rates. For public banks, federal assistance was conditional on their liquidation or privatization. The few banks that remained in the public sector were transformed into development agencies or restricted to transparent, arm's-length relationships with state governments.

Banking sectors were also widely opened to foreign participation. In Brazil, the failure of a large domestic bank was resolved through its sale to a foreign bank. Similarly, in Argentina and Mexico, there

Box 5.4. Vulnerabilities from Offshore Banking

In Latin America, as elsewhere, poorly regulated or unregulated offshore financial institutions (OFIs) present a potential risk to the financial systems within which they operate. In some cases, nonregulated OFIs operate effectively as parallel banking structures that are part of larger financial entities. These entities may increase banking system vulnerability by exploiting regulatory arbitrage opportunities by, for example, transferring nonperforming assets from the regulated bank to the unregulated bank. A focus on only the regulated bank could lead to erroneous conclusions about the risk exposure of the banking system. The problem may be exacerbated if a regulator is not aware of the links between two financial entities or does not have the legal capacity to supervise one of them, which could lead to the risk of contagion being seriously underestimated. In Ecuador, for instance, the 1998–99 banking crisis turned out to be more serious than originally envisaged after apparently sound onshore banks were discovered to be much weaker when supervisors performed consolidated supervision that included closely linked but poorly regulated OFIs. In Uruguay, the absence of consolidated supervision and formal information sharing between Uruguayan and Argentine supervisors contributed to an underestimation of the vulnerability of the Uruguayan banking system and, subsequently, to the seriousness of the 2002 crisis.

In order to minimize the risks associated with OFIs, supervisors in Latin America have sought to impose conditions or restrictions on them to facilitate more adequate supervision. A number of jurisdictions have legislation that permits supervisors to refuse authorization to those banks with "unsupervisable" corporate structures or to revoke existing authorizations. For example, in Panama and Brazil, it is very difficult for banks to be granted licenses if they are chartered in jurisdictions where local supervisors are not able to perform consolidated supervision. In Guatemala, where OFIs account for 30 percent of the local private banking sector, new regulations introduced in 2002 will prohibit the operation of OFIs not formally associated with locally licensed financial conglomerates. In addition, OFIs must comply with their home-country prudential regulations or those of Guatemala, whichever are stricter.

There has also been growing consolidated supervision of financial entities and formal information-exchange agreements. Supervisors in Central America are improving the level of communication among themselves. Panama, for example, has exchange-of-information agreements with many other countries in Latin America, and its supervisors perform on-site inspections throughout Central America of banks that are chartered in Panama and have activities in those jurisdictions. In addition, supervisors in the region are moving toward consolidated supervision of conglomerates. Beginning in 2001, Brazil has conducted consolidated supervision of Brazilian banks, including those that have activities in foreign jurisdictions. To further strengthen the supervision of parallel banking structures that operate in several jurisdictions, it would be important for the relevant supervisory bodies to appoint, where possible, a lead supervisor to supervise the multinational structure on a consolidated basis. Alternatively, a supervisor should consider either forcing a group restructuring or limiting as much as possible the exposure of a domestic bank to related parallel banks or members of the corporate group.

was little protection of large domestic banks from foreign ownership, in contrast with the experience in earlier decades or even that in industrial countries. Internationalization was also seen as a way of importing good regulation and supervision as embodied in the business practices of foreign banks operating in developing countries. The high degree of international financial integration in Central America has resulted in part from such considerations, though it has also created new risks (Box 5.5). It was also expected that foreign banks would have better access to external finance than domestic ones when access to capital markets closed.

These reforms were successful in helping most Latin American countries avoid banking crises during the Asian crisis in late 1997 and 1998. The strengthening of prudential regulation, restructurings, and privatizations helped to raise the quality of banks' balance sheets, while a more cautious approach to lending in the wake of the crisis in the mid-1990s also lessened banks' credit exposures. In-stead, banks tended to hold government securities, reflecting either their recapitalization or a decision to reallocate loan portfolios toward safer assets. In Brazil, large portfolios of interest rate- and exchange rate-indexed government debt insulated banks against the monetary policy tightening implemented to defend the exchange rate band after the Russian default in 1998, as well as against the large devaluations that accompanied the subsequent float of the currency in 1999, the impact of the Argentina crisis in 2001, and the election-related confidence crisis in 2002.

In a number of countries, however, risks related to dollarization received little attention in these reforms, and several dollarized banking systems eventually suffered a second wave of crises. During 2001, concerns about public debt sustainability and an extended recession in Argentina triggered a systemic bank run and loss of reserves, ended only by the abandonment of the convertibility regime and a comprehensive deposit freeze. The high capitaliza-

---

Box 5.5. Cross-Border Financial Integration: Banking in Central America

The changing structure and concentration of the banking system in Central America has been accompanied by growing foreign participation. Central American governments opened their banking systems to the entry of foreign banks during the 1990s, removing restrictions on foreign ownership. Although, according to legal criteria, foreign ownership in banking would not appear to be very widespread, extensive cross-border integration has taken place through informal "ownership relations" between local and foreign banks (see table).[1] Banks have also become increasingly intertwined with other financial and nonfinancial institutions, including the in-house financing arms of large conglomerates.

The process of internationalization and consolidation entails important benefits as well as potential risks. Larger, more international banks enjoy economies of scale and scope, and may be able to better diversify risks across asset classes and countries, both of which help enhance profitability and soundness. Risk exposure may initially increase, however, as banks engage in new activities in different countries and under different regulatory regimes. In particular, these risks might arise from

- a lack of comprehensive prudential regulation and oversight, while regulatory and supervisory frameworks adjust to the complexities (not helped by the lack of transparency) and new risks entailed by consolidation, conglomeration, and internationalization;

- heightened contagion created as substantial losses in one country lead banks to change their strategies and operations in other countries where they operate; and

Cross-Border Banking Relationships in Central America
(In percent of system assets)

	Foreign Ownership	Foreign Relationship
Panama	59	70
El Salvador	13	89
Costa Rica	19	31
Guatemala	4	82
Honduras	4	35
Nicaragua	4	61

Sources: National bank supervisory agencies; and Bank for International Settlements.

- conflicts of interest, since banks that are part of conglomerates may engage in excessive in-house lending with inadequate risk management.

Given that banking-system vulnerabilities have increased, efforts are needed to ensure benefits from financial integration. Empirical analysis suggests that although consolidation has improved bank profitability in recent years, the probability of individual bankruptcies remains high in some countries.[2] Greater efforts are needed to address and contain the heightened risks associated with cross-border financial integration and to deliver the intended benefits. In particular, legal frameworks need to be strengthened to allow banking supervisors to implement comprehensive consolidated supervision. It is also crucial to increase regional cooperation among supervisors and move toward the harmonization of regulatory and supervisory standards across countries.

---
[1]A number of "ownership relationship" indicators signal that a local bank may be part of a parallel banking structure including foreign financial institutions (BIS, 2003): the adoption by a domestic bank of a particular strategy similar to that of a foreign bank; an unusually high level of reciprocal correspondent banking between a domestic bank and a foreign bank; or similar names of a domestic bank and a foreign bank.

[2]Druck and Prat (2003).

---

tion of Argentine banks, extensive foreign ownership, and earlier regulatory reforms meant that the banking system was able to withstand heavy pressures for an extended period, but, in the end, these could not prevent the crisis.[127] In early 2002, the deposit run spread to Uruguayan banks, where many

Argentines held accounts and where Uruguayan residents quickly became concerned about a deposit freeze in their own heavily dollarized banking system. Bolivia and Paraguay also suffered episodes of heavy pressures from deposit withdrawals in the following months. By contrast, the Peruvian banking system was much less affected despite its high dollarization, reflecting the strong macroeconomic framework, including reserve coverage of dollar deposits exceeding 100 percent.

---
[127]For more details on the unfolding of the crisis and the policy response, see Collyns and Kincaid (2003) and IMF (2003).

Lessons, Policy Responses, and Challenges

Experience since the early 1990s has clearly demonstrated the key importance of achieving sound and resilient financial systems to reduce Latin America's vulnerability to crisis and to support sustained economic growth. Notwithstanding efforts to strengthen financial systems, many countries have sustained major crises that have undermined confidence and precipitated severe economic contractions. Moreover, even after the financial system is stabilized, credit growth has remained limited, seriously constraining investment and economic activity.

Against this background, most Latin American countries are continuing their efforts to strengthen bank supervision and regulation. Often these efforts have drawn on Financial Sector Assessment Programs (FSAPs) prepared by the staffs of the IMF and the World Bank.[128] A key task has been to tighten loan-classification and provisioning standards, which ideally should involve more forward-looking (instead of historical) risk models. Moreover, capital-adequacy guidelines have been tightened, with the aim of achieving Basel standards; and prompt corrective-action frameworks are being introduced to ensure faster responses to emerging problems (e.g., in Argentina, Bolivia, Brazil, and Ecuador). Also, the power and independence of financial regulators are being bolstered, including to provide greater immunities from prosecution in the execution of their duties and to extend their jurisdictions to cover nonbank financial activities and to pay greater attention to tasks related to cross-border financial integration.

At the same time, greater use needs to be made of market mechanisms, complementing the role of the financial regulators, to ensure prudent behavior. Key steps in this regard include limiting coverage of deposit-insurance systems and improving the availability of information on financial institutions through stronger accounting and auditing standards (e.g., in Brazil and Mexico).

Countries that have experienced systemic banking crises in recent years will need to continue their efforts to rehabilitate or resolve weak or failed banks, recover value from the efficient disposal of nonperforming loans (e.g., Argentina, Ecuador, and Uruguay), and thus reduce the high exposure of the public sector (e.g., Argentina). These tasks are often slow, given the complexity of the issues involved, including allocating losses fairly among depositors and creditors, and determining the appropriate role for the public sector in potentially cushioning losses, often in the face of binding fiscal constraints. The uncertainties that linger while such sick financial institutions remain unresolved, however, can hold back the growth of healthier ones as well as delay restructuring by borrowers. Also, in several countries, an important task is to make sure that remaining publicly owned banks are efficiently and transparently run and do not provide a source of future quasi-fiscal losses (for example, in Argentina).

A broader range of initiatives is also needed, and efforts are under way to encourage the expansion of more efficient and longer-term credit intermediation. These include the development of more effective information-sharing mechanisms for credit assessment (in Brazil), strengthening bankruptcy legislation and judicial procedures to enhance recovery of value from bad loans (in Bolivia, Brazil, and Mexico), and encouraging the expansion of microfinancing (in Bolivia, Brazil, and Peru). Another necessary task is to reduce current distortionary taxation of financial intermediation, which will require the development of alternative sources of revenue.

Continuing efforts are needed to deepen capital markets. Important progress is being made in a number of countries (including Brazil, Chile, Colombia, and Mexico). Pension reforms have helped to establish a group of large institutional investors, but it will be important to ensure that pension funds have adequate scope to invest their assets to maximize returns and are not unduly subject to requirements to invest in potentially high-risk government paper. Strides are also being made toward the development of deeper and more efficient government debt markets, which can provide useful benchmarks for corporate debt as well as a stable means of meeting government's financial requirements, especially using local currency-denominated paper.

The particular problems faced by dollarized financial systems may pose the greatest challenges, since such systems are particularly prone to instability. These issues are discussed in detail in the next section.

References

Agénor, Pierre-Richard, Joshua Aizenman, and Alexander Hoffmaister, 2000, "The Credit Crunch in East Asia: What Can Bank Excess Liquidity Assets Tell Us?" NBER Working Paper No. 7951 (Cambridge, Massachusetts: National Bureau of Economic Research).

Bank for International Settlements, 2003, *Quarterly Review* (June).

Basel Committee on Banking Supervision, 2003, *Parallel-Owned Banking Structures* (Basel, Switzerland: Bank for International Settlements).

---

[128]So far, FSAPs have been completed or planned for in 16 Latin American countries.

Belaisch, Agnès, 2003, "Do Brazilian Banks Compete?" IMF Working Paper 03/113 (Washington: International Monetary Fund).

———, Laura Kodres, Joaquim Levy, and Angel Ubide, 2001, "Euro Area Banking at the Crossroads," IMF Working Paper 01/28 (Washington: International Monetary Fund).

Berróspide, J., and J. Dorich, 2001, "Aspectos Microeconómicos de la Restricción Crediticia en el Perú: 1997–2000" (Lima: Banco Central de Reserva del Perú).

Braun, Miguel, and Eduardo Levy Yeyati, 2000, "The Role of Banks in the Transmission of Shocks: Micro Evidence from Argentina, 1996–1999" (unpublished; Buenos Aires: Universidad Torcuato Di Tella).

Burki, Shahid Javed, and Guillermo E. Perry, 1997, *The Long March: A Reform Agenda for Latin America and the Caribbean in the Next Decade* (Washington: World Bank).

Caprio, Gerard, and Daniela Klingebiel, 2003, "Episodes of Systemic and Borderline Financial Crises" (unpublished; Washington: World Bank).

Carrasquilla, Alberto, A. Galindo, and D. Vásquez, 2000, "El Gran Apretón Crediticio en Colombia: Una Interpretación," *Coyuntura Económica*, Vol. 30 (March), pp. 1–9.

Catão, Luis, 1997, "Bank Credit in Argentina in the Aftermath of the Mexican Crisis: Supply or Demand Constrained?" IMF Working Paper 97/32 (Washington: International Monetary Fund).

Coelho, Isaias, Liam Ebrill, and Victoria Summers, 2001, "Bank Debit Taxes in Latin America: An Analysis of Recent Trends," IMF Working Paper 01/67 (Washington: International Monetary Fund).

Collyns, Charles, and G. Russell Kincaid, 2003, *Managing Financial Crises: Recent Experiences and Lessons from Latin America*, IMF Occasional Paper No. 217 (Washington: International Monetary Fund).

Druck, Pablo, and Jordi Prat, 2003, "Banking System Effects of Financial Integration in Central America" (unpublished; Washington: International Monetary Fund).

Federación Iberoamericana de Bolsas de Valores, 2002, *Estadísticas Anuales* (Buenos Aires).

Fischer, Stanley, 2003, "The Importance of Financial Markets in Economic Growth," paper presented at the International Derivatives and Financial Markets Conference of the Brazilian Mercantile and Futures Exchange, Campos do Jordao, Brazil, August 21.

Herrera, Santiago, and Guillermo Perry, 2003, "Tropical Bubbles: Asset Prices in Latin America," in *Asset Price Bubbles*, ed. by W. Hunter, G. Kaufman, and Michael Pomerleano (Cambridge, Massachusetts: MIT Press), pp. 127–62.

Hoelscher, David, and Marc Quintyn, 2003, *Managing Systemic Banking Crises*, Occasional Paper No. 224 (Washington: International Monetary Fund).

Instituto Brasileiro de Geografia e Estatísticas (IBGE), 1997, "Sistema Financeiro: Uma Análise a Partir das Contas Nacionais—1990/1995" (unpublished; Rio de Janeiro, Brazil).

International Monetary Fund (IMF), 2003, "Lessons from the Crisis in Argentina" (Washington: International Monetary Fund).

Kim, Hyun, 1999, "Was Credit Channel a Key Monetary Transmission Following the Recent Financial Crisis in the Republic of Korea?" World Bank Policy Research Working Paper No. 2103 (Washington: World Bank).

Krugman, Paul, 1998, "What Happened to Asia?" (unpublished; Cambridge, Massachusetts: Massachusetts Institute of Technology, Department of Economics).

Labán, Raúl, and Felipe Larraín, 1998, "The Return of Private Capital to Chile in the 1990s: Causes, Effects, and Policy Reactions," Development Discussion Paper No. 627 (Cambridge, Massachusetts: Harvard Institute for International Development).

Lora, Eduardo, 2001, "Las reformas estructurales en América Latina: Qué se ha Reformado y Cómo Medirlo," IADB Working Paper No. 462 (Washington: Inter-American Development Bank).

McKinsey & Company, 1998, *Productivity—The Key to an Accelerated Development Path for Brazil* (São Paulo, Brazil: McKinsey Global Institute).

Pimintel Puga, F., 1999, "The Brazilian Financial System: Recent Restructuring, International Comparisons, and Vulnerability to the Exchange Rate Crisis" (unpublished; Rio de Janeiro, Brazil: Brazilian Development Bank).

Rojas-Suarez, Liliana, and Steven R. Weisbrod, 1994, "Financial Market Fragilities in Latin America: From Banking Crisis Resolution to Current Policy Challenges," IMF Working Paper 94/117 (Washington: International Monetary Fund).

World Bank, 2003, *Investment Climate Survey* (Washington).

VI Financial Dollarization in Latin America

The financial systems of many Latin American countries have become increasingly dollarized in the past decade, making Latin America one of the most dollarized regions in the world (Table 6.1).

Following a severe economic crisis, dollarization can help to discourage capital flight and encourage residents to keep their savings in the domestic financial system. Yet dollarization can add to the vulnerability of the financial system by increasing liquidity and solvency risks, and it can limit the scope for an independent monetary policy.[129] During the 1990s, more emphasis may have been placed on the benefits. The recent financial crises of Argentina, Uruguay, and other countries with highly dollarized financial systems, however, have made policymakers more aware of the drawbacks and have underlined the importance of taking steps to manage the risks of dollarization and encourage the use of domestic currency.

This section examines Latin America's experience with partial dollarization of the financial system, which affects many countries in the region. It does not seek to assess the option of full, official dollarization, which has been adopted by only a few countries. The first subsection discusses the causes of partial financial dollarization. The second subsection reviews the steps taken in the highly dollarized countries to manage the risks of dollarization. The third subsection concludes with some lessons and challenges.

Causes

The extent of dollarization varies widely among Latin American countries. In many countries, dollarization began as a response to periods of particular uncertainty—often associated with high inflation—that undermined confidence in the local currency. By the end of 2001, financial dollarization was significant in Argentina, Bolivia, Costa Rica, Nicaragua, Paraguay, Peru, and Uruguay. In all these countries,

Table 6.1. Dollarization Indicators, 2001[1]
(In percent)

	Ratio of Foreign Currency Deposits to Total Deposits	Ratio of Foreign Currency Deposits to GDP
Latin America	56.4	21.1
Transition economies	47.7	8.8
Other low-income countries	26.3	7.8

Source: IMF staff estimates.
[1]Unweighted average for each region.

foreign currency deposits and loans accounted for at least 40 percent, and in some cases more than 90 percent, of total loans and deposits (Table 6.2). Moreover, the degree of dollarization increased during the 1990s in all these countries, as well as in the Dominican Republic, Guatemala, and Honduras, even though their rates of inflation have declined significantly (Figure 6.1).[130]

In some of the highly dollarized countries, residents also hold currency in both U.S. dollars and the national money (known as currency substitution), and pay for goods and services in both currencies (known as real dollarization), although the extent of currency substitution and real dollarization are very difficult to measure. Ecuador and El Salvador recently decided—each under very different circumstances—to adopt full, official dollarization by requiring all financial transactions and payments for goods and services to be denominated in U.S. dollars

---

[129]The benefits and costs of financial dollarization are discussed fully in Baliño, Bennett, and Borensztein (1999).

[130]In Guatemala, reported onshore deposits in U.S. dollars understate the extent of dollarization. The offshore banking system, which was unregulated before 2003, is fully dollarized and is estimated to be equivalent to one-third of the onshore financial system. Costa Rica also has a sizable offshore sector that is fully dollarized, subject to limited supervision, and not captured in the reported data.

Table 6.2. Selected Latin American Countries: Deposit and Loan Dollarization
(In percent)

	Share of Foreign Currency Deposits in Total Deposits		Share of Foreign Currency-Denominated Loans in Total Loans
	1990	2001	2001
Argentina	47.2	73.6	71.6
Bolivia	80.7	91.4	97.1
Brazil	0.0	0.0	0.0
Chile	16.3	12.1	14.0
Colombia	0.3	0.3	11.0
Costa Rica	26.8	43.8	67.2
Dominican Republic	2.2[1]	20.0	27.6
Ecuador	13.3	100.0	100.0
El Salvador	4.1	100.0	100.0
Guatemala	0.0	5.1	13.3
Honduras	1.8	33.1	22.3
Mexico	10.1	8.1	20.5
Nicaragua	40.3	71.0	83.6
Paraguay	33.9[1]	64.3	52.4
Peru	62.5	74.3	80.3
Uruguay	88.6[2]	92.5	69.0
Venezuela	...	0.3	0.5

Sources: Central banks; and IMF staff estimates.
[1]For the Dominican Republic and Paraguay, 1996 data were used.
[2]Loan ratio for Uruguay includes only lending to residents.

and removing the central bank's authority to issue local currency.[131] By contrast, Mexico, Chile, and Colombia have been able to contain and reduce foreign currency deposits and loans, while virtually all financial transactions in Brazil and Venezuela are in local currency.

The high degree of financial dollarization seen in many Latin American countries is the legacy of severe economic crises in the 1980s and 1990s that destroyed confidence in economic policies and in holding savings in domestic currency. During the 1980s, Bolivia and Nicaragua experienced hyperinflation, while Argentina, Uruguay, and Peru suffered years of very high and unstable inflation. Interest rates on deposits in domestic currency were unable to compensate depositors for inflation, leading to significant losses on savings held in domestic currency (Figure 6.2). Moreover, in some countries, such as Bolivia, residents were required to convert their foreign currency deposits into local currency and then incurred sizable losses owing to subsequent currency depreciations.

Some countries (Brazil, Chile, Colombia, Mexico, and Venezuela) have managed to avoid, or achieve a significant reduction in, financial dollarization in recent years. Although they were not immune to economic difficulties during the past two decades, a variety of influences have helped sustain the use of domestic currencies. These include the following:

- Macroeconomic policies in Chile, Colombia, and Mexico had sufficient credibility to help limit dollarization. Faal and Thacker (2003) found that the declines in dollarization in Mexico since 1986 have been attributable in large part to increased credibility of macroeconomic policies and structural reforms.

- Since 1980, real interest rates on domestic currency deposits have remained positive in Brazil, Chile, and Colombia (Figure 6.3).

- Financial instruments indexed to inflation were made available in Brazil, Chile, Mexico, and Colombia. In Brazil, treasury bonds with their face value adjusted for past inflation were intro-

---

[131]Ecuador introduced full dollarization in 2000 to bring the economy out of a severe crisis, while El Salvador made this shift in 2001 in an effort to lock in stability that had already been achieved and to promote growth. Panama has been officially dollarized since 1904.

Figure 6.1. Selected Latin American Countries: Deposit Dollarization and Inflation, 1990–2001[1]

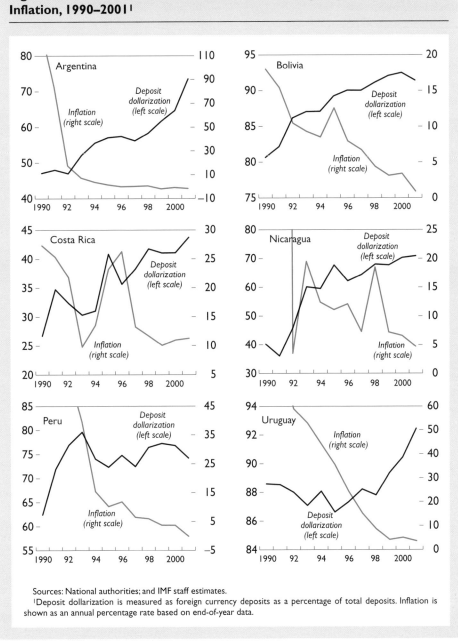

Sources: National authorities; and IMF staff estimates.

[1]Deposit dollarization is measured as foreign currency deposits as a percentage of total deposits. Inflation is shown as an annual percentage rate based on end-of-year data.

duced in 1964. During the years of high inflation, all financial contracts became indexed to these bonds, and monetary policy was geared toward helping banks meet their demand for reserves to avoid any liquidity squeeze during the period of high and unstable inflation (Goldfajn, Hennings, and Mori, 2003). Moreover, exchange rate-indexed financial instruments are issued by the government, which constitutes a form of dollar-

ization, but there are no bank deposits or loans indexed to the exchange rate. Chile's UF (or Unidad de Fomento), introduced in 1967, is a unit of account indexed to past inflation. Since Chile's severe recession of 1982–83, many real, as well as financial, transactions have been denominated in UF (Shiller, 1998). In 1971, Colombia introduced the UPAC (Unidad de Poder Adquisitivo Constante)—a unit of account

Figure 6.2. Real Interest Rates in Selected Highly Dollarized Countries
(In percent)

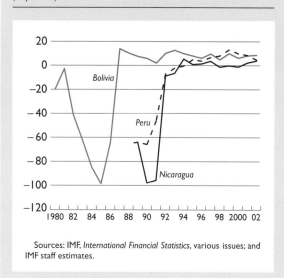

Sources: IMF, *International Financial Statistics*, various issues; and IMF staff estimates.

Figure 6.3. Real Interest Rates in Non-Dollarized Countries
(In percent)

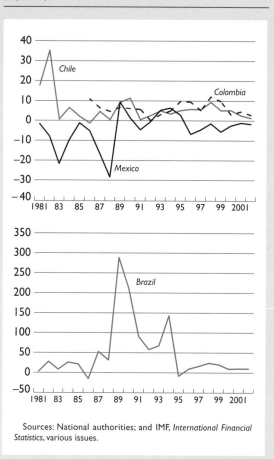

Sources: National authorities; and IMF, *International Financial Statistics*, various issues.

similar to the UF—mainly to protect the housing finance system from inflation. Given the relative stability of Colombia's inflation, indexation has not spread to other parts of the financial sector.

• Brazil, Chile, Colombia, and Mexico have enforced strict regulations on financial transactions in foreign currency, out of a concern that these operations could increase the vulnerability of the financial system (Table 6.3). In particular, foreign currency lending to the nontraded goods sector may add to credit risk, because the cost of borrowing may not adequately reflect the possible risk of exchange rate movements. Foreign currency deposits can increase liquidity risk if banks lack sufficient liquid assets denominated in foreign currency with which to meet large deposit withdrawals.

In some cases, the relatively limited extent of dollarization has partly reflected residents' holdings of foreign currency deposits abroad (Table 6.4). Nevertheless, in most of the nondollarized economies, total foreign exchange deposits (both domestic and abroad) have been considerably less than in the highly dollarized countries. Moreover, with foreign currency deposits held abroad, the balance-sheet risks associated with financial dollarization have been kept outside the country. A notable exception is Venezuela, where residents' deposits in banks reporting to the Bank for International Settlements (BIS) constituted more than double total deposits held in domestic banks throughout the 1990s. These

sizable deposits abroad likely reflected the country's economic difficulties and frequent use of exchange controls.

The highly dollarized countries continued to experience growth in foreign currency deposits and loans during the 1990s, even though inflation had declined to single-digit levels by the late 1990s (see Figure 6.1). To a considerable extent, this experience reflected a policy framework that did little to discourage financial transactions in foreign currency:

• Until recently, many of these governments often accepted or encouraged dollarization in the hope that it would help remonetize the economy, accelerate financial development, and reverse capital flight (Savastano, 1996). For example, Argentina took measures to promote dollarization of the banking system to ease the liquidity squeeze following the tequila crisis and, in principle, to try to enhance the credibility of the con-

Table 6.3. Selected Latin American Countries with Low Dollarization: Risk-Management Arrangements

	Brazil	Chile	Colombia	Mexico
Credit risk	Foreign currency loans prohibited, except for onlending	Banks have strict currency mismatch regulations	Foreign currency loans prohibited, except for onlending	Limits on loans to individual borrowers
Liquidity risk Differential liquidity/ reserve requirements	Ban on foreign currency deposits	Yes	Ban on foreign currency deposits	Yes
		(In percent of eligible deposits)		
If yes, the requirements		13.6–19 on foreign currency; 3.6–9 on local currency		
Lender of last resort Foreign currency operations	No	Yes	No	No
		(In percent of bank capital)		
Limits on banks' foreign exchange positions Long position Short position	60 60	80 20	20 8	15 15
Partial deposit insurance	Yes	Yes	Yes	Yes
Indexed domestic currency instruments available	Yes, prior to 1995	Yes	Yes	No

Source: IMF staff estimates.

vertibility scheme, while Uruguay encouraged foreign currency deposit holdings as part of its efforts to promote the country as a regional financial center.[132]

• Demand policies have not been sufficiently strong for a long enough period to restore confidence in holding domestic currency. By 2000, fiscal deficits in the highly dollarized countries remained high in relation to GDP and larger in several countries than their average during the 1980s, which may have kept residents aware of the possibility of a collapse in the value of the local currency and a return to high and unstable inflation (the "peso problem") (Figure 6.4). In view of the large losses incurred by many residents, decades of strong policies may be required to restore confidence sufficiently. Also,

large fiscal deficits in some countries, such as Costa Rica, put upward pressure on domestic currency interest rates, contributing to the incentive to borrow in U.S. dollars.

• The structure of the banking system has also influenced the extent of dollarization (Catão and Terrones, 2000). In dollarized countries, the credit market has tended to be segmented between large, high-quality firms with their own access to credit lines abroad and other borrowers (such as households and medium-sized and small enterprises) without such access. With some competition in the domestic banking market, banks have lent in foreign currency to the high-quality firms to retain their business. With a large share of their funding coming from foreign currency deposits, banks have also sought to preserve their market shares by expanding foreign currency lending to the other borrowers.

• Dollarized countries have tended to limit fluctuations in their exchange rate—either through a crawling peg or a managed float—to help control inflation and to avoid an increase in the cost of servicing loans in U.S. dollars. The limited

---

[132]Indeed, by 1999–2000, there was a growing body of research that pointed to the benefits of full, official dollarization for many Latin America countries (Calvo, 2001 and Alesina, Barro, and Tenreyro, 2002). There is also some evidence that dollarization has been somewhat successful at retaining financial depth during periods of high inflation (see De Nicolo, Honohan, and Ize, 2003).

Table 6.4. Latin America: Offshore Deposits
(In percent)

	Offshore Deposits as a Share of Total Deposits		Total Foreign Currency Deposits as a Share of Total Deposits
	1995	2001	2001
Nondollarized countries			
Brazil	10.7	18.4	18.4
Chile	19.2	20.6	32.7
Colombia	44.0	43.0	43.3
Mexico	38.6	32.0	40.1
Venezuela	222.6	226.8	227.1
Other countries			
Argentina	44.1	31.8	105.3
Bolivia	13.4	6.3	97.8
Costa Rica	196.4	44.4	88.2
Dominican Republic	27.2	12.3	32.3
Nicaragua	12.9	58.6	129.6
Paraguay	26.4	25.7	90.0
Peru	29.0	24.0	98.3
Uruguay	62.3	38.4	130.9

Sources: Bank for International Settlements; IMF, International Financial Statistics database; and IMF staff estimates.

Figure 6.4. Public Sector Deficits in Highly Dollarized Countries
(In percent of GDP)

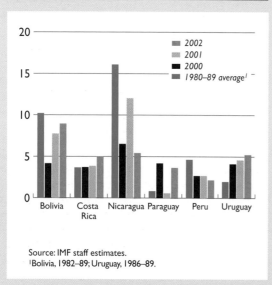

Source: IMF staff estimates.
[1]Bolivia, 1982–89; Uruguay, 1986–89.

local currency. Indeed, the volatility of the real bilateral exchange rate has been less than the volatility of inflation in highly dollarized countries (Figure 6.5).[133]

• The possibility of hysteresis (or some form of nonreversibility in the process of dollarization) may also play a role. This could emerge because of factors such as the sizable transactions costs involved in switching money holdings from foreign currency back to domestic currency (Guidotti and Rodriguez, 1992; Uribe, 1997) or the gradual development of financial instruments and institutions during sustained high-inflation episodes that then become permanent parts of the landscape even after inflation decreases (Dornbusch and Reynoso, 1989; and Dornbusch, Sturzenegger, and Wolf, 1990). Hysteresis does not explain sustained growth in dollarization, however; and it may imply that countries should have adopted even stronger incentives to encourage switching back to domestic currency.

exchange rate volatility has made it easier for residents to keep their savings in foreign currency while paying for goods and services in

---

[133]See Ize and Levy Yeyati (1998) and De Nicolo, Honohan, and Ize (2003) for econometric support for this observation.

Figure 6.5. Selected Latin American Countries: Inflation and Real Bilateral Exchange Rate Volatility, 1990–2002
(In percent; volatility measured as standard deviation)

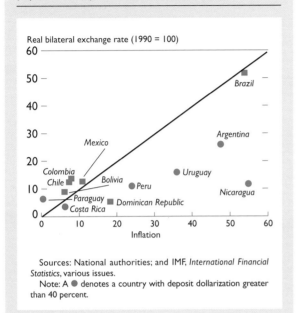

Sources: National authorities; and IMF, *International Financial Statistics*, various issues.
Note: A ● denotes a country with deposit dollarization greater than 40 percent.

Figure 6.6. Selected Latin American Countries: Reserved Coverage of Foreign Currency Deposits
(Average for 1996–2001)

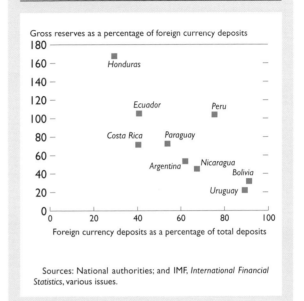

Sources: National authorities; and IMF, *International Financial Statistics*, various issues.

Managing the Risks

The persistence of high dollarization, even after sustained declines in inflation, suggests that it has been very difficult to reverse dollarization once it has become established. It is thus important for the highly dollarized countries to manage the effects of dollarization on the vulnerability of the financial system and on the conduct of monetary policy.

Financial System

The key risks for the financial systems arising in highly dollarized countries have come from increased susceptibility to liquidity squeezes caused by deposit runs and an underpricing of credit risk that have, in several cases, undermined the solvency of the banking system and destabilized economies.

Liquidity Risk

The limited backing of banks' U.S. dollar liabilities by U.S. dollar assets has exposed dollarized countries' financial systems to episodes of large deposit withdrawals. These episodes were triggered by many factors, including a loss of confidence in economic policies (Mexico in 1982, Argentina in 2001), political uncertainty (Bolivia in 2002–2003) or con-

tagion (Uruguay and Paraguay in 2001–2002). Such withdrawals have tended to be sizable, because a small share of depositors often account for a large share of deposits.[134] In Uruguay, a significant share of deposits was held by Argentines, who withdrew their funds during 2001–2002 to meet their liquidity needs at home and out of concern that deposits also would be frozen in Uruguay. Uruguayan banks had been allowed to lend these deposits to Uruguayan residents, which accentuated the liquidity squeeze.[135]

In general, financial systems in these countries have had insufficient protection from the effects of liquidity risk:

• Although foreign currency deposits in these countries are typically subject to reserve or liquidity requirements—ranging from 10 percent in Costa Rica to 26 percent in Paraguay—this level of backing has usually offered little protection in the face of large deposit withdrawals (Table 6.5). Highly dollarized countries have hesitated to set

---

[134]In Bolivia, for example, fewer than 4,500 holders of deposits higher than US$100,000 account for almost half of total deposits.

[135]Loans to nonresidents financed by nonresident deposits incurred no reserve requirements. Loans to residents financed by nonresident deposits, however, had a higher reserve requirement.

Table 6.5. Selected Highly Dollarized Latin American Countries: Risk-Management Arrangements

	Argentina	Bolivia	Costa Rica	Nicaragua	Paraguay	Peru	Uruguay
Credit risk	No specific limits	No specific limits	No specific limits	No specific limits	No specific limits	No specific limits	No specific limits
Liquidity risk Differential liquidity/ reserve requirements	No	No	No	No	Yes	Yes	No
				(In percent of eligible deposits)			
If yes, the requirements					26.5 on foreign currency; 15 on local currency	20 on foreign currency; 6 on local currency	
Lender of last resort Operations in foreign currency	Yes	Yes	No	No	No	Yes	Yes
Limits on banks' foreign exchange position		*(In percent of capital)*					
Long position	Depended	80			4[1]	100	150
Short position	on currency	20			4[1]	2.5	150
Indexed domestic currency instruments available	No	UFV[2] introduced in 2002	No	No	No	Yes, but use limited	

Source: IMF staff estimates.

[1]As percent of total risk-weighted assets, with some adjustments.

[2]UFV denotes *la unidad de fomento de vivienda*, a daily cost of living index using the consumer price index (CPI) base.

higher liquidity requirements out of concern that this action by itself could trigger capital flight.

- Lender-of-last-resort facilities—except in Peru—have often lacked sufficient resources because of central banks' inability to issue foreign currency. Although some countries (Argentina, Bolivia, Peru, and Uruguay) have had explicit arrangements to provide liquidity assistance in foreign currency, these operations were not backed by international reserves. Although most highly dollarized countries hold some gross international reserves, only Peru (among the highly dollarized countries) has sufficient reserves to completely back its foreign currency deposits (Figure 6.6).

- Interest rate defenses against deposit withdrawals have been difficult to engineer in most dollarized economies, because the central banks have often lacked monetary instruments denominated in foreign currency. Moreover, banks have often been reluctant to raise their deposit interest

rates, which could be interpreted as a sign of weakness, exacerbate deposit withdrawals, and result in a wave of loan defaults. In Uruguay and Paraguay—where central banks do not have dollar-denominated monetary instruments—U.S. dollar deposit interest rates did not rise in response to the recent deposit withdrawals. Argentina and Bolivia, where dollar-denominated monetary instruments exist, were able to raise deposit interest rates somewhat, but it is not clear that such a policy would provide an adequate defense against a protracted deposit run.

Credit Risk

Credit risk has tended to be underpriced in highly dollarized financial systems. The highly dollarized economies apply the same prudential guidelines to lending in both foreign currency and domestic currency and, in particular, impose no limits on foreign currency lending to the nontradable sector. In Argentina during the 1990s, such guidelines might have signaled doubts about the sustainability of the convertibility regime. As a result, in many of these countries, the nontradable sector received a significant share of banks' lending in foreign currency (in mid-2002, more than two-thirds in Bolivia, 50 percent in Costa Rica, 60 percent in Peru, and 80 percent in Paraguay).

Exchange rate and prudential policies in dollarized countries have often led borrowers to understate the true cost of borrowing in foreign currency. Interest rates on foreign currency loans have tended to be well below rates on domestic currency loans. Borrowers have perceived little or no exchange risk on foreign currency loans, because central banks in these countries have usually limited exchange rate fluctuations, partly to protect the financial system. At the same time, banks' direct exposures to currency risk have generally been limited by prudential restrictions on their net foreign exchange positions.[136] In this situation, banks have not directly borne much exchange risk and have probably underestimated this risk to their borrowers' capacity to repay.

This arrangement worked as long as the exchange rate remained stable. In the event of external shocks or large deposit withdrawals, however, currencies often came under downward pressure. Initially, central banks were prepared to lose international reserves to defend the currency and to protect the financial system. In many cases, however, the central bank was forced to let the currency depreciate, and borrowers in the nontraded goods sector experienced difficulties servicing their debts, threatening the solvency of the financial system and possibly aggravating the economic crisis.

Monetary Policy

Another potential drawback of high financial dollarization is that it may limit the independence of monetary policy. Highly dollarized countries have tended to operate like small, open economies with inflexible exchange rates and high capital mobility, in which capital flows quickly offset the effects of shifts in domestic credit on monetary aggregates. In highly dollarized countries, a central bank's ability to influence conditions in domestic credit markets using instruments denominated in foreign currency depends on the private sector's willingness to hold central bank liabilities denominated in foreign currency, which, in turn, depends on the adequacy of

the international reserve position. In many dollarized countries, the central banks are not authorized to conduct monetary operations in foreign currency or lack the capacity for these types of operations. In this situation, monetary authorities in highly dollarized countries have sought, as one means of limiting inflation, to keep their currencies on a steady course, which is consistent with the evidence that the pass-through from exchange rates to prices is greater in highly dollarized countries.[137]

Lessons, Policy Responses, and Challenges

Dollarization has appeared to provide a means for economies with low macroeconomic policy credibility to resist capital flight and keep savings in the domestic financial system. The recent experience has shown, however, that highly dollarized economies are particularly prone to crisis, because heightened liquidity and credit risks mean that confidence can be quickly lost and limited lender-of-last-resort facilities do not provide much defense against deposit runs.

The experience of the highly dollarized countries shows that partial dollarization has been very difficult to reverse, once it has become established. In countries that have had severe economic crises, residents may require many years, and perhaps decades, of strong policies to regain confidence in holding domestic currency. Also, dollarization has tended to be self perpetuating, as attempts to limit exchange rate fluctuations have encouraged the growth of foreign currency lending, which, in turn, has increased the incentives for the authorities to seek exchange rate stability.

Against this background, policymakers in highly dollarized countries have encountered difficult policy choices. They face risks to financial system stability and obstacles to conducting an independent monetary policy, yet there are no quick or easy solutions to these problems. Full official dollarization is sometimes suggested as an alternative, but is unlikely to be a durable solution unless criteria for a common currency area with the United States are satisfied or a country is prepared to absorb the cost of having a limited capacity to use monetary policy to respond to shocks.

Policymakers in highly dollarized countries have also recognized that outright prohibition of dollar-

[137]See Honohan and Shi (2001). According to this study, a 10 percentage point increase in dollarization is associated with an 8 percent increase in the pass-through coefficient.

ization could have counterproductive effects. For countries that are trying to restore confidence in their local currencies, experience has shown that very tight regulations on dollarization (for example, requiring that the counterparts to dollar deposits be kept, in full, at the central bank or abroad, or restricting credit to the nontradable sector) encourage capital flight and further constrain the supply of credit to the domestic economy. In this situation, approaches to the problem need to rely on changing incentives to encourage a progressive shift back to use of the domestic currency while containing the short-term risks and building a track record of macroeconomic stability:

- The cornerstone of such an approach is to achieve a more sustained application of strong macroeconomic policies to bolster confidence in holding and transacting in domestic currency. Most countries in Latin America have, indeed, made important progress, particularly in controlling inflation. Nevertheless, experience suggests that it may take many years to reestablish confidence in domestic currencies, especially where there are other weaknesses in the macroeconomic framework, including unsustainable fiscal situations. To limit short-term risks of dollarization, countries have also sought to build up international reserves and arrange lines of credit that could be drawn upon in emergency situations.

- To discourage dollarization, countries have sought to adjust prudential rules to reflect the particular risks associated with dollar-based financial intermediation. For example, some countries—such as Paraguay and Peru—have introduced differential liquidity requirements, requiring that higher reserves be held against foreign currency-denominated deposits. Other prudential measures, such as higher capital and provisioning requirements on foreign currency loans, would also help to ensure that lending conditions accurately reflect the true risks involved.

- A gradual shift to a more flexible exchange rate policy would also make the risks of foreign currency lending more apparent. Such a policy would, however, need to be introduced gradually to avoid the risk of abrupt changes in real exchange rates triggering bankruptcies.

References

Alesina, Alberto, Robert Barro, and Silvana Tenreyro, 2002, "Optimal Currency Areas," NBER Working Paper No. 9072 (Cambridge, Massachusetts: National Bureau of Economic Research).

Baliño, Tomás, Adam Bennett, and Eduardo Borensztein, 1999, *Monetary Policy in Dollarized Economies*, IMF Occasional Paper No. 171 (Washington: International Monetary Fund).

Calvo, Guillermo, 2001, "Capital Markets and the Exchange Rate, with a Special Reference to the Dollarization Debate in Latin America," *Journal of Money, Credit and Banking*, Vol. 33, No. 1, pp. 312–34.

———, and Carmen M. Reinhart, 2002, "Fear of Floating," *Quarterly Journal of Economics*, Vol. 117 (May), pp. 379–408.

Catão, Luis, and Marco Terrones, 2000, "Determinants of Dollarization: The Banking Side," IMF Working Paper 00/146 (Washington: International Monetary Fund).

De Nicolo, Gianni, Patrick Honohan, and Alain Ize, 2003, "Dollarization of the Banking System: Good or Bad?" IMF Research Department Seminar Series No. 2003-103 (Washington: International Monetary Fund).

Dornbusch, Rudiger, and Alejandro Reynoso, 1989, "Financial Factors in Economic Development," NBER Working Paper No. 2889 (Cambridge, Massachusetts: National Bureau of Economic Research).

Dornbusch, Rudiger, Federico Sturzenegger, and Holger Wolf, 1990, "Extreme Inflation: Dynamics and Stabilization," *Brookings Papers on Economic Activity: 2*, Brookings Institution, pp. 1–84.

Faal, E., and Nita Thacker, 2003, "Dollarization in Latin America: Is Mexico Different?" (unpublished; Washington: International Monetary Fund).

Goldfajn, Ilan, Katherine Hennings, and Helio Mori, 2003, "Brazil's Financial System: Resilience to Shocks, No Currency Substitution, But Struggling to Promote Growth," Central Bank of Brazil Working Paper No. 75 (Brasilia).

Guidotti, Pablo E., and Carlos A. Rodriguez, 1992, "Dollarization in Latin America: Gresham's Law in Reverse?" *Staff Papers*, International Monetary Fund, Vol. 39 (September), pp. 518–44.

Gulde-Wolf, Anne-Marie, David Hoelscher, Alain Ize, David Marston, and Gianni De Nicolo, 2004, *Financial Stability in Dollarized Economies*, IMF Occasional Paper No. 230 (Washington: International Monetary Fund).

Honohan, Patrick, and Anqing Shi, 2001, "Deposit Dollarization and the Financial Sector in Emerging Economies," Policy Research Working Paper No. 2748 (Washington: World Bank).

Ize, Alain, 2002, "Financial Dollarization in Central America: What to Do About It" (unpublished; Washington: International Monetary Fund).

———, and Eduardo Levy Yeyati, 1998, "Dollarization of Financial Intermediation: Causes and Policy Implications," IMF Working Paper 98/28 (Washington: International Monetary Fund).

———, 2003, "Financial Dollarization," *Journal of International Economics*, Vol. 59 (March), pp. 323–47.

Savastano, Miguel A., 1996, "Dollarization in Latin America: Recent Evidence and Some Policy Issues," in *The Macroeconomics of International Currencies: The-*

ory, Policy, and Evidence, ed. by Paul Mizen and Eric J. Pentecost (Cheltenham, United Kingdom: Edward Elgar), pp. 225–55.

Shiller, Robert J., 1998, "Indexed Units of Account: Theory and Assessment of Historical Experience," NBER Working Paper No. 6356 (Cambridge, Massachusetts: National Bureau of Economic Research).

Uribe, Martín, 1997, "Hysteresis in a Simple Model of Currency Substitution," *Journal of Monetary Economics*, Vol. 40 (September), pp. 185–202.

VII   External Vulnerabilities

Relatively low trade openness and high financial openness are common characteristics of many Latin American countries. Indeed, Latin America and the Caribbean is the only developing region in which the proportion of countries that are financially open exceeds the proportion that are open to trade (Figure 7.1).

This section explores how the combination of low trade openness and high financial openness—in the context of volatile capital inflows—amplified crisis vulnerabilities in Latin America. The first subsection surveys the considerable range of measures undertaken during the 1990s to liberalize trade and move away from the long-standing strategy of import substitution. The next subsection discusses why, despite these efforts to open the region to trade, Latin America remains relatively closed. The reasons include a number of persistent barriers to trade, the impact of regional trade agreements on outward orientation, and the effects of repeated episodes of macroeconomic instability. The next subsection discusses Latin America's relatively high financial openness and, in particular, the resurgence in capital flows to the region in the 1990s and the continued high volatility of these flows. The channels through which low trade openness and volatile capital flows amplified crisis vulnerabilities are then examined. The final subsection concludes with lessons from the 1990s regarding trade and financial integration, and reviews ongoing efforts and future challenges.

Disappointing Outcomes of Trade Liberalization

Efforts to Liberalize Trade

Trade liberalization has been at the heart of the reform process in Latin America, marking a break with the past strategy of import substitution.[138] Over the

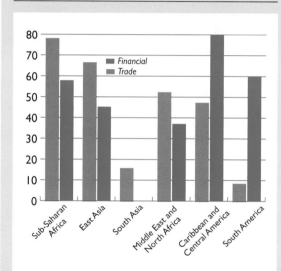

Figure 7.1. Trade and Financial Integration Across Developing Regions, 1975–99[1]
(In percent of open economies)

Sources: Morsink and others (2002); IMF, *World Economic Outlook,* various issues.
[1]For 1975–99, the average share of countries in each region that are open to trade or financial flows. In each year, a country is classified as open if its degree of integration is greater than the median. Trade openness is the sum of exports and imports of goods and services, divided by GDP. Financial openness is the sum of external assets and liabilities of foreign direct investment and portfolio investment, divided by GDP.

last fifteen years, many Latin American countries made progress in implementing measures to liberalize trade, although they undertook such efforts at different times.[139] Chile was the first Latin American country to embark on a program of trade liberalization. Its trade reforms were launched in the early 1970s, and by the end of the decade, the economy had become relatively open. Further trade reforms were implemented in Chile during 1983–91. Most other Latin American countries introduced trade liberalization in

---

[138]Considerable cross-country empirical evidence has shown trade openness is associated with higher productivity and income per capita, and that trade liberalization contributes to growth. Empirical evidence on the positive connection between trade and growth is discussed in Berg and Krueger (2002).

[139]For further details, see, for example, Burki and Perry (1997).

a more abrupt manner. Countries typically implemented trade reform measures over one or two years, beginning in the mid-1980s with Bolivia, Mexico, and Venezuela, followed by Argentina, Brazil, Colombia, and Peru in the late 1980s and early 1990s.

Reducing applied tariff rates was a key component of trade policy reform in Latin America. Tariff rates in Latin America fell from an average of around 49 percent in the mid-1980s to around 11 percent in the late 1990s.[140] Tariff reductions were particularly steep in Brazil and Colombia, where average tariff rates were more than 80 percent in the mid-1980s (Figure 7.2). Tariff dispersion in Latin America also declined from around 30 percent in the mid-1980s to its current level of around 10 percent. From an international perspective, by the end of the 1990s, tariff rates for a sample of six Latin American countries (Argentina, Brazil, Chile, Colombia, the Dominican Republic, and Mexico) were similar to those in East Asian economies and European transition economies.[141]

A number of other policy initiatives also aimed at creating more open trade regimes in Latin America.[142] First, the frequent use of nontariff barriers (NTBs) was scaled back, which improved transparency and eliminated many incentives for rent seeking and corruption. On average, the coverage of NTBs was reduced from nearly 40 percent of imports in the late 1980s to about 6 percent in the 1990s.[143] By the end of the 1990s, the use of NTBs in Latin America was similar to that in Asian emerging market countries.[144] More subtle forms of nontariff measures have emerged, however; and, as discussed later, these are obstacles to promoting greater trade opening.

Second, since the mid-1980s, 15 Latin American countries have joined the General Agreement on Tariffs and Trade (GATT) and its successor, the World Trade Organization (WTO). Adhering to the rules of these multilateral agreements has helped them to cre-

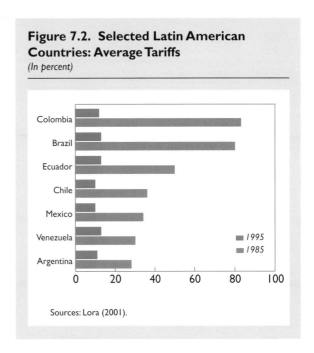

Figure 7.2. Selected Latin American Countries: Average Tariffs
(In percent)

Sources: Lora (2001).

ate more transparent trade regimes. The Uruguay Round negotiations, which took place during 1986–94, focused on improving market access by reducing obstacles to trade in goods and services and on ensuring that the resulting expanded market access would become legally binding under WTO rules. For Latin America, participating in these negotiations further expanded commitments to reduce import barriers.

Third, the "new regionalism" reflected in broader regional trade agreements contributed to lowering average levels of protection and boosting exports within the region, although their broader impact on development of exports to markets outside of the region has been less positive.[145] Since 1990, more than 30 such initiatives were developed, ranging from free trade areas to customs unions (Table 7.1). Notably, Mercosur, established in 1991, included Argentina, Brazil, Paraguay, and Uruguay in a common market with a common external tariff and trade policy. Overall, these many agreements included commitments to liberalize and introduced a large number of mutual concessions, schedules for tariff phase-outs, and a relatively high degree of reciprocity.[146]

---

[140]Based on evidence from Lora (2001).

[141]Estimates are from Laird and Messerlin (2003).

[142]Many Latin American countries also used export-promotion schemes (for example, import-duty drawbacks, export-processing zones, and marketing and insurance support) to foster and develop export markets. As discussed in Macario (2002), however, with the exceptions of Chile and Mexico, export promotion was relatively ineffective in boosting export growth.

[143]Estimate based on 11 Latin American countries for which data are available. For further details, see IADB (1996).

[144]Evidence in Burki and Perry (1997) shows that the weighted incidence of nontariff measures in Latin America fell from more than 30 percent in the 1980s to around 5 percent in the early 1990s, which was just above the level in the Asian newly industrializing countries. Nontariff restrictions are measured as the weighted percentage of tariff-code lines covered by various types of nontariff barriers (such as licenses, quotas, and prohibitions) as a percentage of all tariff code lines, using as weights the countries' respective shares in world trade.

---

[145]For a detailed examination of regional trade agreements in Latin America, see IADB and Iglesias (2002).

[146]See for example, Devlin and Estevadeordal (2002). The objectives of the "new regionalism" go well beyond reducing trade protection. Other equally important objectives of these arrangements include supporting structural economic reforms; providing new opportunities for exports and diversification, which can serve as stepping stones to improved global competitiveness; attracting foreign direct investment; and fostering regional cooperation. For a detailed discussion, see IADB and Iglesias (2002).

Table 7.1. Latin America: Regional Integration Initiatives, 1990–Present

Completed Agreements (Year Signed)	Negotiations in Progress
Intraregional Agreements	**Intraregional Agreements**
Southern Cone Common Market-Mercosur (1991)	Mercosur-Andean Community
Chile-Venezuela (1993)	Costa Rica-Panama
Colombia-Chile (1994)	Mexico-Panama
Costa Rica-Mexico (1994)	Mexico-Peru
Group of Three (1994)	Mexico-Ecuador
Bolivia-Mexico (1994)	Mexico-Trinidad and Tobago
Chile-Mercosur (1996)	
Bolivia-Mercosur 1996	**North-South Agreements**
Mexico-Nicaragua (1997)	Free Trade Area of the Americas (FTAA)
Central American Common Market-Dominican Republic (1998)	Mercosur-European Union
Chile-Peru (1998)	Chile-European Free Trade Association
Chile-Central American Common Market (1999)	Caribbean Community-European Union
Chile-Mexico (1999)	Central America–4-Canada
Mexico-Northern Triangle of Central America (2000)	Central American Common Market-United States
Caribbean Community-Dominican Republic (2000)	Uruguay-United States
Costa Rica-Trinidad and Tobago (2002)	Mexico-Japan
El Salvador-Panama (2002)	Chile-Republic of Korea
North-South Agreements	**Others**
Mexico-North American Free Trade Agreement (1992)	Brazil-China
Chile-Canada (1996)	Brazil-Russia
Mexico-European Union (1999)	
Mexico-European Free Trade Association (2000)	
Mexico-Israel (2000)	
Costa Rica-Canada (2001)	
Chile-European Union (2002)	
Chile-United States (2003)	

Source: Inter-American Development Bank and Iglesias (2002).

Disappointing Results

With these considerable efforts to liberalize trade, some progress was made in diversifying countries' exports and raising the shares of trade in their GDPs. Overall, however, integration with the global economy has proceeded very slowly. Latin American economies remain much less open than those in the rest of the world. Latin American exports as a share of GDP rose from around 15 percent at the start of the 1990s to 21 percent a decade later, but this ratio remains well below those of other developing countries (Figure 7.3).[147] In part, persistent limited trade openness reflects the closed character of Latin America's economies prior to the reforms. Moreover, export growth in Latin America following the reforms has consistently lagged that in the Asian emerging market countries. For example, although export volume growth in Latin America nearly doubled to about 7 percent during the 1990s relative to

[147]Figures for emerging Asia exclude Hong Kong SAR and Singapore, where exports considerably exceed 100 percent of GDP.

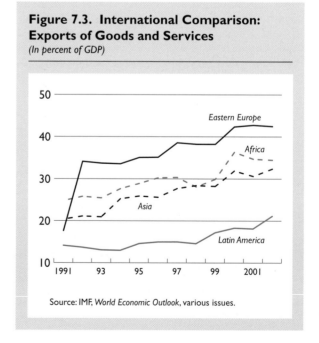

Figure 7.3. International Comparison: Exports of Goods and Services
(In percent of GDP)

Source: IMF, *World Economic Outlook*, various issues.

Table 7.2. International Comparison: Export Performance in Latin America and Asia[1]

	Export Volume (Annual percent change)		U.S. Dollar Export Value (Annual percent change)		Exports (In percent of GDP)	
	1980–90	1990–2000	1980–90	1990–2000	1980–90	1990–2000
Argentina	5.04	6.38	2.84	7.52	8.96	9.05
Brazil	5.59	7.34	4.73	6.41	10.10	9.04
Chile	6.09	9.34	5.43	8.01	27.23	29.54
Colombia	7.37	3.68	5.03	6.08	15.07	17.00
Mexico	7.67	11.36	8.22	9.98	16.96	25.20
Peru	−7.74	8.05	−1.57	7.65	16.74	13.38
Venezuela	2.33	2.41	−0.72	6.28	27.49	27.75
Latin American average[2]	3.76	6.94	3.42	7.42	17.51	18.71
Hong Kong SAR[3]	13.11	9.22	14.65	9.27	110.70	139.86
Indonesia	1.15	10.44	3.35	8.87	25.06	31.68
Korea, Republic of	10.87	15.76	13.97	10.86	41.56	34.18
Malaysia	9.65	9.79	8.83	13.10	59.32	96.21
Philippines	3.57	9.25	5.03	13.72	24.17	40.96
Singapore[3]	9.44	11.00	10.77	10.30	179.55	172.00
Thailand	12.39	10.95	14.73	9.93	26.61	46.25
Emerging Asia average[2]	8.60	10.87	10.19	10.74	66.71	79.90
Excluding Hong Kong SAR and Singapore	7.53	11.24	9.18	11.30	35.34	49.86

Source: Catão (2002).
[1]Exports of goods and nonfactor services.
[2]Unweighted averages.
[3]Exports including re-exports.

the 1980s, it remained lower than in emerging Asia (Table 7.2).

This general picture of lagging trade openness in Latin America masks underlying differences across the region with respect to the openness and diversity of trade structures (Figures 7.4 and 7.5).[148] Although Paraguay and Chile have trade shares greater than 60 percent of GDP, most countries in the region are classified as relatively closed to trade. Some countries—such as Colombia—have relatively diverse export structures, while others—such as Ecuador and Venezuela—have highly concentrated export structures with exports in a few primary commodities, such as oil and metals, accounting for a relatively high share of overall exports (Figure 7.6). Nonetheless, it is evident that during the 1990s, countries made progress in diversifying their export structures—for example, Mexico and a number of Central American countries have increased manufactured goods' share of total trade.

Latin America's persistently low and lagging trade openness is another factor explaining its low growth performance over a long period. There is abundant empirical evidence that the more open an economy is to trade with the outside world, the better is its growth performance relative to others. For example, a recent study, Warcziarg and Welch (2003), of 133 countries between 1950 and 1988 demonstrated that countries that liberalized their trade regimes enjoyed higher annual growth rates after liberalization.[149]

Explaining Disappointing Results

Why did the trade-liberalization efforts of the 1990s not deliver more open economies in Latin America? Geographical location, the size of the economy, the level of economic development, and other influences outside the direct control of policymakers explain why Latin American countries remain relatively closed. Yet, even correcting for these determinants of trade in the context of a gravity

---

[148]Relatively open economies are typically defined as those that have a total trade-to-GDP ratio of greater than 50 percent. The concentration of exports in product categories is measured by a Herfindahl index of concentration of export shares. An index above 0.28 is consistent with a concentration of 50 percent or more of exports in one of 10 product categories.

[149]Warcziarg and Welch (2003). See also Krueger (2004).

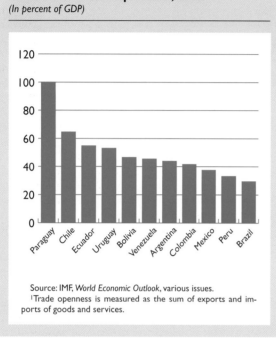

Figure 7.4. Selected Latin American Countries: Trade Openness, 2002[1]
(In percent of GDP)

Source: IMF, *World Economic Outlook*, various issues.
[1]Trade openness is measured as the sum of exports and imports of goods and services.

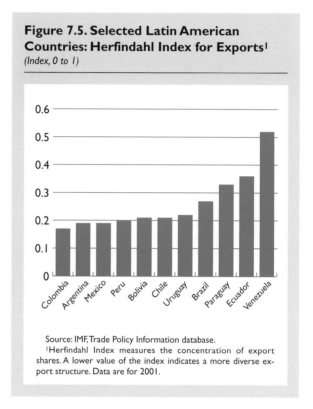

Figure 7.5. Selected Latin American Countries: Herfindahl Index for Exports[1]
(Index, 0 to 1)

Source: IMF, Trade Policy Information database.
[1]Herfindahl Index measures the concentration of export shares. A lower value of the index indicates a more diverse export structure. Data are for 2001.

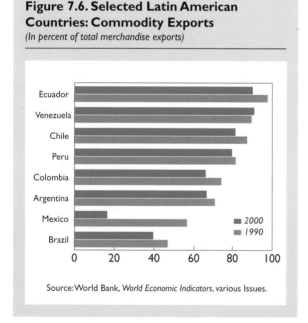

Figure 7.6. Selected Latin American Countries: Commodity Exports
(In percent of total merchandise exports)

Source: World Bank, *World Economic Indicators*, various Issues.

model, Latin American countries tend to trade less, on average, than would be expected.[150]

A broad range of factors, which are further explained later in this section, explain why Latin America remains relatively closed. These include the considerable scope that remains to lower protective barriers, disappointing results from regional trade arrangements, persistent barriers to trade in industrial countries, the lack of effective trade institutions, and the region's persistently volatile macroeconomic environment.

Further Room to Lower Protective Barriers

Although Latin America's average tariff rates declined dramatically over the 1990s, there is still room to lower tariffs and the level of effective protection. First, a high degree of tariff escalation persists in the region. Tariff escalation describes instances where more protection is given to higher-value-added products than to raw materials or less-processed inputs. Thus, even though tariff rates overall have been reduced, the prevalence of tariff escalation means that effective protection of manufactured goods remains high.[151] Over time, such tar-

---

[150]Evidence on undertrading in Latin America is based on conventional gravity model estimates, and is discussed in

Morsink, Helbling, and Sgherri (2002). Such quantitative evidence may overstate undertrading owing to illegal and unreported trade activity.

[151]One prominent example of tariff escalation is the tariff schedule for Mercosur, which affects the trade of some of the

iff escalation discourages higher-value-added exports, leading to a concentration on agricultural goods and raw materials—products that have been hurt by negative terms of trade shocks, high levels of protection in importing countries, and slow growth of world demand. This export structure also tends to insulate these economies from the investment and technology transfers that often accompany trade in more sophisticated manufactured goods.

Second, despite the progress made, nontariff barriers in the form of licensing requirements, government monopolies, quotas or import bans, and trade-related investment measures remain a hindrance to trade. Moreover, countries increasingly are resorting to alternative forms of protection, such as initiating antidumping investigations or invoking the use of technical standards. These more subtle forms of protection are particularly difficult to quantify and could undermine the positive benefits of the trade liberalization that has taken place. Estimates in Inter-American Development Bank (IADB and Iglesias, 2002) suggest that the use of nontariff measures is the highest in Argentina, Colombia, and Mexico.[152]

Third, considerable scope remains to liberalize trade in essential infrastructure services, such as communications, transportation, and finance, which are important inputs into production and trade. Estimates of barriers to trade in business services indicate that liberalization would significantly reduce the cost of production and exports. For example, Stern (2000) cites studies that find a tariff equivalent on business services of more than 30 percent in Brazil, and similar price differentials for telecommunications and financial services in other Latin American countries. Since most business-service exports are delivered through the establishment of foreign firms in the export market, liberalizing trade in services implies a significant liberalization in the rules that affect foreign direct investment.

Regional Trade Arrangements[153]

Although regional trade arrangements in Latin America boosted intraregional trade, they did not vigorously promote export growth outside of the region. The boost to exports from regional agreements was concentrated among major trading partners in South America including Mercosur (Argentina, Brazil, Paraguay, and Uruguay) and the Andean Community (Bolivia, Colombia, Ecuador, Peru, and Venezuela).[154] Indeed, intraregional trade for the Mercosur countries increased from about 7 percent of total trade in 1992 to around 20 percent in the late 1990s, and for the Andean Community from about 8 percent to 11 percent during the same period. These principal agreements were designed as common markets (which require members to have common external tariffs), however, rather than free-trade areas (where each member has flexibility to choose its policy toward nonmembers). When the common external tariff is relatively high, these arrangements can result in costly trade and investment diversion.

The effect of establishing customs unions on members' incentives for multilateral liberalization and on the barriers faced by outsiders seeking market access is the subject of ongoing research and policy debate. Evidence with regard to Mercosur—the largest of the region's customs unions—suggests that its efforts to stimulate economic growth among its members have fallen short. The dismantling of internal trade barriers may have increased trade among members of Mercosur. The imposition of common external tariffs may, however, have lowered welfare overall as members shifted imports away from competitive extraregional suppliers toward suppliers that benefited from the agreement.[155] In addition, there is evidence that Mercosur may have led to specialization in products that were not competitive in international markets, which acted to reduce the dynamism of extraregional exports.[156]

To maximize the benefits of regional trade agreements, a number of issues need to be addressed. First, there are particular benefits from trade integration with advanced economies, including increased investment flows and technology transfers. Moreover, benefits to developing countries also arise from integration with an industrial-country partner with more demanding regulatory standards. In the case of the North American Free Trade Agreement (NAFTA), Mexico has benefited from integration with Canada and the United States in many areas, including investment and competition policies,

---

largest countries in the region. Region-wide studies suggest that there is significant tariff escalation in important product chains, including processed food, textiles and clothing, tobacco, wood products, and automobiles. See, for example, Laird, Cernat, and Turrini (2002).

[152]IADB and Iglesias (2002) estimates are based on data compiled by the United Nations Conference on Trade and Development (UNCTAD) and the IADB under the project TRAINS for the Americas. Estimates include both quantitative restrictions and technical standards, with the latter being particularly difficult to measure.

[153]For an overview on the debate about preferential trade arrangements, see Krueger (1999).

[154]In addition, similar regional integration took place among Central American and Caribbean countries with, for example, the formation of the Central American Common Market and the Caribbean Community.

[155]For example, Chang and Winters (2002) analyze the impact of Mercosur on the pricing of nonmembers' exports to Brazil and conclude that the observed decline in export prices can be attributed to the effects of trade diversion.

[156]See, for example, Yeats (1997).

services regulation, and government procurement practices (Box 7.1).[157]

Second, regional trade agreements would have a greater positive impact if they were more comprehensive in scope. In addition to liberalization of trade in manufactured products, for example, only a few arrangements include trade in services or agreements on foreign direct investment regulations, competition policy, and other kinds of regulatory infrastructure that facilitate exchange and bring certainty to the economic environment. Binding these policy changes in an international agreement tends to better anchor the policy environment and to ensure that the reforms result in positive externalities for trade with partners that are not members of the arrangement.

The most important free trade initiative in the hemisphere is the Free Trade Agreement of the Americas (FTAA). Negotiations are under way among 32 countries in the region, led by the United States and Brazil, with a target date for agreement of 2005. Negotiations were initially to cover trade restrictions on manufactured goods, agriculture, and services, and to establish hemisphere-wide rules regarding intellectual property rights, subsidies, antidumping, countervailing duties, government procurement, investment, competition policy, and dispute settlement. There are considerable obstacles to overcome in these negotiations, however; and, as a result, the agenda has been scaled back from its original objectives. Following the Miami meeting in November 2003, a "menu-driven" approach is emerging, allowing each FTAA member to pick and choose from a list of commitments that has yet to be established. This may entail a correlation between benefits and obligations, undermining nondiscriminatory treatment not only vis-à-vis nonmembers but also within the FTAA. This new approach suggests a diminished, yet complex FTAA with some common standards and a set of plurilateral agreements. Nonetheless, the FTAA is still likely to yield fairly broad coverage of non-agricultural market access and help to chip away at remaining protective barriers in Latin America.

Barriers to Industrial Country Markets

Latin American countries continue to face significant barriers to their exports, and particularly agricultural products, to industrial country markets.[158] Agricultural support in major industrial countries

tends to encourage the overproduction of agricultural products and result not only in fewer imports into industrial countries but also depressed international prices. Industrial country support includes market price supports; a variety of payments to farmers based on output, area planted, input use, historical payments, or farm income; and export subsidies. Total support to agriculture in member countries of the Organization for Economic Cooperation and Development (OECD) amounted to about US$305 billion—or 1.3 percent of OECD countries' GDP—in 2001.[159]

Estimates suggest that agricultural protection in industrial countries is particularly costly for Latin America. For example, estimates based on a general-equilibrium model of the international economy suggest that if U.S. agricultural subsidies and tariffs on field crops were cut by 50 percent, exports of these products from Latin America—Argentina and Brazil in particular—would rise by 9 percent.[160] Moreover, if Canada, the European Union, and Japan also cut subsidies and tariffs by 50 percent, Latin American exports of field crops would rise by about 20 percent. Latin American sugar producers would also benefit from further industrial country liberalization: if the United States removed 50 percent of the barriers to the U.S. sugar market, Latin American sugar exports would rise by 10 percent; and if Canada, the European Union, and Japan also removed 50 percent of their sugar barriers, the region's exports would rise by nearly 40 percent.

More broadly, although the conclusion of the Uruguay Round resulted in an overall reduction in tariff rates in developed countries, Latin American countries continue to face the effects of very high tariff rates—that is, tariff peaks and tariff escalation.[161] Developed countries have continued to have import tariff peaks not only in the agriculture sector but also in such sectors as processed foods, textiles and apparel, footwear and leather products, automotive and transport equipment, and electronic products.

Weak Domestic Trade Institutions and Infrastructure

Establishing the institutions and infrastructure to support international trade plays a critical role in developing a successful and competitive export sector. Weaknesses in these areas have tended to be obsta-

---

[157]Despite the positive results attributed in part to NAFTA, scope remains for further negotiations and liberalization under the agreement, particularly for rules of origin and manufacturing trade, agriculture, and the use of antidumping and countervailing-duty measures. For a detailed discussion, see World Bank (2003a).

[158]NAFTA has been the exception and has illustrated the benefits of improved market access on export growth.

---

[159]See OECD (2003).

[160]The model used for these estimates was the Global Trade Analysis Project (GTAP). For further details, see MacDonagh-Dumler, Yang, and Bannister (2002). Field crops include rice, wheat, grains, and oilseeds.

[161]See, for example, ECLAC (2003).

Box 7.1. NAFTA: Benefits and Challenges[1]

The North American Free Trade Agreement (NAFTA), signed by Canada, the United States, and Mexico in January 1994, was the first comprehensive free-trade agreement among advanced and developing countries. The agreement created the world's largest free-trade area in terms of total gross domestic product (GDP) and the second largest in terms of total trade volume, after the European Union.

NAFTA was broad in scope, eliminating the majority of tariffs and other trade barriers in its first 10 years and phasing out most remaining tariffs by 2008. Various provisions were included covering investment flows, financial services, government purchases, and protection of intellectual property rights. NAFTA also established a variety of unique mechanisms for resolution of disputes that supplemented existing World Trade Organization (WTO) mechanisms and also included side agreements on labor and environmental issues.

How has NAFTA affected Mexico?

- Separating the effects of NAFTA from the positive and negative shocks that affected Mexico over the past decade is difficult. Following the agreement, the U.S. economy experienced a prolonged boom, followed by the 2000 stock market collapse and subsequent recession. The Mexican economy also suffered a major financial crisis in the mid-1990s, from which the banking sector has slowly recovered. Subsequently, the implementation of sound domestic economic policies and the strength of the U.S. economy have played important roles in boosting growth in Mexico.
- Nonetheless, most studies suggest that NAFTA spurred a dramatic increase in trade and financial flows. (See the relevant figure.) For example, Mexico's exports to the United States and Canada tripled in dollar terms between 1993 and 2002. Although the growth of trade has slowed since 2000, Mexico's trade (exports *plus* imports) with its NAFTA partners accounted for about 40 percent of its GDP in 2002. The agreement also appears to have significantly altered the nature of trade flows, with a substantial increase in intra-industry trade between Mexico and its NAFTA partners. Similarly, NAFTA helped boost foreign direct investment (FDI) flows to Mexico, which rose from $12 billion during 1991–93 to roughly $54 billion during 2000–2002, with the share of NAFTA partners in total FDI flows to Mexico increasing from 50 percent in 1994 to roughly 80 percent in 2002.
- Increased trade and financial linkages have affected the dynamics of economic growth in Mexico in several ways. (See the relevant figure.) Contributions of exports and investment to GDP growth have increased substantially following the introduction of the agreement. In particular, the contribution of investment to GDP growth reached 3 percentage points during 1996–2002 as the average growth rate

of investment rose to more than 8½ percent. Recent studies suggest that NAFTA induced a sizable increase in total factor productivity in Mexico, helping double GDP growth from an annual average of 2 percent during 1980–93 to 4 percent during 1996–2002.

How Has NAFTA Affected Mexico?

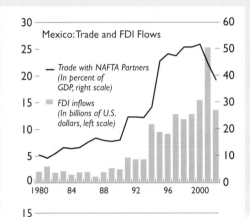

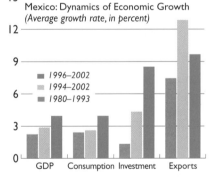

Source: Kose, Meredith, and Towe (forthcoming).
Notes: FDI denotes foreign direct investment. NAFTA denotes North American Free Trade Agreement.

---

[1]This box draws on Kose, Meredith, and Towe (forthcoming).

Box 7.1 *(concluded)*

• NAFTA appears to have been associated with significant changes in the Mexican business cycle. (See the relevant figure.) Mexico's output volatility has decreased by almost 30 percent, and the volatility of investment has fallen by more than 40 percent, since 1996. Business cycles in Mexico and the United States have become significantly more synchronized, with marked increases in the cross-country correlations of the major macroeconomic aggregates.

What challenges lie ahead for Mexico, and what are the lessons for other developing countries?

• Mexico's trade with NAFTA partners has slowed in recent years, and Mexico's output growth has also fallen sharply. This has reflected cyclical factors, including the U.S. recession and the initially halting recovery. At the same time, however, structural factors have been important. Mexico has been adversely affected by the health of the U.S. manufacturing sector, which has been the destination for most of Mexico's exports, as well as by the rapid expansion of the market shares of emerging market economies, particularly China, in the United States.

Mexico's experience under NAFTA illustrates that structural reforms are needed to sustain the benefits of comprehensive trade agreements. In Mexico's case, although there has been considerable progress in attaining financial and macroeconomic stability, there is also a clear need for measures to boost competitiveness in a number of areas. For example, Mexico has among the most rigid labor market institutions in Latin America, which discourage the development of the formal labor sector. The energy sector is another key concern, and measures are needed to facilitate investment and exploitation of new opportunities. Telecommunications remain highly regulated, driving up business costs. In the institutional area, judicial reforms are needed that would provide greater certainty to the legal process and enhance the rule of law. Finally, comprehensive tax reform is essential to reduce dependence on oil revenues and generate the resources needed to improve public infrastructure and education.

---

cles to trade in some Latin American countries. For example, with regard to institutions, despite progress made in recent years, improvements in customs administration are needed in a number of countries. Clearing customs efficiently is important for containing costs, particularly for assembly of products for re-export. Moreover, the proliferation of regional trade arrangements has complicated the process by adding requirements to administer rules of origin, preferential duties, and other discriminatory rules. As a result, the average delay in customs in Latin America is about nine days, compared with just five days in East Asian and Pacific countries.[162]

Other institutional weaknesses that have hindered trade flows include legal uncertainty about the enforceability of trade documents, such as bills of lading and letters of credit; corruption, particularly with regard to clearing customs; and complex and nontransparent administrative procedures. In addition, although many Latin American countries belong to international institutions such as the WTO, they participate less than fully in a number of agreements and make extensive use of developing country exemptions, restraining the momentum of liberalization.[163] Also, countries have been slow to adopt and enforce a number of scientific, technical, and phytosanitary standards that can be critical in promoting exports, particularly of agricultural products.

Trade-related infrastructure needs to be strengthened to facilitate the movement of goods across borders. Trade-related transactions costs are important in determining how successful a country is in participating in global trade.[164] Problems that add to trade costs include frequent reloading of goods; port congestion owing to inadequate facilities; the limited use of e-commerce, which adds to the cost of processing information; and relatively weak service sectors. For example, even in Chile, where exporters are less hindered than elsewhere in Latin America, weaknesses in infrastructure—such as the absence of tunnel access through the Andes in winter and inadequate port facilities—have held back export growth.[165] In many Latin American countries, further investment is needed to expand port facilities, implement new technology, and develop other infrastructure services. In this regard, the entry of foreign service providers can prove helpful in introducing new technologies and management practices to the domestic service industry. Latin America's reluctance to undertake meaningful market access com-

---

[162]World Bank (2003b).

[163]One aspect of this special treatment is the wide gap between tariff levels committed to ("bound") in the WTO and those actually applied, which further increases the uncertainty about future market access conditions.

[164]Evidence in World Bank (2003b) suggests that transport cost barriers to trade generally outweigh tariff barriers and that improvements in service-sector infrastructure would provide large gains from trade.

[165]See Macario (2000).

mitments under the WTO's General Agreement on Trade in Services (GATS) has not helped it to realize the full potential of such investment.[166]

Weaknesses in Macroeconomic Environment

Latin America's macroeconomic environment has also contributed to the region's disappointing trade performance. Overvalued real exchange rates and financial volatility have been particularly important. As discussed in Section IV, although exchange rate-based stabilization programs arrested inflation in the 1990s, a common result was persistent appreciation of the real exchange rate, which, in turn, promoted investment in nontradable goods and discouraged exports. Macroeconomic volatility also undermined investment and trade.[167] The volatility was driven not only by external developments, such as fluctuations in the terms of trade and capital flows, but also by domestic policy inconsistencies and recurring financial crises.

Capital Flows to Latin America

While the ratio of trade to GDP expanded modestly during the 1990s, channels of external financing reopened and capital flows to the region surged from the very depressed levels of the 1980s.

In a number of Latin American countries, capital account liberalization either accompanied or predated trade liberalization measures.[168] Capital accounts in Latin America were opened up beginning in the 1970s, with initial steps taken in Argentina, Chile, and Mexico. In the mid-to-late 1970s, capital account openness was further encouraged by large bank-based inflows related to recycling of Organization of Petroleum Exporting Countries (OPEC) oil surpluses that dominated flows to the region. Key capital account reforms centered on eliminating exchange controls and ending restrictions on foreign direct investment (FDI) and other capital flows.

During the 1980s debt crisis in Latin America, many countries imposed capital controls to forestall capital outflows. These controls were largely ineffective, and capital flight continued throughout most of the decade. Following these difficulties, efforts to

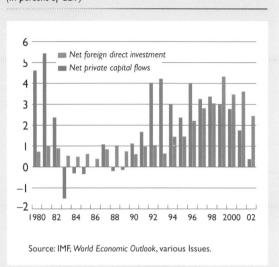

Figure 7.7. Latin America: Net Private Capital Flows
(In percent of GDP)

Net foreign direct investment
Net private capital flows

Source: IMF, *World Economic Outlook*, various Issues.

liberalize capital accounts resumed in the late 1980s. In Mexico, for example, restrictions on foreign capital participation in investment were liberalized substantially; nonresidents were allowed to buy shares on the Mexico Stock Exchange; and resident firms were allowed to issue stocks in foreign markets, provided that they were registered on the national stock registry.[169] Subsequently, nonresidents were permitted to hold Mexican government bonds and privatization of banks was allowed.

Capital flows returned to the region beginning in the early 1990s owing to both domestic and international developments (Figure 7.7).[170] The return of private capital reflected, in part, the new structural reform agendas that had been put in place—including improvements in financial sector regulation. Privatization and increased scope for foreign ownership, particularly in the financial and energy sectors, also encouraged increased inflows. Moreover, improved macroeconomic policies in a number of countries succeeded, at least initially, in reducing inflation, narrowing budget deficits, and contributing to a more stable exchange rate. Together, these improvements in the domestic environment increased the creditworthiness of Latin American borrowers. At the same time, the Brady debt restructuring initia-

---

[166]See Adlung (2000).

[167]See, for example, Rodrik (1999).

[168]Empirical evidence on the economic benefits of capital account liberalization is mixed. Based on a survey of the literature, Edison and others (2002) conclude that the evidence does not strongly point to a general result regarding the consequences of capital account liberalization, although there is some mixed evidence that liberalization boosts long-term economic growth. These effects seem to be most pronounced in East Asian countries.

---

[169]For a detailed discussion of capital account liberalization in Mexico and other countries, see Ishii and Habermeier (2002).

[170]For a detailed discussion of the behavior of capital flows to Latin America over the last two decades, see Fernandez-Arias and Panizza (2001) and Griffith-Jones (1998).

Figure 7.8. Selected Latin American Countries: Net Foreign Direct Investment (FDI) Flows

(In percent of total net FDI flows to Latin America)

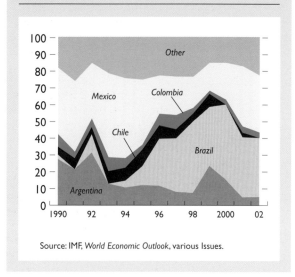

Source: IMF, *World Economic Outlook*, various Issues.

tives reduced the debt overhang, which increased confidence in countries' economic prospects and improved their market access.

International developments also boosted capital flows to Latin America. Recessions in the industrial countries in the early 1990s and the decline in U.S. interest rates created abundant international liquidity, prompting investors seeking higher returns to channel more funds to emerging markets, including Latin America.[171] Financial liberalization in the industrial countries and the trend toward international diversification of institutional portfolios also improved the availability of funds to the region.

Together, these factors resulted in a surge of capital flows to Latin America on a scale similar to that observed in the 1970s. Compared with the 1980s, the inflows in the 1990s were concentrated more in portfolio flows (both debt and equity) and substantially less in bank borrowing.

In addition, FDI rose as a share of inflows, particularly in the second half of the 1990s (see Figure 7.7)—an encouraging development, since empirical evidence has shown that FDI can have a positive impact on growth.[172] Foreign direct investment in

Latin America increased from an average of about ¾ of 1 percent of GDP in the 1980s to around 1 percent in the first half of the 1990s and then jumped to around 2½ percent of GDP in the second half of the 1990s before peaking at more than 4 percent in 1999. Although privatization was a key development fueling the pickup in FDI, the foreign acquisition of assets—that is, foreign investment in large private domestic enterprises in the manufacturing, electricity, and oil sectors—was important as well. On a country basis, Mexico accounted, on average, for about one-third of net FDI flows to Latin America over the 1990s, although this share varied from a high of 50 percent in 1993 to a low of around 20 percent for several years following the 1994–95 Mexico crisis (Figure 7.8). By the end of the 1990s, net FDI flows to Brazil accounted for a large share of the total flow to Latin America.

Volatility in capital flows continued in the 1990s, again subjecting the region to costly reversals and "sudden stops." When access to capital markets closed, real activity collapsed as credit dried up and production came to a halt. The crises inside and outside the region—the Mexican peso crisis in 1994–95, the Asian crisis and its after-effects during 1997–99, and the Argentine crisis beginning in 2001—were all accompanied by sharp retrenchments in flows, often with severe macroeconomic effects. For example, Fernandez-Arias and Panizza (2001) estimate that the difference in Latin America's GDP growth rates between years when it had access to financial markets and years when it did not was about 2 percentage points.

Some of the volatility of capital inflows reflected weaknesses in prudential guidelines in developed markets, which did not encourage adequate differentiation among emerging market borrowers according to risk. When risk perceptions worsened, the reversal of flows was immediate, with important contagion effects across countries. In addition, lenders tended to reduce apparent risks by investing in short-term and/or foreign currency debt or sovereign debt. Shifting market-risk exposure to governments did not reduce overall risk, however, but instead transformed it into (less visible) default risk. When the implications were belatedly recognized in markets, a sharp drop in market access and jumps in yield spreads led to crises.

The opening of capital accounts in a number of Latin American countries took place before other structural reforms—particularly with regard to the financial sector—were firmly in place.[173] As dis-

---

[171]For a discussion of how movements in the supply of external financing have triggered lending booms in emerging market countries, and in Latin America in particular, see Calvo, Reinhart, and Leiderman (1996) and Arora and Cerisola (2001).

[172]FDI can have a positive impact on growth, especially in countries where education levels are high, thereby allowing FDI spillover effects to be exploited. The pickup in FDI flows was not

unique to Latin America, since other emerging market countries were also recipients. See, for example, IMF (2001).

[173]For a detailed discussion of capital account liberalization, see Ffrench-Davis (2000); Edwards (2001); Hanson (1995); and Arteta, Eichengreen, and Wyplosz (2001).

cussed in Section V, the confluence of increased access to capital markets, weak regulatory and accounting standards, and inadequate banking supervision resulted in an increase in risky loans in financial systems, heightening vulnerability to economic shocks. Moreover, capital account liberalization occurred in some countries where the macroeconomic policy regime was insufficiently robust to manage the strains associated with volatile capital flows. Sudden reversals of capital flows typically exerted heavy pressure on the foreign exchange market and forced the authorities to devalue or abandon the exchange rate anchor altogether, as discussed in Section IV. Experiences in Latin America, and other regions as well, have illustrated the importance of sequencing and coordinating capital account liberalization with other policies, and particularly with strengthening of domestic financial systems to improve the ability of financial and non-financial entities to manage the risks associated with capital inflows.[174] The optimal sequencing of capital account liberalization is complex, however, and varies widely depending on the initial country conditions.

Low Trade Shares and Volatile Capital Flows Amplified Vulnerabilities

Weak trade opening and volatility in external financing flows—individually and in combination—amplified crisis vulnerabilities in Latin America. The structure of trade in Latin America heightened the region's vulnerability to external shocks. First, as already discussed, in a number of countries exports remained concentrated in a few primary commodities. With relatively high volatility in world commodity prices, economies generally remained highly vulnerable to terms of trade shocks that amplified underlying macroeconomic weaknesses. Second, increases in trade flows among close neighbors resulting from regional arrangements raised the exposure and vulnerability of these countries to common shocks and spillovers. The relatively high intraregional trade flows, therefore, may have amplified, rather than eased, shocks to the region.

More broadly, Latin America's relatively low trade openness was a key source of vulnerability in the region. Indeed, evidence based on the experience of the last twenty-five years suggests that financial crises have occurred more frequently in countries that are less integrated into the world trading system.[175]

Why does higher trade openness tend to reduce the frequency of crisis?[176] First, openness to trade tends to force an economy to become more flexible and thereby build greater resilience with respect to shocks. Second, trade integration can play an important role in increasing a country's ability to service its external debt. With a higher export-to-GDP ratio, a given exchange rate depreciation will provide a country with a greater opportunity to earn additional foreign exchange to service debt denominated in foreign currencies. Thus, a higher export ratio enhances the likelihood that a country will be able to service its foreign currency debt and, therefore, reduces the prospects of a reversal in capital inflows. The level of Latin America's external debt was similar to, if not lower than, those of other regions (Figure 7.9, top panel). The external debt was, however, primarily concentrated in public, rather than private, debt (Figure 7.9, middle panel); and the ratio of Latin America's total external debt to its exports far exceeded that of emerging Asia (Figure 7.9, bottom panel), with Uruguay and Argentina registering debt-to-export ratios in excess of 500 percent (Figure 7.10).

Crisis vulnerabilities were further exacerbated by a strong "fear of floating" in the region. Governments generally resisted exchange rate depreciation, owing to their past experience with exchange rate pass-through fueling inflation and the potential adverse liquidity and solvency consequences of highly dollarized balance sheets. With exchange rates in Latin America constrained, adjustments in trade competitiveness would have required significant declines in nominal domestic wages and prices.

Lessons, Policy Responses, and Challenges

Although Latin America made considerable progress in liberalizing trade during the 1990s, the extent of integration remains limited. Moreover, in many Latin American countries, the mismatch between a high degree of capital account openness and a low degree of trade openness left the region ill-equipped to deal with shocks and, in particular, the

---

[174]See Ishii and Habermeier (2002) and Nsouli, Rached, and Funke (2002) for a discussion of coordinating and sequencing capital account liberalization.

[175]As noted in Morsink, Helbling, and Sgherri (2002), developing countries that are less integrated are about 20 percent more likely to experience a debt default and 30 percent more likely to have a currency crisis than the average developing country. Sgherri (2002) shows that the inverse relationship between trade integration and crises remains robust under alternative econometric specifications.

[176]This subsection draws on Catão (2002).

Figure 7.9. International Comparison: External Debt

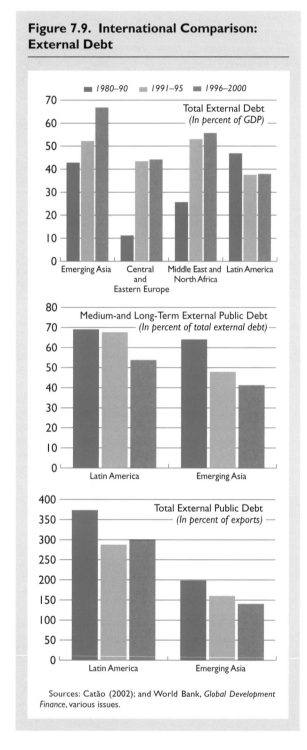

Sources: Catão (2002); and World Bank, *Global Development Finance*, various issues.

Figure 7.10. Selected Latin American Countries: External Debt, 2000
(In percent of exports)

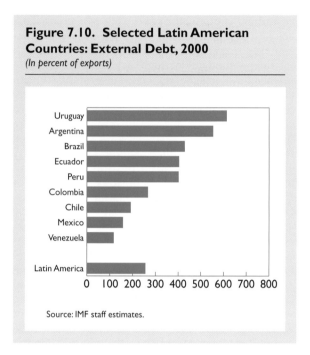

Source: IMF staff estimates.

years, however, considerable progress has been made in addressing these underlying vulnerabilities, with efforts made to liberalize trade and create greater financial resilience.

Building on the progress they made during the 1990s, Latin American countries have pushed ahead with trade liberalization in recent years. Many countries have continued to pursue liberalization through multilateral, bilateral, and unilateral channels— efforts that bear fruit by contributing to trade openness and by spurring broader reforms.

• The greatest potential benefit would arise from successful multilateral trade negotiations that could bring improved access for key Latin American exports, such as agricultural and textile products, in advanced countries. Indeed, many Latin American countries have actively participated in WTO negotiations. Recently, there has been a renewed momentum in the talks, with Brazil and other Latin American countries taking a prominent role in the search for common ground. The importance of a successful Doha round cannot be overstated. Estimates of the total gain from a Doha round agreement range from several hundred billion to a trillion U.S. dollars over the next decade or so, with the principal beneficiaries being developing countries.[177]

volatility inherent in capital flows. The relatively low level of exports in Latin America made it more difficult to achieve trade surpluses through exchange rate depreciation, while capital outflows could quickly be triggered by a loss of confidence, making debt payment more difficult. In recent

---

[177]Krueger (2004).

• Bilateral trade agreements can also play a beneficial role in expanding trade. For example, Chile's Free Trade Agreement with the United States, which became effective in January 2004, eliminates more than three-quarters of all tariffs immediately, with the rest to be phased out over 12 years. In addition, in mid-2004, five Central American countries (Costa Rica, El Salvador, Guatemala, Honduras, and Nicaragua) and the Dominican Republic signed the U.S.-Central American Free Trade Agreement. Other countries have also signaled their interest in similar agreements with the United States; and negotiations have begun with Colombia, Peru, and Ecuador.

• Further steps have been taken in forging trade agreements between the European Union (EU) and many Latin American countries. For example, the EU signed free-trade agreements with Mexico (1999) and Chile (2002), while negotiations between Mercosur and the EU have continued. Furthermore, it is expected that negotiations will be opened between the EU and Central America and the Andean Community.

• Progress continues on broader regional trade negotiations including the Free Trade Agreement of the Americas, which would progressively eliminate barriers to trade and investment among countries in the Western Hemisphere.

Aside from progress in designing and finalizing multilateral and bilateral agreements, there remain considerable scope and benefits for Latin American countries to encourage trade opening by unilaterally easing their own restrictions, particularly with regard to tariff escalation, nontariff barriers, and the significant remaining restrictions on services trade. Unilateral liberalization may have been slowed in recent years by the ongoing regional and multilateral negotiations.

More broadly, further development of trade institutions, as discussed in this section, will also help to support trade growth and openness. The importance of such infrastructure, including institutions to establish or adapt standards and promote conformity, is illustrated by the experience in Central America. For example, efforts in Costa Rica have yielded a comprehensive infrastructure for assessing conformity to technical standards. Progress is also under way in developing customs-administration capacity. For example, in Brazil, a number of important trade-related institutional improvements have been implemented, including a centralized electronic system to register, monitor, and control foreign trade operations. Further development of transportation infrastructure—including roads and ports—will help alleviate bottlenecks in a number of countries.

The full impact of increased trade openness will depend on the progress made on complementary reforms, especially to entrench a more enabling business environment that would enhance labor mobility across economic activities, in Latin America. At the same time, trade reform also requires the implementation of well-targeted and temporary adjustment-assistance programs to compensate workers in sectors that will not benefit from the expected changes in relative prices. In many cases, adjustment-assistance programs should be focused on households or small firms that are *net* producers of import-sensitive agricultural commodities and/or on policies to enable the diversification of regions where these commodities are produced.

To better cope with the volatility of capital flows, progress continues to be made across the region in strengthening financial systems and underlying macroeconomic frameworks:

• As discussed in Section V, many countries have taken critical steps toward improving risk-management practices of financial institutions by shoring up prudential regulations and supervision.

• For example, central banks and supervisors are generally acquiring increased authority to deal with problem banks; initial capital requirements are being raised for the opening of new banks; and banks are being required to implement risk-control systems. Moreover, the broader institutional framework of the financial sector has been strengthened. For example, Mexico improved accounting standards, and Brazil required external account audits with strict rotation rules.

• More flexible exchange rates in many Latin American countries have contributed substantially to improving macroeconomic flexibility and the ability of countries to better weather the strains associated with surges and reversals in capital flows.

Looking ahead, Latin America's progress toward greater trade openness and strengthened financial systems and underlying macroeconomic frameworks is likely to contribute to greater resilience with respect to external shocks—and, in particular, to volatile capital flows—than was seen in the past.

References

Adlung, Rudolf, 2000, "Services Trade Liberalization from Developed and Developing Country Perspectives," in *GATS 2000: New Directions in Services Trade Liberalization*, ed. by Pierre Sauvé and Robert Stern (Washington: Brookings Institution Press).

Arora, Vivek, and Martin Cerisola, 2001, "How Does U.S. Monetary Policy Influence Sovereign Spreads in Emerging Markets?," *Staff Papers*, International Monetary Fund, Vol. 48, No. 3, pp. 474–98.

Arteta, Carlos, Barry Eichengreen, and Charles Wyplosz, 2001, "When Does Capital Account Liberalization Help More Than It Hurts?" NBER Working Paper No. 8414 (Cambridge, Massachusetts: National Bureau of Economic Research).

Berg, Andrew, and Anne O. Krueger, 2002, "Trade, Growth, and Poverty: A Selective Survey," paper presented at the Annual World Bank Conference on Development Economics, Washington, April 29–30.

Bouzas, Roberto, and Saul Keifman, 2003, "Making Trade Liberalization Work," in *After the Washington Consensus*, ed. by Pedro-Pablo Kuczynski and John Williamson (Washington: Institute for International Economics), pp. 156–79.

Burki, Shahid Javed, and Guillermo Perry, 1997, *The Long March: A Reform Agenda for Latin America and the Caribbean in the Next Decade* (Washington: World Bank).

Calvo, Guillermo, Carmen Reinhart, and Leonardo Leiderman, 1996, "Inflows of Capital to Developing Countries in the 1990s," *Journal of Economic Perspectives*, Vol. 10 (Spring), pp. 123–39.

Catão, Luis, 2002, "Debt Crises: What's Different About Latin America?" Chapter II in *World Economic Outlook: A Survey by the Staff of the International Monetary Fund, April*, World Economic and Financial Surveys (Washington: International Monetary Fund).

Chang, Won, and L. Alan Winters, 2002, "How Regional Blocs Affect Excluded Countries: The Price Effects of Mercosur," *American Economic Review*, Vol. 92 (September), pp. 889–904.

Connolly, Michelle, and Jenessa Gunther, 1999, "Mercosur: Implications for Growth in Member Countries," *Current Issues in Economics and Finance,* Federal Reserve Bank of New York, Vol. 5, No. 7, pp. 1–6.

Devlin, Robert, and Antoni Estevadeordal, 2002, "What's New in the New Regionalism in the Americas?" IADB Working Paper No. 6 (Washington: Inter-American Development Bank).

Economic Commission for Latin America and the Caribbean (ECLAC), 2003, *A Decade of Light and Shadow: Latin America and the Caribbean in the 1990s*, ed. by José-Antonio Ocampo and Juan Martín (Santiago, Chile: United Nations).

Edison, Hali, Michael Klein, Luca Ricci, and Torsten Sløk, 2002, "Capital Account Liberalization and Economic Performance: Survey and Synthesis," IMF Working Paper 02/120 (Washington: International Monetary Fund).

Edwards, Sebastian, 2001, "Capital Mobility and Economic Performance: Are Emerging Economies Different?" NBER Working Paper No. 8076 (Cambridge, Massachusetts: National Bureau of Economic Research).

Fernandez-Arias, Eduardo, and Ugo Panizza, 2001, "Capital Flows to Latin America: New Issues and Old Concerns," paper presented at the conference on Domestic Finance and Global Capital in Latin America, Federal Reserve Bank of Atlanta, November 1–2.

Ffrench-Davis, Ricardo, 2000, *Reforming the Reforms in Latin America: Macroeconomies, Trade, Finance* (New York: St. Martin's Press).

Griffith-Jones, Stephany, 1998, *Global Capital Flows* (New York: Macmillan).

Hanson, James, 1995, "Opening the Capital Account: Costs, Benefits, and Sequencing," in *Capital Controls, Exchange Rates, and Monetary Policy in the World Economy*, ed. by Sebastian Edwards (Cambridge, United Kingdom: Cambridge University Press).

Inter-American Development Bank (IADB), 1996, *Report on Economic and Social Progress in Latin America* (Washington).

———, and Enrique V. Iglesias, 2002, *Beyond Borders: The New Regionalism in Latin America* (Washington).

International Monetary Fund (IMF), 2001, "International Financial Integration and Developing Countries," Chapter IV in *World Economic Outlook: A Survey by the Staff of the International Monetary Fund, October*, World Economic and Financial Surveys (Washington).

Ishii, Shogo, and Karl Habermeier, 2002, *Capital Account Liberalization and Financial Sector Stability*, IMF Occasional Paper No. 211 (Washington: International Monetary Fund).

Kose, Ayhan, Guy Meredith, and Christopher Towe, forthcoming, "How Has NAFTA Affected the Mexican Economy? Review and Evidence," in *Monetary Policy and Macroeconomic Stabilization in Latin America*, ed. by Dennis Snower (Berlin: Springer).

Krueger, Ann O., 1997, "Trade Policy and Economic Development: How We Learn," NBER Working Paper No. 5896 (Cambridge, Massachusetts: National Bureau of Economic Research).

———, 1999, "Are Preferential Trading Arrangements Trade-Liberalizing or Protectionist?" *Journal of Economic Perspectives*, Vol. 13 (Fall), pp. 105–24.

———, 2004, "Trade, Jobs, and Growth: Why You Can't Have One Without the Others," paper presented at Reuters Trade, Globalization and Outsourcing Conference, New York, June 15.

Laird, Sam, Lucian Cernat, and Alessandro Turrini, 2002, "Back to Basics: Market Access Issues in the Doha Agenda," United Nations Conference on Trade and Development (New York: United Nations, Trade Analysis Branch).

Laird, Sam, and Patrick Messerlin, 2003, "Trade Policy Regimes and Development Strategies: A Comparative Study," in *Bridges for Development: Policies and Institutions for Trade and Integration*, ed. by Robert Devlin and Antoni Estevadeordal (Washington: Inter-American Development Bank).

Lora, Eduardo, 2001, "Structural Reforms in Latin America: What Has Been Reformed and How to Measure It," IADB Working Paper No. 466 (Washington: Inter-American Development Bank).

Macario, Carla, 2000, *Export Growth in Latin America: Policies and Performance* (Boulder, Colorado: Lynne Rienner Publishers).

MacDonagh-Dumler, Chris, Yongzheng Yang, and Geoffrey Bannister, 2002, "Recent U.S. Trade and Agricultural Policies and Their International Implications," in *United States: Selected Issues*, IMF Country Report 02/165 (Washington: International Monetary Fund).

Michalopoulos, Constantine, 1999, "Trade Policy and Market Access Issues for Developing Countries: Implications for the Millennium Round," Policy Research Working Paper No. 2214 (Washington: World Bank).

Morsink, James, Thomas Helbling, and Silvia Sgherri, 2002, "Trade and Financial Integration," Chapter III in *World Economic Outlook: A Survey by the Staff of the International Monetary Fund, September,* World Economic and Financial Surveys (Washington: International Monetary Fund).

Nagarajan, Nigel, 1998, "La Evidencia sobre el Desvio de Comercio en el Mercosur," *Integración y Comercio*, Vol. 2 (September–December), pp. 257–88.

Nsouli, Saleh, Mounir Rached, and Norbert Funke, 2002, "The Speed of Adjustment and the Sequencing of Economic Reforms: Issues and Guidelines for Policymakers," IMF Working Paper 02/132 (Washington: International Monetary Fund).

Organization for Economic Cooperation and Development (OECD), 2003, "Agricultural Policies in OECD Countries: Monitoring and Evaluation, 2001" (Paris: OECD Committee for Agriculture).

Rodrik, Dani, 1999, "Why Is There So Much Economic Insecurity in Latin America?" (unpublished; Cambridge, Massachusetts: Harvard University).

Sgherri, Silvia, 2002, "Trade, Financial Openness, and Volatility: Some Interactions" (unpublished; Washington: International Monetary Fund).

Stallings, Barbara, and Wilson Peres, 2000, *Growth, Employment, and Equity: The Impact of Economic Reforms in Latin America and the Caribbean* (Washington: Brookings Institution Press).

Stern, Robert, 2000, "Quantifying Barriers to Trade in Services," Discussion Paper No. 470, Research Seminar in International Economics, School of Public Policy (Ann Arbor, Michigan: University of Michigan).

Wacziarg, Romain, and Karen Horn Welch, 2003, "Trade Liberalization and Growth: New Evidence," NBER Working Paper No. 10152 (Cambridge, Massachusetts: National Bureau of Economic Research).

World Bank, 2003a, "Lessons from NAFTA for Latin America and the Caribbean," Latin America and the Caribbean Regional Studies (Washington).

———, 2003b, *Global Economic Prospects 2004* (Washington).

Yeats, Alexander, 1997, "Does Mercosur's Trade Performance Raise Concerns about the Effects of Regional Trade Agreements?" Policy Research Discussion Paper No. 1729 (Washington: World Bank).

VIII   Lessons and Priorities for Future Agenda

The aim of this study has been to take stock of the achievements and disappointments in Latin America since the start of market-based reforms in the early 1990s, a period that also witnessed growing democratization in the region. This concluding section draws lessons from this period and, based on this experience, discusses policy priorities and the future roles of the major players involved—the policymakers in Latin America; the international institutions, and especially the IMF; and industrial country governments—in order to make a decisive break from the region's long history of recurrent crisis and to entrench growing prosperity.

Looking Back

When Latin America's experience since the early 1990s is viewed against the backdrop of the 1980s—an unsettled period for the region—it is clear that much has been achieved. This study has pointed to the following principal achievements.

Policy Performance

The 1990s saw the establishment of low inflation, a major achievement for much of Latin America, given its past record of high and volatile inflation. An important reason has been the emergence of widespread public awareness of the need to bring inflation down, leading to popular resistance to policies that would risk reigniting inflationary pressures. Thus, for example, the deep economic and financial crises of Argentina and Uruguay resulted in only a temporary acceleration of inflation, followed quickly by a return to single-digit rates. Similarly, strenuous efforts have kept inflation low in Bolivia despite fiscal and financial imbalances in a situation of political difficulty. Nevertheless, in many countries across the region, the sustainability of low inflation still needs to become fully entrenched, which will require sustained progress to bring down public debt and to address concerns raised by financial dollarization.

Policy Flexibility

The adoption of much more market-determined exchange rates by many Latin American countries in recent years has greatly improved the flexibility of the macroeconomic policy frameworks. In parallel, the region is also successfully developing a new basis for monetary policy by moving away from exchange rate anchors and toward placing growing reliance on inflation-targeting regimes, which has contributed to successful inflation outcomes. The shift to inflation targeting has underscored the importance of central bank autonomy and encouraged greater transparency in communicating the rationale for monetary policy decisions to the wider community.

Role Models

The region has yielded important role models. The experiences of Chile and Mexico in delivering sustained and less volatile growth, improving policy flexibility, and striving for social consensus have become important examples for the region. Both countries have established sound macroeconomic frameworks and open trade regimes that have allowed them to successfully avoid the financial difficulties affecting other countries in the region during recent years. Moreover, they offer valuable lessons on the benefits of containing public debt, implementing an inflation-targeting framework, and building a strong regulatory and supervisory framework for the banking system. Other countries in the region have also demonstrated successes in important areas that can be followed by others—for example, Brazil's success in building a strong set of institutions for fiscal management.

Crisis Resolution

Although financial crises have recurred in the region, the speed with which the affected countries have been able to recover has generally exceeded expectations. For example, Brazil has endured two periods of high stress since 1998, but, each time, the government's commitment to low inflation and fiscal prudence has fostered a rapid stabilization of the situation and return of the country's access to international markets. Elsewhere in the region, Argentina and Uruguay have now returned to growth faster than had been anticipated, although recessions were very deep after their crises in 2002. Thus, countries in the region have generally been better positioned to benefit from the global recovery over the past year.

Speed of Response

The international community has also demonstrated its ability to act swiftly and comprehensively in addressing crisis situations. IMF-led support packages were assembled in record time in many cases, incorporating increasing safeguards against moral hazard. An important feature of recent IMF-led official assistance in many Latin American countries has been the ability to support economic policy continuity, thereby smoothing political transitions. Thus, in different ways tailored to individual circumstances, recent IMF-supported programs in Argentina, Brazil, Bolivia, Guatemala, and Paraguay have helped maintain macroeconomic stability through periods of political change. There have also been improvements in the role of the private sector in crisis resolution. Uruguay was able to complete a debt exchange in record time last year, and collective-action clauses have become standard in new emerging market bond issues.

Disappointments

Nevertheless, the past decade has also witnessed many disappointments. Most importantly, in contrast to objectives set at the start of the 1990s, a number of Latin American countries have not been able to boost growth in an enduring way and to reduce the recurrence of financial crises. Moreover, efforts to address the region's high poverty and income inequality have had very disappointing results, leading to concerns about the political sustainability of reforms.

Key Disappointments

The revival of growth and initial improvements in poverty in the early 1990s were not generally sustained. Since the latter part of the decade, per capita income has increased very little, thereby extending for another decade the stagnation of the 1980s. Repeated episodes of financial instability again proved to have lasting adverse effects in terms of lost output and rising poverty and income inequality. Overall, no clear trend emerged toward reducing the region's

high poverty rates and income inequalities. As a result, the gap in living standards with North America has grown over the past decade, and Latin America has continued to fall behind fast-growing economies in Asia.

Prolonged Use of IMF Resources

The period since the early 1990s was marked by continued and prolonged use of IMF resources. Argentina and Bolivia—together with Honduras, Nicaragua, Panama, and El Salvador in Central America—had almost continuous financial arrangements with the IMF in this period. They were not alone, however, since virtually all countries in the region—with the exception of Chile—made substantial use of IMF resources.

Political Economy Factors

The disappointments of the 1990s have had important political economy implications for a number of countries in the region. There has been a risk that popular support for reform programs would be seriously undermined by repeated adjustment programs. Moreover, there has been a growing sense, in many countries, that the benefits of global integration have been unevenly distributed, accruing primarily to those in upper-income brackets although the costs have been borne by the less wealthy majority. In a few countries, there has even been a growing militancy among disenfranchised groups. Thus, the experience of the last decade has emphasized to policymakers and the international community that much more needs to be done to secure and maintain a domestic consensus on continuing economic reforms. In many countries, new or enhanced dialogues with civil society are now under way—auguring well for maintaining the consistency of the reform process in the future.

Explanatory Factors

Although external factors certainly played a role in explaining the recent disappointments in Latin American economic performance, this study suggests that shortfalls in domestic policies bore the principal responsibility. Three types of problems have been identified: policy imbalances, the lack of policy resilience ("crisis proofing"), and the need for more sustained reforms.

Policy Imbalances

The study points to a number of inconsistencies and imbalances in the stabilization and reform programs adopted by Latin American countries in the 1990s:

- *Macroeconomic imbalances.* With public debt rising, rather than falling, during the 1990s, a key vulnerability was allowed to persist, constraining overall macroeconomic policy. Fiscal policy remained procyclical; and monetary policy was constrained, first by the fixed exchange rate regimes and then by the events surrounding the disorderly exits from these regimes, including financial-system pressures and strains.

- *Financial systems.* The liberalization of financial systems that occurred in the early 1990s was not accompanied by consistently strong regulatory and supervisory frameworks and effective strategies to curtail fiscal dominance. As a result, financial systems remained exposed to systemic risk from public debt and dollarization, which, in turn, created balance-sheet mismatches owing to exchange rate fluctuations. Even well-regarded financial systems, such as that of Argentina, harbored vulnerabilities, especially exposure to public debt and government interference, that were not adequately addressed.

- *Structural reforms.* Notwithstanding the ambitious plans of the early 1990s, progress on structural reforms was inconsistent and unbalanced. As indicated earlier in this paper, Latin America's financial liberalization and capital-market opening in the early 1990s proved to be faster than the adoption of key supporting reforms. Thus, trade opening moved ahead more slowly, and labor and key product markets remained inflexible, with the result that adjustment of trade balances in response to external shocks proved much more difficult than it had been, for example, in Asian economies in the aftermath of the Asian crisis of 1997–98.

Need for "Crisis Proofing"

Latin America's failure to provide greater insurance against shocks can be attributed to its persisting macroeconomic vulnerabilities, especially in fiscal policy and public debt. In a number of countries, crisis proofing probably weakened, rather than strengthened, as public debt climbed to an average of 60 percent of GDP, despite the Brady debt-restructuring initiative and large-scale privatization programs in many countries that helped to reduce their debts in the early 1990s. Moreover, the debt was often foreign currency-denominated or indexed and issued at short maturities. This debt structure contributed to vulnerabilities, especially when a loss in market confidence entailed higher interest rates or exchange rate depreciation.

The lack of progress with crisis proofing reflected underlying weaknesses in spending and revenue systems and institutions. In addition, there were the heavy costs of dealing with vulnerabilities in banking systems and the recognition of "fiscal skeletons" whose existence was initially hidden in off-budget accounts. Overall, for many countries in the region, "debt intolerance" rose again.[178]

Sustainability of Reforms

Sustainability of reforms was another problem. Even where reforms were implemented, too often the supporting institutional structures remained weak. Sustainability problems were evidenced in the persistence of informal dollarization because of the continued lack of credibility of macroeconomic policy frameworks. Sustainability issues were most important in the public finances, where problems in tax administration contributed to low collections despite high rates (especially for income taxes and indirect taxes). Low revenues, combined with high revenue volatility and expenditure earmarking, increasingly limited resources for infrastructure and growth while imparting a procyclical bias to fiscal policy and raising the public debt. Structural reform policies, however, also were subject to sustainability problems. In a number of reform areas—including, for example, privatization—the results fell short of expectations because of a lack of complementary policies to strengthen regulations or to ensure an adequately competitive business environment.

Priorities for Future Agenda

In looking at the future agenda for Latin America, the focus needs to be much broader than short-run policies alone. It needs to embrace institutional change that will enhance the sustainability of policy frameworks. Thus, when policymakers are reviewing the priorities in each of the major areas of macroeconomic and structural policies, they need to emphasize institutional change.

Macroeconomic Policies

Monetary and Exchange Rate Policies

Many countries have exited fixed exchange rate systems and have adopted inflation-targeting regimes that offer promising frameworks for imple-

---

[178]Reinhart, Rogoff, and Savastano (2003) make the point that once a country slips into being a serial defaulter, it generates a high level of debt intolerance that is difficult to shed. A corollary of this point is the difficulty countries face in graduating from prolonged use of IMF resources.

menting monetary and exchange rate policies in the region. Inflation targeting has the key strength of focusing the policy debate on what monetary policy can do on a sustainable basis—that is, controlling inflation—rather than on what it cannot do—raising output growth or boosting external competitiveness. It also provides a suitable framework for implementing flexible exchange rate regimes, which provide greater resilience in the face of shocks. Two important challenges remain, however. First, in those countries that have already adopted inflation targeting, how can the institutional framework for inflation targeting be reinforced to improve implementation and, therefore, entrench credibility? And, second, how can suitably robust frameworks for monetary and exchange rate policies be developed for those countries that choose to pursue alternative policy approaches?

To ensure the credibility of inflation targeting, it is important to establish a clear framework for central bank autonomy. A number of countries have already made good progress toward this goal. This progress can be reinforced by developing stronger central bank laws that clearly assign monetary policy responsibility to senior bank officials; provide appropriate objectives, incentives for performance, and budgeting independence; and further reduce fiscal dominance and financial sector vulnerabilities. Regarding implementation, an important task is to increase transparency about the decision-making process and generally progress further in putting in place all the enabling conditions for full-fledged inflation targeting. This includes the publication of regular reports that discuss the outlook for inflation and the consistency of policy settings with meeting the inflation target. Such an approach would help to convey to markets how the authorities intend to meet their objectives, especially in the face of shocks such as sudden, sharp exchange rate movements.

In contrast to countries with inflation targeting and flexible exchange rate regimes, a number of countries in the region, especially in Central America, continue with less flexible exchange rate systems in which monetary policy is geared toward exchange rate objectives. For many of these countries, priority must be given to developing an institutional and policy framework that will gradually allow for greater flexibility in an orderly way. Some countries, however, may choose to remain with an inflexible exchange rate system or to progress toward full dollarization. Choice of the latter regime typically reflects a country's circumstances, including trading patterns, degree of dollarization, and past record of inflation control. Countries making such choices must then ensure that fiscal policy is sufficiently robust to support such a regime while making sure that

structural policies provide sufficient flexibility in the economy to absorb shocks.

Fiscal Policy and Public Debt

Debt burdens in many Latin American countries are above prudent levels and must be brought down. Reinhart, Rogoff, and Savastano (2003) suggest that the safe range needs to be particularly low for countries with a history of default and high inflation. At the same time, historical experience has taught us that such a transition does not become credible simply through the running of large primary budget surpluses. The pursuit of surpluses needs to be demonstrably sustainable and rigorously implemented, ensuring that—in particular—it is not based on unrealistic spending cuts and distortionary taxes inimical to efficiency and growth. More generally, the pursuit of debt sustainability must be based on a broader agenda to raise growth and implement structural reforms, especially institutional reforms, that can set in motion a virtuous circle of improving confidence, lower interest rates, and higher growth. Short-run policy adjustments that are not accompanied by efforts to achieve broader institutional change are unlikely to bring about such a virtuous circle or be sustained and, therefore, are not likely to succeed in bringing the public debt ratio down in an enduring way.

Institutional weaknesses in fiscal systems identified in this study include reliance on distortionary taxes, low effective tax rates, revenue volatility, and expenditure earmarking and other budgetary rigidities. Raising the effective tax rate depends on addressing tax avoidance and strengthening weak tax administration. Revenue volatility can be dampened by reducing the reliance on the taxation of commodity exports and broadening the tax base. Expenditure earmarking and special wage regimes for protected public sector employees raise difficult issues requiring, in many cases, constitutional changes to implement reforms.

Broader reforms to the overall fiscal framework may also be helpful in instilling fiscal discipline. Legislation to impose conservative and sustainable debt limits may be useful, particularly in countries where strong political forces are driving spending decisions, or where their natural resource revenues are subject to wide short-term swings, but experience has shown that such rules can all too easily be circumvented. Chile's success with fiscal consolidation in the 1990s illustrates the effectiveness of a range of institutional reforms to support prudent fiscal policy decisions. Important factors that contributed to debt reduction in Chile included giving more power to the finance ministry than to other ministries or the legislature; prohibiting the central bank from extending credit to the government; and preventing lower levels of government from borrowing, thus eliminating the subnational free-rider problem. Brazil's recent success in strengthening its fiscal position and consistently meeting fiscal objectives has also benefited from a series of fundamental improvements in the budgeting process and the structure of center-state relations in the context of a fiscal responsibility law.

Improving the composition of debt is as important as reducing the level of debt. Specifically, countries should take every opportunity to replace short-term, floating-rate, and foreign currency-linked debt with longer-term domestic debt. Otherwise, countries are left vulnerable to high rates of rollovers and changes in credibility and global financial conditions. To this end, domestic debt must be made more attractive to investors, which requires working to entrench a sound framework for sustaining macroeconomic stability. Inflation indexing domestic debt would reduce the risk of fluctuations in real value, both to lenders and borrowers. This approach has succeeded in promoting longer-term domestic financial intermediation in Chile and Colombia. In addition, experience—especially in Mexico—underlines the importance of maintaining an active investor-relations program, especially to provide transparency and transmittal of information on economic and debt developments.

Structural Reforms for Raising Growth and Reducing Poverty

Latin America has suffered from a chronically weak growth performance, with the structural reforms of the 1990s providing only a temporary reprieve from disappointing outcomes. To improve growth and poverty reduction, macroeconomic policy strengthening needs to be supported by a broad-based structural reform agenda and, in particular, institutional reform. What should be the priorities?

Financial Systems

Achieving sound and resilient financial systems is a key element in reducing Latin America's vulnerability to crisis and sustaining long-term economic growth. In particular, financial systems across the region require strengthening to enable them to deliver the steadily rising financial intermediation that is needed to support sustained growth. Argentina's experience shows, however, that even a well-regarded financial system is not safe as long as public debt remains a key vulnerability. Although considerable progress was made during the 1990s in strengthening banking systems, there is a continuing need to improve banking regulation and supervision. It will be important to encourage provisioning require-

ments based on more forward-looking risk assessments and to ensure that these requirements are reviewed and enforced, minimizing the need for regulatory forbearance as much as possible. Moreover, further efforts are needed to implement crisis-management and bank-resolution frameworks, to improve legal protection for bank supervisors, and to monitor risks arising from cross-border financial integration. In some countries, the legacy of financial crisis persists in the form of nonperforming loans that remain to be efficiently liquidated and public banks that need to be restructured.

Enhancing the transparency of financial activities would help to promote prudent decision making and risk taking. Accounting and auditing standards need to be strengthened to improve the availability and reliability of information to the public while encouraging the emergence of formal credit rating of borrowers, which would help to reduce the cost of lending for banks. Moral hazard implied by deposit-insurance systems would be contained by introducing explicit limits on payouts and restricting benefits to small depositors.

Lack of suitable financing remains an important constraint on growth in Latin America. Sustained credit creation would be encouraged by reducing the costs of dealing with defaults on problem loans. A key step toward achieving this objective is to strengthen lenders' ability to recover value from distressed loans. In many countries, antiquated bankruptcy laws favor borrowers over creditors, making it difficult to appropriately resolve claims in cases of default. Increasing the operational efficiency of banks, especially of public banks; enhancing competition; and allowing lenders to make more informed decisions would help deepen financial intermediation. It is also important to develop alternative vehicles of financing—for example, through the deepening of capital markets and expansion of microfinancing initiatives.

Trade Opening

Despite considerable efforts to liberalize trade during the 1990s, Latin America remains much less open than other dynamic regions of the world. Reforms to further liberalize trade are critical to stimulating growth and reducing vulnerabilities. The greatest benefits would flow from successful multilateral trade negotiations, which could bring countries improved market access for their key exports, such as agricultural products and textiles. Even if progress on the multilateral front were slow, there would remain considerable scope and benefit for Latin American countries to encourage trade opening, including within the region, by doing the following:

- curtailing still-widespread protectionist practices in Latin America—in particular, the use of nontariff barriers, high tariffs on processed goods, and restrictions on trade in services;

- addressing the shortcomings of existing regional trade agreements to make them more comprehensive in scope in terms of the products and types of policies (investment, regulatory, etc.) covered; and

- advancing bilateral trade agreements with industrial country trading partners—as well as agreements within the region—that would help to reduce problems of trade diversion and bring a number of advantages, including increased investment flows and technology transfers.

For these initiatives to bear fruit, however, it will be important for Latin American countries to maintain a stable macroeconomic environment with appropriate exchange rates and to further develop trade-related institutions and infrastructure. In particular, improvements are needed in port and customs administrations, which currently impose costly delays and inefficiencies in many countries. Other institutional weaknesses that have hindered trade flows—including legal uncertainties and corruption—and need to be remedied to permit sustained growth are discussed more broadly in the next subsections.

Labor Markets

Labor market reforms—which were notably absent from the reform agendas of most Latin American countries in the 1990s—assume even greater significance in the context of increased trade liberalization. International experience suggests that this is a key step toward increasing flexibility, private investment, and growth in the economy. Recent research has stressed that reaping the full benefits of trade integration depends upon the flexibility within economies for labor to move across employment sectors—from less productive to more productive ones.[179] Institutional arrangements in the form of high severance costs and restrictions on hiring temporary workers act as significant barriers to entry and exit and, therefore, to such flexibility. Elevated nonwage labor costs are also an impediment to employment. Although initial political obstacles must be overcome, labor market reforms that make it more attractive to hire workers will, over time, yield broad-based benefits, including more rapid growth of employment in the formal sector, that would, in turn, likely increase popular support for the reform process. The state has an important role, in this context, in providing for efficient mechanisms to deal

with transitional problems associated with intersectoral mobility, and to invest in workers' training and skill upgrading, especially in the context of increased external trade openness.

Role of State in Governance and Institutional Reforms

In a number of Latin American countries, weak institutions of governance have undermined market activity; support for broad-based reforms; and, ultimately, growth. Institutional reforms are needed to confront these weaknesses, create a firmer foundation for economic activity, and thereby sustain growth.[180] The task is arguably more difficult now, since institutions in the region have been successively weakened by a history—in many countries—of recurrent crisis.[181]

Corruption has tended to hamper economic growth and foreign investment, which relies on investors' perceptions of contract viability, ease of profit repatriation, and the probability of payment without delay. The poor have been hardest hit by corruption, given their greater reliance on public services and inability to pay the high costs of bribery or fraud. Visibly reducing corruption would provide a positive impetus to growth and help to sustain support for the reform process. For example, fostering greater accountability of the public sector—for example, by assuring public access to government information—would help to deter corruption.

Reforms are also needed in the judicial system, which is often regarded as weak and highly politicized rather than impartial in predictably enforcing laws. The absence of a strong judicial system tends to undermine investor confidence and property rights, hindering the introduction of new reforms, increasing lending risk, and ultimately restraining economic activity. Establishing an independent and responsible judiciary is central to increasing the credibility of the rule of law and improving the environment for the operation of market forces. Strengthening the judicial process will require improving the accountability of judges—including through publishing information

---

[179]For example, Chapter II in IMF (2004) discusses the implications of China's integration for the international economy.

[180]In the context of Chile's experience, Foxley (2004) explains the importance of institutional reforms for sustaining poverty reduction.

[181]Rodrik (2003) emphasizes the importance of institutional reforms for *sustaining* growth, as opposed to igniting economic growth. Many of the specific components of institutional reforms that he discusses—sound monetary policy, debt sustainability, and the rule of law—are also crucial for attracting private investment, especially the domestic private investments that are necessary for the *acceleration* phase. In any case, his distinction between accelerating and sustaining growth is less relevant in the context of Latin America, where there have been frequent false starts and recurring macroeconomic volatility.

on judicial performance. Judicial efficiency could be improved by simplifying legal procedures and establishing specialized court systems—such as bankruptcy and commercial courts—or alternative dispute-resolution mechanisms.

Many of these concerns directly affect the business environment, which is crucial for attracting and increasing private investment. As previously discussed, Latin America generally does less well than other, more rapidly growing regions in providing the key ingredients of a friendly investment climate. A number of surveys have shown the increased deadweight costs associated with heavy regulation of the entry and exit of businesses, labor force management, and contract enforcement. These costly distortions in the regulatory and incentive structures in many Latin American countries divert domestic capital and investment overseas, and often hit hardest small and medium-sized enterprises and those in rural areas, which typically face greater difficulty than urban enterprises in accessing public services. Improving the investment climate can directly help attract new private investment that is crucial for productivity and growth; and provided the improvements are equitably implemented within countries, they can also help to integrate the small enterprises and the rural economy—thereby reducing income inequalities and poverty. The state has a crucial role in improving regulatory governance and better securing property rights to help establish a more enabling investment climate.

IMF Role: Supporting Growth Agendas

Faced with the economic and financial crises in Latin America, as well as in other emerging market countries, over the past decade, the IMF has understandably emphasized crisis resolution and prevention. Much progress has been made, especially in drawing lessons from these crises in emerging markets, expanding the tools of crisis prevention, and deepening IMF surveillance of key risks and vulnerabilities.

Taken together, the various initiatives have already brought about a sea change in the role of the IMF:

• The need to reduce vulnerabilities to crises has led the IMF to emphasize developing a framework of internationally agreed standards and codes for monetary, fiscal, and financial transparency (reflected in countries' preparation of reports on standards and codes, or ROSCs); encourage deeper cooperation on financial sector issues, including through the Financial Stability Forum; emphasize greater transparency of IMF staff work, including through the publication of country reports and policy papers; and deliberately focus on the social costs of crises and their alleviation.

• The IMF has also been at the center of the continuing debate on crisis resolution that has led to the widespread acceptance of collective-action clauses (CACs) in new bond issues with no evidence of any additional interest premium resulting from their use. The increased issuance under local law of international sovereign bonds including CACs in New York, where they had not been the market standard, has been a major positive development since 2003.

• The IMF's stronger focus on potential vulnerabilities, with more rigorous and candid assessments of debt sustainability, exchange rate arrangements, and balance-sheet exposures have raised the bar for surveillance and Article IV consultations.

Although they are still being consolidated, these initiatives have helped to catalyze stronger and more transparent policymaking in Latin America, which has already had a considerable impact on markets. There is evidence that contagion risks have lessened; the dispersion of spreads on emerging market debt has increased; and cross-country correlation of financial market developments has been reduced—all evidence of greater market discrimination between countries.

The agenda for the region's future includes, in particular, sharpening the IMF's surveillance role, particularly in countries that have had a succession of IMF-supported programs, and increasing the focus on entrenching growth. Several aspects of these issues warrant further discussion:

• The experience in Latin America of prolonged dependence on IMF arrangements and financial assistance, in a situation of recurrent financial crisis, has exposed the need for the surveillance process to include "a fresh pair of eyes." This applies to both sides of the dialogue. Prolonged use of IMF resources has probably also been inimical to a process of widening contact in the community and building awareness for longer-term institutional change, given the typically small group of officials charged with the responsibility of putting together IMF-supported programs in times of crisis. In particular, the IMF's surveillance role, carried out through the Article IV consultation process, should be strongly maintained even while the country has a current IMF-supported program.

• A parallel challenge for the IMF lies in sharpening its focus on promoting growth. A growth-focused agenda will have many dimensions—

including infrastructure investment, the corporate sector, the labor market, and other issues that lie outside the IMF's core expertise—and thus heighten the need for effective coordination with the other relevant international financial institutions (IFIs)—the World Bank and the Inter-American Development Bank. To be sure, in recent years, a number of important initiatives have already helped to improve such coordination— such as the poverty reduction strategy paper (PRSP) process for low-income countries and the broadening use of Financial Sector Assessment Programs (FSAPs). There is room, however, for expanding collaboration in the higher-income countries in the region, where PRSPs are not prepared, and especially in helping identify and raise funds for efficient public investments and coordinating technical assistance.

- Institutional reforms have been a recurring theme of this paper. Recent IMF research indicates that institutional factors—including those related to governance and corruption issues—are more important than capital-labor ratios in explaining cross-country differences in per capita incomes. Institutional strengthening is seen as crucial to build and foster increased levels of "crisis proofing," improve the business climate, attract private investments, and support growth. Achieving the priority objectives for Latin America that were discussed in the previous subsections will depend heavily on achieving institutional change. Such an approach will also place increased demands on closer coordination among the IFIs.

Experience in Latin America over the last decade and a half suggests two important lessons for the IMF and the other IFIs to keep in mind as they increase their emphasis on institutional change and reform:

- first, broad country ownership of the institutional policy agenda will be even more essential, since political interests would be directly involved; and

- second, external incentives or anchors can play a crucial role in catalyzing the process of domestic institution building in Latin America.

Establishing country ownership of institutional change will, most likely, prove to be an even more daunting challenge than doing so for ownership of prudent short-run macroeconomic management— particularly since it involves even greater political sensitivities and trade-offs. In addition, institutional reforms do not always lend themselves to "best-practice" formulations because of the diversity of individual circumstances and conditions.[182] The pay-

offs from doing this would be considerable, however, most notably because tensions over short-run policies could be reduced. The shift to inflation targeting is a good example of an institutional change that has generally reduced controversy over short-run monetary policy. Accordingly, conditionality in IMF lending programs will need to evolve further and emphasize institutional change rather than short-term policy adjustment. In many countries, such a shift would be regarded as politically intrusive. The ground therefore needs to be carefully prepared by an outreach strategy that is well coordinated among the IFIs. Such an outreach strategy could include the following elements:

- *Contacts with national congresses.* The IFIs could present coordinated seminars for members of congress in selected countries to encourage greater understanding of the policies that the IFIs are advocating and improve the IFIs' understanding of the concerns of lawmakers and the constraints that they face.

- *Contacts with civil society.* In the course of their country work, staff members of the IFIs need to find opportunities to explain policy options to civil society. These contacts are essential to ensure that the IFIs fully understand the issues facing a country and communicate effectively the logic behind IFI policies to as wide an audience as possible, thereby helping encourage ownership. It is especially important to explain the need for civil service reforms; and, toward this end, the IFIs will need to undertake presentations to groups—such as teachers, health service workers, and the military—that typically have special wage and/or pension regimes.

Finally, an improved set of external incentives or anchors can play an important role in supporting the process of domestic institution building in Latin America. International trade offers clear possibilities for such anchors and incentives:

- Greater trade openness in Latin America would—in addition to its other benefits—help to strengthen institutions. The opening up of markets can play an important role in weakening vested interests and reducing economic rents associated with long-standing economic and institutional arrangements. Trade can thus spur improvements in domestic institutions that otherwise would not have been possible.

- International agreements can be an important external anchor and catalyst for institutional change by breaking through domestic impediments to reforms. For example, participation in NAFTA has helped to build stronger institutions in Mexico than might otherwise have been possi-

[182]Rodrik (2003) stresses this point.

ble. The emerging trade agreements with the United States that are under consideration—such as the U.S.-Central American Free Trade Agreement—are likely to provide a boost to institutional development in a number of countries. From a broader perspective, membership requirements of the World Trade Organization will also contribute to reforms.

Access to IMF arrangements that rewards good policies and, thereby, strengthens the incentives for good practice is also likely to continue to be very beneficial as an external anchor. Although prolonged use of IMF resources may have perversely reduced program ownership in many countries, well-designed instruments that reward good behavior could catalyze the opposite effect.

References

Foxley, Alejandro, 2004, "Successes and Failures in Poverty Eradication: Chile," paper presented at the World Bank conference on Scaling Up Poverty Reduction: A Global Learning Process held in Shanghai, May 25–27.

International Monetary Fund (IMF), 2004, *World Economic Outlook: A Survey by the Staff of the International Monetary Fund, April*, World Economic and Financial Surveys (Washington).

Reinhart, Carmen, Kenneth Rogoff, and Miguel Savastano, 2003, "Debt Intolerance," *Brookings Papers on Economic Activity, 1*, Brookings Institution, pp. 1–74.

Rodrik, Dani, 2003, "Growth Strategies" (unpublished; Cambridge, Massachusetts: John F. Kennedy School of Government).

Recent Occasional Papers of the International Monetary Fund

239. GEM: A New International Macroeconomic Model, by Tamim Bayoumi, with assistance from Douglas Laxton, Hamid Faruqee, Benjamin Hunt, Philippe Karam, Jaewoo Lee, Alessandro Rebucci, and Ivan Tchakarov. 2004.

238. Stabilization and Reforms in Latin America: A Macroeconomic Perspective on the Experience Since the Early 1990s, by Anoop Singh, Agnès Belaisch, Charles Collyns, Paula De Masi, Reva Krieger, Guy Meredith, and Robert Rennhack. 2005.

237. Sovereign Debt Structure for Crisis Prevention, by Eduardo Borensztein, Marcos Chamon, Olivier Jeanne, Paolo Mauro, and Jeromin Zettelmeyer. 2004.

236. Lessons from the Crisis in Argentina, by Christina Daseking, Atish R. Ghosh, Alun Thomas, and Timothy Lane. 2004.

235. A New Look at Exchange Rate Volatility and Trade Flows, by Peter B. Clark, Natalia Tamirisa, and Shang-Jin Wei, with Azim Sadikov and Li Zeng. 2004.

234. Adopting the Euro in Central Europe: Challenges of the Next Step in European Integration, by Susan M. Schadler, Paulo F. Drummond, Louis Kuijs, Zuzana Murgasova, and Rachel N. van Elkan. 2004.

233. Germany's Three-Pillar Banking System: Cross-Country Perspectives in Europe, by Allan Brunner, Jörg Decressin, Daniel Hardy, and Beata Kudela. 2004.

232. China's Growth and Integration into the World Economy: Prospects and Challenges, edited by Eswar Prasad. 2004.

231. Chile: Policies and Institutions Underpinning Stability and Growth, by Eliot Kalter, Steven Phillips, Marco A. Espinosa-Vega, Rodolfo Luzio, Mauricio Villafuerte, and Manmohan Singh. 2004.

230. Financial Stability in Dollarized Countries, by Anne-Marie Gulde, David Hoelscher, Alain Ize, David Marston, and Gianni De Nicoló. 2004.

229. Evolution and Performance of Exchange Rate Regimes, by Kenneth S. Rogoff, Aasim M. Husain, Ashoka Mody, Robin Brooks, and Nienke Oomes. 2004.

228. Capital Markets and Financial Intermediation in The Baltics, by Alfred Schipke, Christian Beddies, Susan M. George, and Niamh Sheridan. 2004.

227. U.S. Fiscal Policies and Priorities for Long-Run Sustainability, edited by Martin Mühleisen and Christopher Towe. 2004.

226. Hong Kong SAR: Meeting the Challenges of Integration with the Mainland, edited by Eswar Prasad, with contributions from Jorge Chan-Lau, Dora Iakova, William Lee, Hong Liang, Ida Liu, Papa N'Diaye, and Tao Wang. 2004.

225. Rules-Based Fiscal Policy in France, Germany, Italy, and Spain, by Teresa Dában, Enrica Detragiache, Gabriel di Bella, Gian Maria Milesi-Ferretti, and Steven Symansky. 2003.

224. Managing Systemic Banking Crises, by a staff team led by David S. Hoelscher and Marc Quintyn. 2003.

223. Monetary Union Among Member Countries of the Gulf Cooperation Council, by a staff team led by Ugo Fasano. 2003.

222. Informal Funds Transfer Systems: An Analysis of the Informal Hawala System, by Mohammed El Qorchi, Samuel Munzele Maimbo, and John F. Wilson. 2003.

221. Deflation: Determinants, Risks, and Policy Options, by Manmohan S. Kumar. 2003.

220. Effects of Financial Globalization on Developing Countries: Some Empirical Evidence, by Eswar S. Prasad, Kenneth Rogoff, Shang-Jin Wei, and M. Ayhan Kose. 2003.

219. Economic Policy in a Highly Dollarized Economy: The Case of Cambodia, by Mario de Zamaroczy and Sopanha Sa. 2003.

218. Fiscal Vulnerability and Financial Crises in Emerging Market Economies, by Richard Hemming, Michael Kell, and Axel Schimmelpfennig. 2003.

217. Managing Financial Crises: Recent Experience and Lessons for Latin America, edited by Charles Collyns and G. Russell Kincaid. 2003.

216. Is the PRGF Living Up to Expectations?—An Assessment of Program Design, by Sanjeev Gupta, Mark Plant, Benedict Clements, Thomas Dorsey, Emanuele Baldacci, Gabriela Inchauste, Shamsuddin Tareq, and Nita Thacker. 2002.

215. Improving Large Taxpayers' Compliance: A Review of Country Experience, by Katherine Baer. 2002.

214. Advanced Country Experiences with Capital Account Liberalization, by Age Bakker and Bryan Chapple. 2002.

213. The Baltic Countries: Medium-Term Fiscal Issues Related to EU and NATO Accession, by Johannes Mueller, Christian Beddies, Robert Burgess, Vitali Kramarenko, and Joannes Mongardini. 2002.

212. Financial Soundness Indicators: Analytical Aspects and Country Practices, by V. Sundararajan, Charles Enoch, Armida San José, Paul Hilbers, Russell Krueger, Marina Moretti, and Graham Slack. 2002.

211. Capital Account Liberalization and Financial Sector Stability, by a staff team led by Shogo Ishii and Karl Habermeier. 2002.

210. IMF-Supported Programs in Capital Account Crises, by Atish Ghosh, Timothy Lane, Marianne Schulze-Ghattas, Aleš Bulíř, Javier Hamann, and Alex Mourmouras. 2002.

209. Methodology for Current Account and Exchange Rate Assessments, by Peter Isard, Hamid Faruqee, G. Russell Kincaid, and Martin Fetherston. 2001.

208. Yemen in the 1990s: From Unification to Economic Reform, by Klaus Enders, Sherwyn Williams, Nada Choueiri, Yuri Sobolev, and Jan Walliser. 2001.

207. Malaysia: From Crisis to Recovery, by Kanitta Meesook, Il Houng Lee, Olin Liu, Yougesh Khatri, Natalia Tamirisa, Michael Moore, and Mark H. Krysl. 2001.

206. The Dominican Republic: Stabilization, Structural Reform, and Economic Growth, by a staff team led by Philip Young comprising Alessandro Giustiniani, Werner C. Keller, and Randa E. Sab and others. 2001.

205. Stabilization and Savings Funds for Nonrenewable Resources, by Jeffrey Davis, Rolando Ossowski, James Daniel, and Steven Barnett. 2001.

204. Monetary Union in West Africa (ECOWAS): Is It Desirable and How Could It Be Achieved? by Paul Masson and Catherine Pattillo. 2001.

203. Modern Banking and OTC Derivatives Markets: The Transformation of Global Finance and Its Implications for Systemic Risk, by Garry J. Schinasi, R. Sean Craig, Burkhard Drees, and Charles Kramer. 2000.

202. Adopting Inflation Targeting: Practical Issues for Emerging Market Countries, by Andrea Schaechter, Mark R. Stone, and Mark Zelmer. 2000.

201. Developments and Challenges in the Caribbean Region, by Samuel Itam, Simon Cueva, Erik Lundback, Janet Stotsky, and Stephen Tokarick. 2000.

200. Pension Reform in the Baltics: Issues and Prospects, by Jerald Schiff, Niko Hobdari, Axel Schimmel-pfennig, and Roman Zytek. 2000.

199. Ghana: Economic Development in a Democratic Environment, by Sérgio Pereira Leite, Anthony Pellechio, Luisa Zanforlin, Girma Begashaw, Stefania Fabrizio, and Joachim Harnack. 2000.

198. Setting Up Treasuries in the Baltics, Russia, and Other Countries of the Former Soviet Union: An Assessment of IMF Technical Assistance, by Barry H. Potter and Jack Diamond. 2000.

197. Deposit Insurance: Actual and Good Practices, by Gillian G.H. Garcia. 2000.

196. Trade and Trade Policies in Eastern and Southern Africa, by a staff team led by Arvind Subramanian, with Enrique Gelbard, Richard Harmsen, Katrin Elborgh-Woytek, and Piroska Nagy. 2000.

195. The Eastern Caribbean Currency Union—Institutions, Performance, and Policy Issues, by Frits van Beek, José Roberto Rosales, Mayra Zermeño, Ruby Randall, and Jorge Shepherd. 2000.

194. Fiscal and Macroeconomic Impact of Privatization, by Jeffrey Davis, Rolando Ossowski, Thomas Richardson, and Steven Barnett. 2000.

193. Exchange Rate Regimes in an Increasingly Integrated World Economy, by Michael Mussa, Paul Masson, Alexander Swoboda, Esteban Jadresic, Paolo Mauro, and Andy Berg. 2000.

Note: For information on the titles and availability of Occasional Papers not listed, please consult the IMF's *Publications Catalog* or contact IMF Publication Services.